Management, Information Systems and Computers

Other Macmillan books of related interest

J. Harvey, *Modern Economics*, 4th edition
A. Hindmarch, *Accounting — An Introduction*
D. Longley and M. Shain, *Dictionary of Information Technology*
J. D. Radford and D. B. Richardson, *Management of Manufacturing Systems*

Management, Information Systems and Computers

An Introduction

Roy Anderson

Management Consultant, and
Head of the
Department of Computing
and Cybernetics
Brighton Polytechnic

M

First published 1986

Published by
MACMILLAN EDUCATION LTD
Houndmills, Basingstoke, Hampshire RG21 2XS
and London
Companies and representatives
throughout the world

Photoset in Times by
CAS Typesetters, Southampton

Printed in Hong Kong

British Library Cataloguing in Publication Data
Anderson, Roy
   Management, information systems and computers: an
   introduction.
   1. Management information systems   2. Business
   —Data processing
   I. Title
   658.4' 038' 0285   T58.6

ISBN 0–333–39852–1
ISBN 0–333–39853–X Pbk

Cover photograph supplied by Digital Equipment Corporation.

Contents

Preface

The title of this book invites attention to the three principal subject areas with which it is concerned: Business Management, Information Systems, and the application of Computers to them. It is also about Economics, System Theory, Information Technology, and Systems Analysis and Design. It does not purport to provide comprehensive coverage of any of these subjects, but is offered as a useful introduction for anyone intending to pursue studies which require some understanding of the uses of computers. In doing so, the objective is to fill a gap in the available reading material by bringing together study topics which are usually presented separately, so as to provide a coherent explanation of the relationship between economic principles, the organisation and management of business undertakings, the importance of information to effective business management, and the vital role of computers and information technology in the provision and use of that information.

The book begins with an outline of relevant economic and system theory, identifying links between business objectives, the functions of management and decision-making necessary to pursue those objectives, the need for information to aid those decisions and for systems to provide the information required. The following chapters contain an examination of the nature of business systems, of the concepts of efficiency and productivity in the use of human and material resources, and of the paths open towards improvement of information systems and better use of those resources. This leads to a survey of the historical and potential growth in the use of machines for business systems, with illustrations of the range of application of computer-based information systems. The final chapters provide an explanation of some of the practical aspects of computer systems, with some consideration of organisation, economics and planning of such systems.

The book is aimed at four kinds of reader

1. At first-year students taking degree and higher diploma courses in Computer Studies, Information Technology, Systems Analysis and associated subjects. All these students need to complement and precede their specialist studies with some understanding of the purposes and practicalities of computer-based information systems.
2. At other students undertaking vocational courses at Higher Education

Institutions which require some basic understanding of business subjects and computers. It is believed that there are now very few professions and occupations which do not require some understanding of these subjects, and few courses of study which do not need to find a place for such a general introduction as is attempted here.

3. At trainee supervisors, managers and analysts who may be attending shorter courses of study as part of their training within employment, to complement reading on more detailed aspects of management and system studies.

4. At general readers seeking a better understanding of business organisation and systems and of the place of computers in the production of business information.

The reader is not expected to have any previous knowledge of the subject matter, which is presented with as little use of academic theory or educational jargon as possible. Some consideration of theory is unavoidable in examining system concepts, just as jargon is an inescapable feature of computer topics, but wherever any novel terminology appears to be necessary it is accompanied by a brief explanation in the text. This intention to give a practical and realistic view is not only a reflection of experience over three decades of rapid change in management techniques and information technology but also results from a view that the starting point for any study of computers should be rooted firmly in the real world. Managers who see their profession only as an exercise of personal skills, programmers and software engineers who see theirs as an abstract science, and system designers who seek only to refine their technical expertise will not be adequately equipped to meet the demands of their employment. This book cannot be sufficient in itself to turn students into trained managers, software engineers or systems analysts but it is believed that it can help to set them on the right path.

One assumption is made about the reader: that he or she does have a reasonable standard of numeracy and literacy, sufficient for a ready understanding of new concepts and arguments. Although we cannot always take these things for granted at the level of higher education, they are essential for those wishing to achieve their full potential in any employment, and certainly for anyone concerned with management, information systems or computers.

Acknowledgements

My thanks to my friend Stephen Fall for his professional advice and to my wife, Anne, for her invaluable help in the preparation of the text.

November 1985 Roy Anderson

1 Economic Background

The Meaning of Work

Scarce Resources and Unlimited Wants

Classical economic theory offers us the proposition that we live in a world in which resources (that is, the 'land', 'labour' and 'capital' used for production of goods and services) are scarce and wants are without limit, and that the purpose of economic activity is to reconcile those wants and resources. Upon this proposition a whole science of economic theory and application has been built to explain the principles, purposes and mechanisms which govern economic activity in the world. Of course, it is a little rash to describe as a science a subject in which human behaviour is the most important element, just as it is extremely risky to use economic theory to predict outcome when economic activity is so full of unpredictable variables. Fortunately, although it is appropriate to begin the treatment of subjects in the book with this first proposition of scarcity and wants, it is not necessary to explore the whole of economic theory, or to depend on it for valid conclusions. It is sufficient to start with some general principles and to add a few reasonable assumptions.

Work as the Prime Human Activity

From the first proposition that we live in a demand-driven society where resources are scarce, we come to a second proposition: that work is the most important human activity. Work is not simply physical effort or employment, it relates to all economic activity with its organisations, systems, machines and tools: the business of turning those scarce resources into the variety and volume of goods and services needed to please the inexhaustible demand of consumers.

The dominant instinct in human beings — and of all living things, for that matter — is to survive. Because resources are scarce it is necessary to work in order to survive and, for much of the living world, the search for food and defence against predation and other perils absorbs all available time and energy. In the kind of advanced industrial society in which such concepts as Management, Information Systems and Computers are usually assumed to apply, it may be suggested that survival is not the problem. However, one does not have to go very far away from the industrial society to see that survival in face of scarcity can be a problem for mankind. Extreme poverty and starvation can occur even if the fortunate many have concerns and interests other than the provision of basic food and shelter.

Comfortable survival may be the more typical condition, but it does not in any way invalidate the basic economic proposition. One important qualification is that the condition of scarcity is relative as well as absolute. Land and all natural resources are accepted as scarce in economic theory because they are virtually fixed in supply. Labour (the capacity for work) is not scarce because the population can grow as long as it has the means of survival, but the products derived from the use of labour and resources can be scarce in relation to the needs for them.

Needs, however, are whatever mankind determines they will be and needs will usually be greater than the resources available to meet them. If all our wants were magically filled today, then tomorrow we would want more, because needs are a matter of priority. Once the first priority is satisfied we adjust quickly to that as a normal condition and find some fresh need. If today's patterns of expenditure are compared with those of a generation ago, it will be found that the nature of 'consumption' (that is, the acquisition) of goods and services for personal use has changed enormously. (In economic theory the production of goods (tangible) and services (intangible) which results from economic activity is used for two purposes — consumption and saving, the latter linking with the creation of capital resources for further production.) Today it is poverty not to have a television set, or a car, or a centrally heated home. Yesterday it was luxury; the day before such luxuries did not exist. Through successive generations of development of industry and trade, these processes of expanding consumption and production have continued at varying but accelerating pace. Industrial society continues to drive itself onward, creating new technology and new products, solving old economic problems and finding new ones, but always offering more to consume. Yet more is demanded and the 'economic problem' does not become resolved; there is never any stage at which satisfaction is reached and we say "we have enough".

The Pressure for Economic Expansion

However, the purpose of these comments is not to consider the philosophical aspects of society nor to point a moral but to argue a third proposition: that modern economic society is driven by inescapable pressure to expand. Since, in a world in which natural resources are scarce the only way to expand production is to use those resources more effectively, the pressure is also there to be more efficient. It may seem paradoxical when labour is the one resource in ample supply that efforts to become more efficient should focus mainly on improving labour 'productivity' but, if it is recognised that 'labour' is a word for people who both work and consume, it should be apparent that, in the long term, the only way they can consume more is through working more effectively.

It may be argued (as has been in relation to the effect on society of the microprocessor) that we may expect to work less as we grow more prosperous; this argument extends to the fear that advances in technology will lead to a society in which unemployment is endemic because work is of no importance. The implication is that production will level off because all wants have been satisfied and further increases in economic efficiency will result in greater leisure.

In the history of industrial society, there is no evidence of this any more than there is evidence that the application of new technology has more than a transient effect upon employment levels. It is true that working conditions in general are less onerous than they used to be and that working hours in most industries and occupations are continuing to decline, but one will not find evidence that affluent industrial countries always choose leisure in preference to greater wealth. On the contrary, the preoccupation of modern economic society seems to be ever more strongly with growth. Anything less than rapid and continuous expansion of production has come to be regarded as economic and political failure and this is matched equally by the desires of individuals to consume more, and to acquire new and better possessions. Even were we to envisage a condition in which this momentum might slacken, we need only to contemplate the future perils of world over-population and the probable exhaustion of such vital resources as timber and hydrocarbon fuels to believe that there is no imminent possibility of any slackening in the economic drive.

Changes in patterns of consumption are partly a function of the economic advances and new technology which have brought new products within our means; some change is enforced because other goods and services are no longer produced. Work patterns are also different because new products are produced, new methods are employed and also because we are no longer prepared to undertake certain tasks or work under conditions which were acceptable to a previous generation. These changes in production and consumption are largely a consequence of more effective use of labour and also a cause of it because they fuel the pressure to find yet more efficient means of production.

It is a fine point of argument whether or not the chicken or the egg came first: whether technological advances such as the computer came to create fresh opportunities for better use of labour, or whether it was necessary to invent the computer because we could no longer continue as we had. This is all part of the continual process of change in a society moving always to a new base from which comparisons are made and which then becomes the springboard for a further leap forward.

This pressure to expand, improve and advance feeds on itself and — at least so far, in the 20th Century — has shown a tendency to acceleration in many aspects. The consequence has been that for most of us the personal survival objective is redefined as 'prosperity', and prosperity redefines itself with each generation at a higher level of production and consumption (figure 1).

We have, of course, been making work more 'effective' long before Adam Smith (who may be considered as the first economist) talked about division of labour as the way to improve productivity in his *Wealth of Nations* (published in 1776). With a few romantic exceptions, we accept the economic framework within which we live and our discontents spring rather from a view that production is insufficient, or that our share of it is less than we deserve than a belief that we should discard our machines and sophistication and go back to the simple life. Most of us do not need to be told that the 'simple life' would not support more than a tiny fraction of the world population.

Changes in UK, 1962 compared with 1984

	1962	1984
Car licences (millions)	6.6	15.7
Inland telephone calls (billions)	(1955) 4	23
Personal micro sales (millions)	nil	2.1
Video recorders (percentage of households owning)	nil	24

Figure 1   Expanding consumption

The Computer as a Means of Production

It is not the intention in this book to pass judgement on the working of economic systems, or to examine the structure and behaviour of those systems beyond that necessary to establish a link between the basic mechanisms of economic activity and the use of the ultimate business machine — the computer. It is also not the intention to provide a close view of the technology of computers and other business machines. The fourth introductory proposition, on which much of the content of this book is based, is that the computer is only important for what it produces. A prime objective is to root the understanding of computer-based business information systems in the real world of economic activities, to link the organisations, decisions and actions of which it consists with the economic principles from which they spring and with the consequences of the economic pressure continually to operate more effectively. In practical terms, we are concerned with business, with organisation, with information systems and with information technology.

Business: Organised Productive Human Activity

The Meaning of Business

In this book 'business' is defined as organised productive human activity. Business is extraction, manufacture, distribution and services; it is public or private, profit-making or charitable. It is equally appropriate to attach this label to a social club or a Government agency as it is to the activity of a sole trader or large multi-national public corporation; all are concerned with the organised productive human activity. Such apparently different business activities all have certain basic elements in common: they employ people and physical resources and they are concerned with how to use those resources. Whatever difference there may be in the nature or purpose of the business activity and whatever the 'mix' of resources and the method of allocating and using them, all businesses have objectives, organisation structures and information systems.

Objectives, Decisions, Organisation, Information, Systems

This brings us to a fifth proposition which supports the themes explored in this book. The aims, structure and activities of the business undertaking may be described under five related headings — objectives, decisions, organisation, information and systems — which will lead to an understanding of the relation between business management and computers.

The first thing to notice about modern economic society is that it is 'organised'. Each national economy can be seen as composed of a large number of business undertakings: separate (though often connected) structures which have been created to fulfil business purposes — which purposes can be expressed in terms of objectives. To achieve those objectives it is necessary to make (management) decisions; to make those decisions it is necessary to have organisation structures and information; to provide information and implement decisions it is also necessary to have systems.

These concepts are examined in detail, in turn: the nature of organisation structures, the concepts of management responsibility for decisions, and the theoretical and practical nature of business information systems. Following this examination it is then considered how the need to make decisions more effective in response to the pressures for economic gain leads business management to look towards machine systems.

Machines as the Key to Improvement in Business Systems

The final proposition offered in this introduction to the subject matter is that it is the machine which is the necessary key to improvement in business systems. The 19th Century Industrial Revolution was the product of mechanical engineering; the accelerated advances in the 20th Century have come mainly from automotive, electrical and chemical engineering. It is already clear that the economies in the first decade of the 21st Century will be dominated by micro-electronics, telecommunications and (probably) biochemical engineering. Throughout this period it has been largely the introduction of machines which has led to better systems, thence to more effective use of resources and greater production. These processes of change and improvement affect virtually every aspect of business activity and in very few of them is the computer now not a vital element. As a substitute for human or other machine actions, it has provided advances in economy, speed and accuracy in providing information for decision and action. It is tempting to see the invention and rapid development of the computer and other aspects of information technology as something which has appeared almost magically, and which provides an opportunity we only have to grasp to achieve a further revolution in our economic and social condition. The advance of computer technology itself, which brought an apparently abrupt transition from an idea of unseen power to one of universal availability, has added excitement and expectation of easy benefits, tinged with some apprehension about the resultant pace of change and its possible social consequences.

In looking at computers and other business machines in relation to management and information systems, we need to see all these matters in perspective and realise that it is neither chance nor inspiration alone that brings business efficiency, nor is the computer a magic device which gives the power to achieve the results we desire. To understand how we make use of information technology, we must understand also how business organisations and systems work, how we can improve existing systems and how we can create new ones by making use of business machines. In looking at such machines it would be wise to appreciate also that understanding the technicalities of the computer and its operation is not an end in itself. A computer is only useful for what it produces; it can only produce anything of value if its facilities have been chosen and the uses specified and implemented with the greatest care and understanding.

Management

Management has been identified as a key part of the subject matter because management is the function in business of making decisions and thence of determining what follows: how resources are used and what is produced. It is a management responsibility to define the nature of organisation and of systems and how they will operate. It is clearly also a management responsibility to decide why, when, and how to use a computer. If, therefore, those concerned with the management of business undertakings do not have sufficient understanding of computers to make sound decisions about them, there is little chance of achieving their objectives in a world in which the computer-based information system is becoming, above all, the essential business resource.

It also follows that those who have the technical responsibility for design, specification and operation of computer systems, as well as all those who are concerned with implementing business decisions as users of such systems, are themselves likely to be much more effective if they understand the objective, organisation, decision and information system context in which computer facilities are used. Modern business society no longer has room for unprofessional management or ill-informed operatives. The 'convergence' of technology which is a current theme in the world of computing has its parallels in the convergence of business skills, and one purpose of the treatment of business and technical subjects in association is to demonstrate that a sufficient understanding is not difficult to achieve if one sets out to obtain it. This means, among other things, looking behind the action and the decision, seeing these functions in their relationship with other activities and placing reality in importance ahead of theory. There is room and need for specialisation (and the management function itself is a form of specialisation) but general understanding must come first. We need to concern ourselves with what we can achieve with computers and how we can plan their use before acquiring proficiency in using key-boards or in writing computer programs. In this process towards a general understanding, the first question to ask is, "where are we going — what is the objective?"

Check List 1

An understanding of computer-based information systems must itself be built upon an appreciation of the fundamentals of modern business organisations and of how the objectives and requirements of such organisations lead inevitably to the need for ever more sophisticated business machines and systems for information and control.

Economic Propositions

The purpose of economic activity is to reconcile scarce resources and unlimited wants. We live in a demand-driven society.

Work is the most important human activity: the means of turning resources into useful goods and services.

Modern economic society is driven by inescapable pressure to expand, to be more efficient.

The key to economic improvement is effective information systems.

The computer offers a means of achieving greater efficiency but, like other machines, it is useful only for what it produces.

Key Words

Business: organised productive human activity.
Objectives: the expression of the business purpose.
Decisions: means of achieving business objectives.
Organisation: structures created to carry out business activities.
Information: necessary for decisions to be made.
Systems: the means by which information can be produced and decisions implemented.

Further Reading

Clifford, J., *Decision Making in Organizations*, Longman, 1977.

Creedy, J. *et al.*, *Economics — An Integrated Approach*, Prentice-Hall, 1985.

Harvey, J., *Modern Economics*, Macmillan, 4th edn, 1983.

Prest, A. R., *The UK Economy: A Manual of Applied Economics*, Weidenfeld and Nicholson, 1984.

Stanlake, G. F., *Introductory Economics*, Longman, 1983.

2 Objectives

Business Purpose

A business undertaking will be created and will exist for a purpose: to engage in a particular trade or profession, or to provide specified services or facilities. An airline, a bank, a confectioner, an architect, a local government authority, a tennis club, a dogs' home — each may be expected to have a definable set of purposes which give it a general identity and indicate the nature of its activities. Often these purposes will be identifiable from a written constitution which may both limit and protect the legal relationship with owners and with other organisations. Many business undertakings are formally identified by law; public bodies are generally created and governed by statute, private organisations such as registered charities and limited companies are required by law to declare their purposes and be bound by them.

The statutory basis may be more or less significant; in respect of business undertakings operating under the UK Companies Acts, the law permits the objectives to be framed in such a way that many businesses would appear to be able to do anything they fancy. This is not because business organisations are all wilfully amorphous or opportunist but rather because of an understandable desire to avoid constraints that would limit freedom to adapt to changing needs. The typical business does operate under a recognisable label and does behave consistently, although it is exceptional for large organisations to be tidily dedicated to a single purpose or confined to a clearly allied set of activities. Many organisations are in business to manage other businesses, often bringing together widely disparate undertakings. Local Government authorities are mixtures of quite separate activities too, many of which have as their only links that they are financed by taxation and operate in the same geographical area.

Knowing what it is supposed to be doing is obviously an essential prerequisite to understanding a business but (even where the 'label' is clearly legible) this recognition of its purposes will not necessarily go far to explain how a business works and why it behaves in a particular way. One must look at the business in detail and study its organisation, activities and information flows, its history and its relationships with other organisations.

At any one time, of the one-and-a-half million organisations which make up the United Kingdom economy some may just have been created, some may be thriving, others declining and some just on the point of expiry. If one were to look at a new business, it might be possible to see clearly that it had been created for a particular purpose and to relate all elements of the organisation and its activities to that purpose; for an established undertaking it is much more difficult, and one needs to try and see the present in perspective. It is rare to find a business concern which, having been created for a particular purpose, maintains intact its structure and identity as long as that purpose subsists and, when it is fulfilled, is quietly wound up. Business organisations grow and change, absorb and are absorbed by other businesses. They may change their names, their location and their activities. Some have huge populations of employees and great substance in assets and income, but most businesses are either very small and privately owned or are owned by other businesses. Many indeed are just 'shells', 'paper' companies or trade names with no resources or assets other than the names themselves.

In looking at the purpose of an organisation and trying to see where it is intending to go, one must take all these things into account. No organisation can escape its past. The great basic industries such as railways, steel, engineering and shipbuilding, which grew to immense size and power in the Western industrial countries in the Victorian era before settling into their present slow, agonising decline, are as much victims of the past as of the changing economic environment. However much those responsible for management of these industrial businesses may have expressed determination to take advantage of new technology and to change their products, techniques and attitudes, many still have found themselves trapped in the past. They remain influenced by the recollection of the heyday when visiting customers would tiptoe respectfully into dark-panelled, marble-floored entrance halls with their splendid model ships and engines in glass cases, an atmosphere which evokes tradition but which also clings to attitudes with the smell of a museum. It is an atmosphere which breeds caution and a reluctance to change or to face realities, particularly where those realities are grim.

Not all great industries from the beginning of the 20th Century are in decline, but all must be affected by their history. Even where a long-established business has been totally absorbed without apparent trace, the new organisation must itself be altered in some way by the process. There is not some peculiar biochemical effect on business through amalgamation or 'take-over'; the past retains its influence simply because a change of name, of ownership or of any other aspect of identity is rarely accompanied by a total change of people. People always carry with them their own experience with which they influence others, and this influence is probably one of the most important in determining the direction in which an organisation will then go.

In contrast, the new organisation in the new industry (and, often the established organisation in a new market) which has no constraint from experience or tradition may show radically different characteristics of optimism and enterprise, with a willingness to take risks and grasp all opportunities for change. Again, it will reflect the attitudes of the people who constitute its management and operating staff, whose primary aim will be to establish themselves in a flourishing environment. It is in these new areas that the momentum of growth is found, into which the new technology and the new methods are directed and which reflect the mainstream of economic activity.

Overall Objectives

What are objectives? Like all business concepts, objectives are seldom simple and unaffected by external factors and other secondary considerations. Having information about the purposes of a business gives some indication but does not explain why, of two similar businesses, one might be in collapse and the other thriving, or why adjacent Local Government authorities chose quite different kinds of vehicle for refuse collection.

The purpose of a motor manufacturer may be to produce and sell cars, but that is not the objective because it does not tell us whether there should be one or a million produced, or anything about the models, the prices, or any of the other plans and consequent actions which comprise the organisation's activities. An understanding of these matters can be grasped only through an identification of the business objectives: what it wishes to achieve through its activities (as a motor manufacturer) in quantity, quality, time, value or other measurable and recognisable form. By definition, an objective must be specific; otherwise there will be nothing to indicate when it has been reached. Moreover, if the overall objective is to determine all subsidiary decisions and actions, they themselves can be formulated with any precision only if they fit within the framework. This is the essence of the objective: that it identifies the framework within which all elements of the business will be defined and operate.

Objectives may be divided into two tiers: overall objectives which relate to the policy and general direction of the business, and secondary financial and physical objectives which are determined, at successively lower and more-detailed levels of management, in order to secure achievement of the primary overall objectives (figure 2).

These objectives may be categorised in a number of ways but there are five which seem to be of prime importance

- Profit
- Survival
- Expansion
- Equilibrium
- Continuity

Which of these is the most important is less easy to decide.

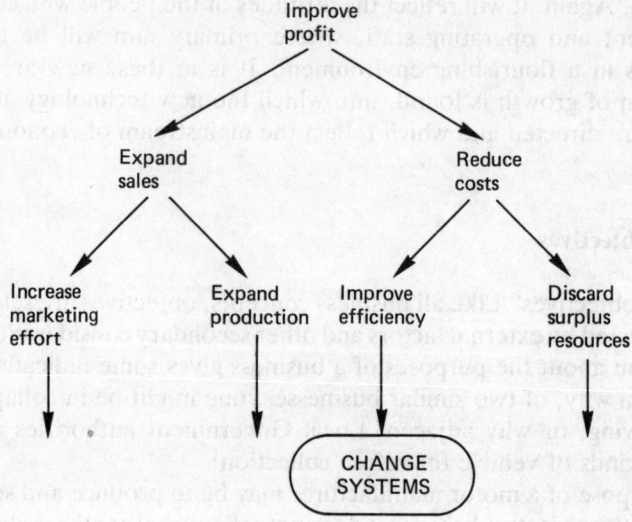

Figure 2   Objective 'tiers'

Profit

If a privately owned trading concern is used as an example of business undertakings, the first instinct is to identify the likely overall objective as profit. We do expect any trading organisation, whether public or private, to operate at a profit and the generation of profit is essential to the viability of all business undertakings.

An objective, to be meaningful, must be capable of clear definition and measurement; 'profit' by itself is too vague. If profit were defined as 'maximum profit' that might be sufficient, implying that every action by the organisation would be determined by its expected effect on profit. This could be seen as a likely objective of an entrepreneurial concern but it does not necessarily apply to all privately owned business nor, clearly, does it apply to publicly owned and 'non-trading' business undertakings which probably constitute a substantial majority of the organised business activity in a developed society.

We have to define the concept of profit further. Does 'maximum profit' mean immediate or longer-term profit? Will it mean maximising profit regardless of other consequences, or is there some qualification to the profit objective, some secondary objective which limits it? One can find plenty of examples of maximising profit. The 'pioneers' of property speculation of the 1960s who developed the techniques of 'asset stripping' (the acquiring of a business with the object of selling its assets as a more profitable course than keeping the business as a going concern) presumably were concerned more with profit than survival, as vanished enterprises and empty office blocks testified. Even some outstanding examples of sober trading respectability have decided that making a profit was more important than staying in business when they have found the value of their factory to be greater as a building site than as a going concern. It still is an accepted, although not always undisputed, business practice to abandon the purposes of a business and to sell its assets for their property value.

However, the kind of radical pursuit of maximum profit which involves the disposal of its assets is exceptional. If the objective is maximum profit in the long term, the ultimate intention may not be easily apparent because the route to maximum profit may involve the rejection of short-term gains. For most business undertakings one might conclude that, although profit has some part to play in the objectives, it does not dominate because behaviour is rather related to producing a more modest return.

Survival

The more usual situation is that profit is not the primary concern, and such actions as disposal of assets are more often the consequence of an external 'attack' upon the business rather than the means of fulfilling a declared objective. For the most part the profit objective is likely to be secondary, as a qualification of the principal objective.

It is more realistic to see survival as the main objective. This fits with the opening economic propositions that it is the intention to survive which provides the fundamental motivation for work, and only when survival is assured do we consider other, lesser objectives. Survival, of course, implies a minimal aim of financial viability for any organisation — making sufficient profit, generating sufficient funds to meet necessary expenditure. If any organisation cannot ensure that it has sufficient funds to meet current commitments, then its survival is at risk. The objective of survival, therefore, means that a business will take the decisions necessary to preserve its financial stability. It can also mean ensuring that the business continues to have some purpose even though its original purpose may be gone; this often explains why an organisation appears to change — to integrate, to diversify, to launch new products, to alter location or to adopt new methods. The business that is determined to survive will adapt to changes in its environment and make fresh plans to ensure that it will still exist. Such actions as reinvestment of surpluses in tangible assets (a term used in accounting for accommodation, equipment, vehicles etc. which are held for use by the business — a firm may also have 'intangible assets' in the form of debts owed and investments), introduction of new products or services, and amalgamation with or acquisition of other businesses are usually indications of a survival objective. Such an objective is also demonstrated by a tendency to be cautious and conservative, avoiding decisions which might place survival at risk.

It would be wholly exceptional for any organisation, from the smallest social club to the largest State-owned enterprise, to aim knowingly for liquidation or to accede readily to external pressures which might be seen to threaten its decline. One should not be surprised to find the instinct for survival, which is fundamental to our understanding of natural laws, to be equally applicable to man-made institutions. Most organisations are created without a finite life span in mind and, at any point in time, it usually seems more attractive to go on than to give up. If revenue is too low, it must be increased; if costs are too high, they must be reduced. Whatever the nature of the adversity, those responsible for the management of business affairs will usually try, like good military commanders, to put up a resolute defence. They are, after all, concerned not only with survival of the organisation but also with their own survival. Like generals too, business managers may struggle unsuccessfully, going down 'fighting against overwhelming odds' or prudently abandoning an indefensible position. There are few things which arouse such public fervour as the defence of a moribund bus service or theatre which has been threatened with extinction, or which excite the business manager into uncharacteristic optimism about his failing company's future as the news that someone else wishes to take it over. Had such interest in the survival of these organisations been shown at an earlier stage, perhaps the situations would not have arisen. Ironically, caution itself may be the cause of downfall; defending failure instead of reinforcing success, retrenching instead of innovating, saving instead of investing.

Expansion

Another common business objective which has some link with survival and profit, but yet clearly differs from them, is that of expansion. Expansion is one of the paths a struggling business may follow in seeking survival but it may be the dominant motive of a new business, of a mature but successful trading concern or of an organisation which does not sell its services at market price at all. Growth is a natural objective of organisations whose size and achievement can be measured in terms of quantity or value of output, of membership, number of outlets, or value of assets. It would be a rare curiosity to hear a sales manager declaring the undesirability of increasing sales next year or a financial manager seeking to avoid any increase in next year's profit. Not to do better than last year in many aspects of business is to be regarded as an unqualified failure deserving of condemnation.

Expansion is often also the primary objective in Government where the financial constraints which affect most other attitudes to objectives do not seem to apply. Government, of course, does suffer from the separation between financial and operational responsibilities in its organisational structure. It should not be surprising that its objectives are often concerned with expansion because the pressures upon Government services are almost always to expand — better hospitals, better schools, more pensions, more welfare services. Government services are largely an expression of individual needs, and there is no conceivable limit to our needs for these kinds of things, particularly where we do not pay for them individually and directly. Who would be prepared, personally, to declare a price for a life, or even a limb? Yet the economic reality is that we do, and we must because otherwise there is an implication that we can project longevity to infinity and compensate absolutely for any disablement. This is even beyond projecting the limit of personal wealth to absolute satisfaction because we probably can find someone who has reached that point. For most of us economic satisfaction is a long way off and even those who have enough to eat, a place to live and other reassurances of survival would still like motor cars, video recorders and personal computers; and if we have these things, we would like better ones.

Desire for material benefits, therefore, is behind the drive for expansion but it is not the only personal motivation with which it is fuelled. People are also concerned with status. Managers, even in an age of computers, often relate their importance to the number of subordinates (as well as to the size of their desks or cars). There is nothing which makes an employee so quickly dissatisfied with his wage as to discover that someone else is paid more. The North American ethic which argues the virtues of the biggest, fastest, highest and richest is probably only an exaggerated but honest expression of what society in general feels. Aggrandisement offers emotional as well as financial satisfaction for most people, and the motivation for corporate expansion often may be traced back to objectives of individuals within the organisations concerned. This helps to explain why growth in business sometimes appears to be pursued for its own sake. Once again we come back to the possibility that the origin of a corporate policy can be the personal objectives of those in control rather than an objective assessment of the organisation's needs by the management.

Equilibrium

The fourth of the principal categories of overall objective — achieving equilibrium — also reflects basic human attitudes in that people, generally, do not like change. They tend to prefer stability and security in their environment and although there is always pressure for change there is also a substantial desire for stability at any level of economic and social development. Paradoxically, it can be argued that the greater economic well-being in developed societies means that while there is a desire for stability within, external pressures become fiercer, threatening this stability. In this environment achievement of equilibrium becomes more important, indicating a lack of confidence that things will remain as they are and a consequent fear for continued survival.

Even where survival is not threatened, there is a natural tendency for the restoration of equilibrium to become a principal objective as a consequence of some imposed disturbance: business as usual after the fire or flood, replacing lost markets by opening up others, restoring reserves after a bad year. The concept of organisation itself implies an understanding of the importance of equilibrium: the balance of an organisation which aims to ensure that those who make its decisions are in control of events. If a business is perpetually off-balance, then it really has no objectives at all. Without equilibrium as a starting point it is much more difficult for conditions to be created for survival, expansion or profit.

Continuity

As with any systems concept, the four categories of overall business objective identified so far can be related and subdivided to serve many business situations. However, in the full sense of business covering all economic activities, there are also many situations which would not be clearly identifiable with these categories. A fifth category is needed which is identified under the heading of 'continuity'. Where there are no significant internal or external pressures to change direction and, specifically, where the nature of the organisation itself does not contain a dominating impulse to 'do better', the business may only look forward to a continuation of policies similar to those pursued in the past, with limited adjustment, sufficient only to remain 'on course'.

Continuity, like Equilibrium, is a much less overtly commercial objective than Profit, Survival or Expansion and may be inferred from the behaviour of a business organisation more often than it can be identified as the measured outcome of formal policy decisions. This would be appropriate for many social or Governmental bodies, or for other undertakings which have been created for specific purposes. For example, a sports club or a charitable foundation might see only a need to continue as before unless the fundamental purpose had changed or some event had occurred which threatened the ability of the organisation to meet its commitments.

The objective of continuity may apply also to a private trading organisation, at least for a time. The comfortably profitable organisation in a secure market might well be content to continue on its settled course, although continuity in that sense should more appropriately perhaps be called complacency; in few industries these days would it last very long.

The concept of continuity is, nonetheless, an element appropriate to many aspects of business planning and reflects the significance of experience within the organisation which often dominates management approaches at policy level. In the process of preparing annual financial budgets — a serious and important ritual in the calendar of all large organisations — there are few managers or accountants who would not be confounded if they could not look at last year's financial information before preparing their next year budget estimates. We all feel more confident if we have a reference point, so that we need only be concerned with deciding what difference there will be next year from this. When we have to build up a picture of the future from basic information, using our own judgement with no reference point to guide us, often we tend to flounder.

If there is a valid reason to assume that a present situation truly represents the business at optimum efficiency, and 'other things are equal', then continuity clearly is appropriate as a policy for the future. But the truth is that continuity is easier than another policy because it requires less effort, and because it is believed to carry less risk. Thus an organisation which is running at excessively high cost or is failing to exploit its potential market but is nonetheless viable, may not bother to look objectively at its performance; regarding itself as successful it may see continuity as the appropriate and inevitable objective to follow.

Objectives in Practice

These five, then — survival, profit, expansion, equilibrium and continuity — are the associated primary elements of overall business objectives, one of which may be dominant at any one time. It is possible to identify the theoretical concept by describing situations in which one objective dominates but reality tends to be blurred; the problem is to identify clearly what the objectives are in any business situation at any time. This is made difficult because many organisations behave as if the management themselves do not clearly understand where they are going. The objective behind a policy of acquisition of other businesses, for example, might be thought to be expansion (and expansion through acquisition is one of the accepted ways of achieving growth) but it might be used as a means of protection: in ailing industries to precede rationalisation, or as a defence against absorption by another organisation, by becoming too large a mouthful to swallow. Acquisition may also be directly related to a profit objective: acquiring assets which appear to be under-used with a view to their exploitation, or aiming to achieve a dominant market position from which monopoly powers could be exercised.

Another reason why objectives may not be readily indentifiable is that extremes are the exception. To say that survival is usually the predominant objective, for example, is not meant to imply that most businesses are avoiding insolvency only by judicious use of post-dated cheques and tax avoidance (although such practices are common enough) and, despite what sometimes is said, the great multi-national corporations are not dedicated to squeezing the last ounce of profit out of the unfortunate native populations on whom they batten. On the contrary, they tend to be singularly circumspect and altruistic in their behaviour in comparison with small organisations which have no public reputation to lose. Again, contrary to what we may read, Trade Unions are not solely dedicated to a ruthless pursuit of expanding membership and power. Generally speaking, business organisations in modern complex society tend to behave with moderation, simply because the external pressures upon them are such that any objective represents a compromise. Those responsible for business management see limits in the scope for expansion and dangers in over-reaching for objective goals. They see risks in total dedication to profit; even the largest organisation is usually conscious that circumstances could arise where complacency or recklessness might put survival of the business in jeopardy.

Individuals, of course, do behave recklessly and ruthlessly. It has always been possible for an individual to make a fortune, but not so easy for those who have some regard for the consequences of their actions upon others. It is not unknown for individuals in positions of authority in membership bodies and associations — with or without a charitable status — to use such influence for personal power and aggrandisement. These activities are usually an exaggeration of, or in complete contrast to, the identifiable objectives of the business organisations with which the individuals are associated. So, in studying the overall objectives which determine the succeeding stages of formulating detailed objectives, it is right to look first for ordered structure and rationality in policies, while having in mind that individuals may act foolishly or scurvily to frustrate these objectives by deflecting the organisation from its proper path.

In any consideration of the structure of business organisation (see chapter 4) it is important to recognise the differing influences of people who have some connection with the business — owners, employees, customers and suppliers — those who provide the business income, and those who derive benefits from it. Sometimes those who make the policy are also those who pay and benefit (directly or indirectly) as with the self-employed, taxpayers, and members of social clubs. Sometimes there is a clear difference of identity, and perhaps of interest, between these groups, as with political bodies, charities, and incorporated trading concerns.

Relationship between Business and Employee

This raises the question of the relationship between a business and its employees. It is said by some that the well-being of employees should be considered one of the overall objectives. Leaving aside the social and legal constraints which are imposed on all kinds of business today, this is a dubious proposition. Although a business undertaking may declare its dedication to the good of its employee, and overtly behave accordingly, such an objective is unlikely to be the prime consideration except in the coincidence of ownership and employment, as in a very small entrepreneurial business or closed society. The well-being of employees might be seen as necessary to the achievement of an overall objective such as survival or expansion but, by itself, would be as short-term as the maximising of profit, and probably anarchic and contrary to the basic business purpose. Certainly, assuming objectivity and rationality in the management of the business, its policy-makers will not set the objectives of individuals above those of the organisation where this might lead to instability or threaten survival.

Although it is argued that identifying overall objectives of a business is a key to understanding in more detail its policy and activities, it is an over-simplification to seek to explain all the actions of an organisation in relation to its own economic interests. The State, through its ownership or influence upon many of the United Kingdom's major national industries such as coal, steel, transport and agriculture, as well as through its policy on security of employment in major Government departments might, at first sight, appear to be making the welfare of employees the primary objective since it would seem that few of these industries could survive without substantial financial support from the rest of the community.

However, these are not so much an example of public altruism as a pointer to the importance of economic links between differing organisations and industries, and to the effects that they have one upon another. A business may have a separate legal and physical identity but cannot be considered truly independent where those who make its policy and determine its objectives are also closely involved with other organisations. Thus the State might decide to protect coal or agriculture from collapse because it sees the consequences of such failure, whether economic or political, to be greater than the cost of protecting an individual organisation. It will do the same for privately owned organisations where they are considered sufficiently important to have some impact on the economy. Private businesses will discard an activity or subsidiary function for the sake of the organisation as a whole, but will also protect unprofitable activities if they see them becoming viable in the long term.

Thus, we have four types of interest for consideration — of the business itself, of those involved in it (the employees and decision-makers), of the owners (the shareholders, the tax-payers or the members) and of those concerned with associated organisations.

So far, the examination of objectives has been confined to policy levels — provision of a framework for the general business activity. For a deeper understanding we have to look next at the consequences of overall objectives which give a practical shape to general policy and present each decision level with a clear set of requirements.

Financial Objectives

It is not always easy to identify which overall objective is dominant although it should not be too difficult to see that an organisation is surviving, in a state of equilibrium, expanding and/or profitable because this can be discovered by looking at its financial condition. In the achievement of any overall objective, finance is the primary expression and in any detailed examination of subsidiary objectives it will be seen that financial objectives are vital and specific for both central management and lower tiers of the organisational structure. Financial objectives are unquestionably more important than physical objectives for most organisations, not only because finance is such a useful and universal measure of an organisation's condition and activities but also because financial objectives for the business as a whole will be set by the highest level of management.

The principal financial objectives are identified in terms of relationships between income and expenditure, and between assets and liabilities at the start and end of each period of business activity. They can be seen in five aspects (see also chapter 5)

- Control of cash flow
- Containment of cost
- Achievement of budgets
- Increase in profit margins
- Maximising returns on investment.

Control of Cash Flow

Although its importance may not be immediately obvious, control of cash flow is properly regarded as the first financial objective to be considered. Cash flow is essentially the movement of liquid funds in and out of the business (figure 3). Any business needs cash to set itself up and to provide for expenditure on its operations. To have sufficient funds available to meet expenditure commitments is the basic essential for survival of any business. Since cash is useful only as a means of obtaining other resources, control of cash flow as an objective is essentially one of balance: to ensure that there is enough cash, but no more than is needed at the appropriate time. If, for example, the overall objective were to maximise profit, then the cash flow objective would be to achieve as great an excess as possible of incoming over outgoing funds in the planning period; if to expand, then cash flow policy would be to ensure that sufficient cash was available to fund the expansion in advance of future (expanded) income (see chapter 5 — Financial Accounting).

Containment of Cost

Containment of cost is a necessary part of control of cash flow; it can also be seen as one of the major aspects of financial objectives in its own right and, in

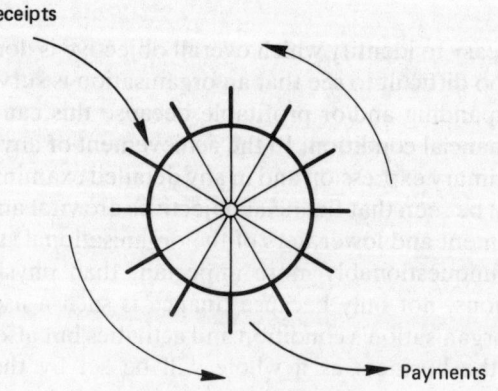

Receipts

Payments

Figure 3   Cash flow

most businesses, containment or reduction of costs will be a financial objective whatever the overall objective. Organisations of all kinds — manufacturing and distributing businesses, clubs and Government bodies — may be expected to be preoccupied with curtailing cost, in good times and in bad. The only notable exceptions are in general, when the economy as a whole is out of financial control and the value of money is falling fast through inflation, and in those favoured few industries such as entertainment, advertising and com- munications media where maximising revenue is more important than minimis- ing costs.

Uncontrolled costs tend naturally to increase; the categories of business which do not depend on profit to survive nominally include cost reduction in their financial objectives but often with insufficient determination to avoid natural increases in costs. Government-controlled bodies and monopoly suppliers of essential commodities and services offer notable examples. An equivocal approach to cost control is often evident also in general business organisations during periods of easy profit; a sudden catastrophic collapse into heavy losses by a well-known business following a change in the economic climate is usually a sign of laxity during the 'good times'.

Nonetheless, cost reduction is a necessary and desirable objective which will find a place in the financial objectives of all well-run organisations. The discipline of prudent and careful use of resources, like restraints in personal consumption, may require constant vigilance in the face of temptation but is much easier, and cheaper, than the 'crash diet' when the absurd wastage from plant closures and redundancies becomes unavoidable because of past profligacy.

Achievement of Budgets

Drastic measures, when cost reduction has become essential for survival, are less likely with non-profit-making organisations, which do not usually face such stark choices in achieving survival because they are influenced by differing criteria. The problem faced by local and national Government organisations is that they find themselves trapped in a cost–inflation spiral because it becomes argued that expenditure must increase each year to avoid an undesirable reduction in the output. They cannot go back without unacceptable political consequences, and each new level of expenditure and activity becomes a base from which there is further pressure to expand. In such organisations expansion tends to be the overall objective and achievement of the budget takes preference over cost control in the list of objectives.

The 'budget' is a financial plan which contains estimates of revenue and expenditure on business activities in the forthcoming financial period. The shape of the plan will be determined by the overall objectives, and the financial estimates contained in budgets will incorporate cash flow, cost control and profit elements as well as reflecting the profit or expansion aims. The concepts and application of budgets are examined more fully in chapter 5. Achievement of budgets as a financial objective means a successful fulfilment of financial plans within which all the operating activities are determined.

Increase in Profit Margins

Increasing profit margins as an objective is, by definition, particular to trading organisations. It does not apply just to private organisations because profit, as a continued positive cash flow, is not needed simply to provide dividends to shareholders. It is essential to meet interest payments on funds advanced to the business from other sources, in order to provide for replacement of assets and to finance expansion. Increasing profit margins may appear as a financial objective in State-owned businesses when interest rates charged for Government borrowing have increased, or where a higher return from a State Industry is considered necessary as an alternative to taxation. Nonetheless, the private organisation is more likely to be concerned with profit margins because the level of profit affects total worth of the business, and this will affect its ability to obtain further funds. A business undertaking which aims to maximise profitability or to expand must achieve increased profits or expectation of increase to fulfil either overall objective.

Maximising Return on Investment

Profit can be seen as the return on investment for the business as a whole or in relation to a particular project. Any organisation, whatever its activities and however owned or managed, must be concerned with the financial return to any investment it makes: any planned expenditure on assets which are to be used in the business would be justified only if the projected return from such investment is at a satisfactory level. One of the more discouraging indicators during the United Kingdom period of inflation and industrial decline in the 1970s was illustrated by the policy of the General Electric Company, which had seemed to demonstrate admirable control over its finances in contrast to many other major organisations, but decided to retain its accumulated large surpluses in 'cash' rather than reinvest them in business ventures. One must assume that this was because the projected return from any business ventures considered was less than that obtainable through the money market. Discouraging though it may be, where we ignore such considerations and emulate those who subsidise unprofitable enterprises or acquire assets for large sums with no prospect of a reasonable return on the investment made, then we are taking an ostrich-like attitude towards clearly defined financial objectives.

The return on an investment is the net benefit which is received as a result of committing given resources to a business venture. It is usually expressed as a percentage relationship to the cost of the investment (figure 4). The interest or dividend received by the lender or shareholder is a return on that investment. In the same way the cost of capital investment in machinery should be evaluated in terms of the net increase in revenue to the business which results

	Investment	Return
	Bank loan	Interest[1]
	Shareholding	Dividend
	Asset purchase	Net revenue increase
	Operating expenditure	Profit

· *Figure 4   Any investment seeks a return*

from that investment. The return to an investment does not have to be in cash or necessarily in any tangible form, although an appraisal is obviously difficult if such benefit cannot be quantified (see chapter 13).

Reconciling Financial Objectives

Any business is likely to have financial objectives under all five of these headings because these all reflect necessary aspects of financial control, whatever overall objectives the business may have. In practice one or other may be dominant but, like overall objectives, any attempt to identify clear-cut financial objectives immediately raises the question of overlap. However, it is not true that different financial objectives identified are all really aspects of the same thing. Consider for example, the question of size and efficiency. Cost reduction and increasing profit margins could be related to improving general efficiency, but they could also be related to excising unprofitable activities or to increasing prices. In many businesses, there is no better way of increasing profits than through first increasing costs: for example, by spending huge sums on advertising and promotion to achieve an even greater increase in revenue.

Quantitative Objectives

Volume

Although every part of an organisation will work within some financial constraint or towards some financial target, it is clearly valid to identify quantitative as well as purely financial objectives. For example, where expansion is the overall objective, a financial objective for the sales function might be expressed in terms of an increase in sales value during a particular trading period. However, in many organisations selling prices are determined by criteria outside sales control and, even where the value of money remains constant, sales objectives need to be defined at the operating level in quantitative terms — in sales volume as well as sales value. It is sales volume which truly identifies sales achievement and determines the resources it requires. It is also projected sales volume which will determine physical objectives and resource requirements for production or supply functions within the organisation.

Objectives for a production function will include financial (cost) elements but the quantitative objectives would again be inescapable. In production one talks about manufacturing or supplying given quantities, at particular costs, not the other way around. Financial and physical objectives are often likely to be related, sometimes one taking primary relationship and sometimes the other. Thus a cost-reduction objective might be expressed firstly as a financial sum which is then interpreted in numbers of people or quantities of material. An expansion objective might start as a volume of production or specification of a physical asset which has then to be priced to form a financial requirement. Restoring equilibrium equally might be mixed in financial and physical terms — changing costs and revenue structures, eliminating surplus resources, or improving systems.

Time

The concept of time as an objective is particularly applicable in project-oriented activities such as engineering, construction and many professional services. Time in such businesses not only determines the organisation and systems followed in handling projects, but also sets the framework for evaluating performance and may be decisive in its influence upon profitability or survival. Use of capacity is an equally vital consideration in businesses which operate at high levels of minimum cost, because the nature of the business requires heavy investment in fixed assets. Hotels are much concerned with occupancy, newspapers with number of copies sold, transport undertakings with load factors.

Capacity

Shipbuilding is a notable example from engineering and construction of an industry which is concerned with both time and capacity: failure to complete delivery of a vessel to the contract time and failure to obtain orders to fill empty construction capacity can be equally disastrous.

In these and many other types of business which provide capacity in advance of sales there will usually be a clear distinction between major objectives in the short and longer term. Organisations which use a high proportion of fixed assets would, in order to achieve an overall objective of expansion, become involved in long-term projects to expand capacity, in order to acquire new plants, new aircraft, etc. When this capacity becomes available — which might be a number of years later — the short-term objective then is to maximise use of this capacity. One does not necessarily follow the other nor is there always a conflict between long and short term objectives, although the one might involve future expansion and the other immediate contraction, or long-term dedication to profitability and short-term disregard of costs.

These elements of cost, volume, time and capacity are key aspects of business objectives which reappear again and again in more detailed questions of management decision-making, and in the design of business information systems.

Personal Objectives

Self-interest

Earlier in this chapter it was said that objectives are influenced by the attitudes and behaviour of people concerned with the business. A particular kind of personal influence is the individual or collective objectives of those in control. The singly owned and controlled entrepreneurial organisation is most likely to be concerned with maximising profit because that objective benefits the entrepreneur personally. The large organisation with separation of ownership and control is likely to aim principally for survival and growth, influenced by the personal interest of its managers who would have no desire to sacrifice their jobs to the greater profit of the owners.

In most business situations, organisational and individual objectives may be compatible but self-interest of the employee does not always coincide with that of the business. There can be substantial variations in attitude within the business undertaking; at one end there may be employees who do not see themselves participating in any benefit from the organisation's prosperity while, at the other, those in charge sometimes fail to distinguish between the company funds and their own purses.

There always will be some influence from individual objectives of individuals not employed by the business, whose personal aims again may be different from those declared for the organisation itself. These influences offer an explanation of the sometimes quixotic or contradictory behaviour of businesses when they act apparently against their own primary interest. Government bodies and social organisations, for example, are particularly susceptible to the influence of special interest groups which may be able to push an organisation in a particular direction because those exerting influence are vociferous and the mass of people (voters or members) are passive.

Motivation

We have to understand people as they are if we are to understand business management and systems, and where we generalise we must also qualify, recognising the range of possibilities and investigating before reaching conclusions. This is no more to suggest that everyone has his 'hand in the till' than to believe that all in positions of authority are guided by altruism and other moral principles. The theories associated with economics, business management and design of systems provide a framework within which the varieties of human behaviour may operate. Thus economic consequences vary, decisions are not always consistent and systems represent a compromise. One word often used in management theory to embrace the variations in human behaviour in business situations is 'motivation'. Why do people urge their own ruin, or work themselves to death for no apparent reward, or otherwise behave rationally or irrationally according to our individual viewpoints? The answer, if it is to be found, lies in that very proposition that people do not all see things in the same way: their 'motivation' will differ.

One of the secrets of successful business is the common identification of all employees with the corporate objective, so that everyone aims in the same direction. Ownership, management, operations ('the work force') and the external environment ('the general public') do not have to exist as separately defined and incompatible groups, with distinct and conflicting interests, and it is an essential feature of modern managing practice that proper attention is given to motivation through the careful cultivation of good public and employee relations.

Determination of Objectives

So far this subject has been taken largely from the viewpoint of an observer, looking at a business organisation from the outside, attempting to identify its objectives and, from that, to understand the way the business is conducted. It is desirable to look also from another viewpoint: that, as a matter of principle, a necessary element of business success is to set a clear objective. It is not enough, for example, to have a general intention to expand. To be able to establish that an objective has been achieved, it must itself be clearly defined, quantifiable and understandable to all concerned. Thus, expansion might be defined in terms of an amount of revenue to be earned or a number of members recruited by the end of the planning review period. From this specific objective, secondary objectives should be identified and thence the resource planning and work allocation.

However, in the general setting of human activity, as one would expect, this is an over-simplification. Boards of Management do not sit down with blank sheets of paper to decide what their objective shall be. The determination of objectives is the sum of influences on attitudes of those involved in the management process, with a leavening of facts about internal and external situations which create a mixture of the subjective and objective. Assuming, for the sake of illustration, that the process of arriving at the overall objectives culminates in a formal decision at a meeting of a Board of Management or other highest level of executive authority, that decision will be affected by any combination and degree of the following influences

- The experience, nature and attitudes of those making the decisions
- The previous policy and policy-making environment of the organisation

- The existing objectives
- The current and historic performance of the business
- Information about external influences on the organisation.

Many overall planning decisions are enforced: a consequence of present circumstances of the business. Survival and restoration of equilibrium are most likely to be reactions to unfavourable influences. Even plans for improved profitability by a confident management looking forward to another good year are often a question of momentum — of continuity, rather than deliberate policy. It is many times more difficult to formulate a coherent long-range corporate plan if one does not have access to the previous plan; the past always exerts a powerful influence.

These are not to be regarded as acceptable situations even for a business which seems to be tackling its problems and facing its prospects sensibly, because there is an implied unnecessary lack of control over events. The determination of objectives has to be made with an understanding both of what is achievable and what is desirable, and furthermore, that understanding should arrive from an appreciation of the strategic aims of the business.

The creators of new businesses — the entrepreneurs or the State — set up their organisations because they identify a market or a need which they believe they can fulfil. They decide upon the aims and bring together the resources they think will be required to achieve those aims. Initial aims are not necessarily precisely determined unless the organisation is intended to have a determinate life; the great majority of businesses are created with the assumption that they may last for ever and the aims indicate a direction if no ultimate destination. The objective, which follows from relating those aims to an appreciation of the current position of the organisation, provides that destination. Usually this destination is only a point on an unending journey, a staging post sufficiently far ahead for practical planning, and sufficiently close to be identifiable and attainable.

Short and Long Term Objectives

In reality, the period to which one looks ahead may vary considerably between one kind of business and another and, for any organisation, there may well be both long and short term plans, representing strategic and tactical objectives. In business one needs to look sufficiently far ahead to consider the outcome of today's decisions or, looked at in another way, to make sure that vital decisions are not neglected because of lack of foresight.

It is said that it takes about seven years or more for aircraft manufacturers to progress from the original concept to the introduction of the new aircraft into operational service. If so, it means that much of the aerospace and air transport industries needs to be looking at least that far ahead: probably longer, since the success of a new aircraft project is determined not only by how many will be bought in seven years time but also how long after that it will be before it is superseded. In forestry, the classical illustration of long-term investment, the period to maturity may be twenty to fifty years; in manufacture of personal computers, a contrasting example from contemporary industry, a new business venture may germinate, blossom and wither in the space of little more than a year.

From these three illustrations it must be evident that there is no universal optimum planning period and, in practice, an organisation needs two complementary approaches to planning. The first is to set long-term objectives relevant to current aims and expected conditions and to the nature of resource-planning decisions. The second is to have a regular pattern of periodic reviews covering the longest manageable period of business activity. This regular review pattern is usually a year, for the obvious reason that the year is the basic cycle of seasons, of trade, of social activity and of legal requirements which affect business. That does not prevent a review of change of direction within the period but business life cannot be only a matter of looking ahead when circumstances demand or of reacting to crises. There must be an ordered approach to business management at the very highest policy level as well as in day-to-day operations.

Some of the essentials for effective business operation can, therefore, be summarised as follows. Those responsible for a business must

- understand why the business was created
- know what it is trying to do
- understand what is required to achieve those aims
- determine objectives compatible with the aims, resource requirements and conditions affecting the business
- within the overall objectives, determine financial and physical objectives appropriate to each organisational and decision level
- undertake appropriate planning reviews to ensure that objectives continue to be desirable and achievable.

Check List 2

The objectives of a business undertaking determine its activities and, from this, its information requirements. The activities of any business need to be seen as patterns of decisions to meet the objectives, for which information is required.

Finance is the key element in organised activities, but profit is not always the main business objective nor are all objectives necessarily financial.

Overall Objectives
Profit.
Survival.
Expansion.
Equilibrium.
Continuity.

Financial Objectives
   Control of cash flow.
   Containment of cost.
   Achievement of budgets.
   Increase in profit margins.
   Maximising return on investment.

Quantitative Objectives
   Volume, time and capacity
   Meeting commitments.
   Fulfilling demands.
   Completing projects.

Personal Objectives
   Motivation.
   Special interests.

Factors in Determination of Objectives
   Experience and attitudes of decision-makers.
   Previous policy.
   Existing objectives.
   Business performance.
   External influences.

Further Reading

Clifford, J., *Decision Making in Organizations*, Longman, 1977.
Drucker, P., *The Practice of Management*, Heinemann, 1955.
Savage, C. and Small, J. R., *Introduction to Managerial Economics*, Hutchinson, 1967.
Torrington, D. and Weightman, J., *The Business of Management*, Prentice-Hall, 1985.

3 Management and Decisions

Functions of Management

In order to achieve the objectives which have been declared necessary to the business purpose, decisions must be made. Making these decisions is an essential function of management. The decisions which determine the objectives in the first place are, of course, a primary responsibility of management at the highest level. They will be formulated at policy level by Boards of Management, and then interpreted and refined as practical financial and physical objectives in strategic and tactical plans by managers responsible for functional and departmental matters.

The kinds of major decision which represent the principal functions of management may be grouped under four headings

- To direct and control the use of resources
- To plan future activities
- To improve the effectiveness of the business
- To link the business with its environment.

Direction and Control of Resources

This is probably the most easily recognised management function, associated with allocation of work and the subsequent action to make sure that it has been accomplished properly. These functions are most readily illustrated by duties such as those of foremen and office managers in direct control of groups of people undertaking manual or clerical tasks. They apply equally to the supervisory function of a Chief Executive in relation to the next reporting level of senior management or to the Sales Manager's responsibility for sales representatives.

Direction and control responsibilities include such matters as providing precise instructions for carrying out a job, monitoring progress as the work is carried out, providing guidance and corrective further instructions, and applying disciplinary measures when instructions are wilfully disobeyed. They include also the important aspects of human relations in business undertakings: of providing help and encouragement and resolution of problems to assist motivation and create a suitable work environment.

30

Comparable responsibilities for direction and control apply to resources other than labour: to machines, accommodation, vehicles, materials for processing, tools and all kinds of other equipment and facilities — to everything used by a business in the production of its goods and services, including information. If any of these resources is idle or misused, it will make the business less effective and imperil achievement of its objectives, and it is a necessary management function to ensure that this does not occur.

Resources which are used by a business include those hired from other organisations as well as those which it owns or of which it is the main or sole employer. A business may use a consultant or contractor as a cheaper, or otherwise more suitable means of achieving an objective than employing its own resources; in some situations, the entire responsibility for managing a business undertaking may be contracted out to another organisation. However, this does not mean an abandonment of management responsibility or removal of the necessity for decisions about direction and control; it simply means that the way it is done is different from the approach adopted for activities which are wholly within the business itself.

Planning Future Activities

Present activities usually are determined by previous planning decisions. Long-range planning — provision of new plant, accommodation, development of new services and creation of new products — may take several years, committing the business in terms of capacity well in advance of actual requirement. Five years would be a typical period for long-range planning in many organisations; for large capital projects such as new aircraft or power stations, the planning period may be much longer. The financial planning associated with allocation of physical resources is, in most businesses, an annual cycle. Within overall plans, there are necessarily detailed adjustments at shorter and shorter periods and one can find many examples of more immediate planning decisions, from day to day, or hour to hour, as one gets closer to the actual direction and control of resources.

Because long-range planning decisions involve anticipation of remote future events, they are necessarily more difficult than short-term decisions. They also carry more risk because they must be made with less factual information, and hence with more estimation and assumption. At the start of the long cycle of development such as that for a new type of civil aircraft there will be basic planning decisions which could be of fundamental importance to all the main parties involved — both to the aircraft manufacturer and to the customer airlines. From a knowledge of current and past conditions in the aviation business, those responsible for planning make forward projections of traffic and operating conditions which lead to conclusions that a vehicle of a particular capacity and characteristics will meet a market need by the time that it could be in service. The manufacturer will attempt to reduce his risks by seeking acceptance of a design from prospective purchasers before any significant investment is committed, but must still accept the chance that the new aircraft may not be sold in sufficient numbers to recover the initial investment. For the customer, the risk is that the aircraft will prove unsuitable or unnecessary when it is eventually brought into service a number of years later. No more telling example can be found in recent years than that of supersonic passenger travel, but even this type of problem probably offers more choice of courses of action than commitments to construction of such facilities as bridges, docks and power stations, in the use of which there is very little choice. It is no coincidence that high-risk capital projects tend more and more to be the decisions of Government, in which the consequences of planning failures do not fall on the planners.

It would give a misleading impression merely to illustrate the importance of planning by reference to the dire consequences of bad planning with major high-risk capital projects. The absence of any planning is likely to bring much more serious risk than would the possibility of drawing wrong conclusions if a planning process had been carried out.

In this examination of business information systems one of the arguments is that there are no 'good' or 'bad' computers, or 'good' or 'bad' computer users; there are good or bad business systems and good or bad investment and implementation plans. In any situation, an instinctive or routine response is appropriate only if all elements in that situation are familiar, and wherever decisions are related to situations which contain new factors — and that applies to most business activities — then planning is a prerequisite even if it involves no more than making a list of tasks to be carried out.

Planning both precedes direction and is a consequence of it at successively lower levels of management decision. At the highest level, the Executive Board will (in association with its decisions about the principal business objectives) make major strategic decisions about the resources that must be available within the short and long term to support the corporate objectives. At the next management level, shorter-term planning decisions will be made to meet 'departmental' objectives. These plans will then be referred further down to the level of individual operating units.

The significance of planning is the extent to which it commits an organisation to subsequent actions and to consequences which become unavoidable. Planning is a matter of considering differing courses of action and evaluating the possible outcome of each. It is also concerned with inaction: consideration of what may happen if no decision is taken to change the present course. In other words, planning is the prerequisite of taking decisions at the right time both as a reaction to events and, wherever appropriate, as an anticipation of events.

Improving Effectiveness of the Organisation

It may be accepted as axiomatic that it is a general management responsibility to run a business effectively, which will be achieved through the quality of decisions about planning, direction and control. This proposition goes farther: that it is a principal function of management, in the context of the economic society in which we live, to improve the effectiveness of the organisation. Any business undertaking which is content with its situation and which sees no possibility of improving performance is potentially moribund. Although a business may achieve its immediate target objective of profitability, equilibrium or growth, it always will be in a position to seek further improvement in its performance. This is a logical consequence of a concept of business objectives which generally demand some improvement over the present situation; it is also a practical necessity if a business is to protect itself from unforeseen future unfavourable factors. If we do not exercise our minds and bodies, they decay; so do our institutions if we do not constantly revitalise them. In the economic world, business organisations (with a very few exceptions) are subject to external pressures more likely to be unfavourable than favourable whether they be economic, legal, social, political, climatic or simply the consequence of business competition. In the natural world, some of these arguments may be difficult to sustain but 'planning' and 'management' are not natural functions and it is because we seek to oppose the operation of 'natural' laws that we must strive for improvement.

Management, by definition, must be good management and therefore it is prudent to assume that any situation is capable of improvement. Management functions should always include the requirement to seek reductions in cost, improvements in revenue, better service standards and other advances which will help to ensure that objectives are met. The fact that such an objective as survival may be a consequence of failures in planning or lack of will to improve effectiveness does not mean that these are not essential functions; on the contrary, where an unsatisfactory situation can be traced to management decisions, it is a clear demonstration of their importance.

Linking the Business with its Environment

It is a function of management to identify, evaluate and anticipate any direct and indirect external influence which might have some bearing on objectives, decisions or organisation. Because information about external factors is inevitably more difficult to obtain than information arising directly from businesses' own activities, external problems can be much more influential and much more dangerous than internal problems.

Environmental links concern Government and society in general, and suppliers and customers in particular (figure 5). Any business is ultimately dependent on its 'customers' whether they are buying goods or services, paying subscriptions or taxes; anything which affects the behaviour of those customers is of vital concern to the business (a basic fact of business life which is forgotten far more often than it should be). People will choose between suppliers of umbrellas because of such considerations as price and quality but they will decide to buy umbrellas because of the weather, or because of the choice made

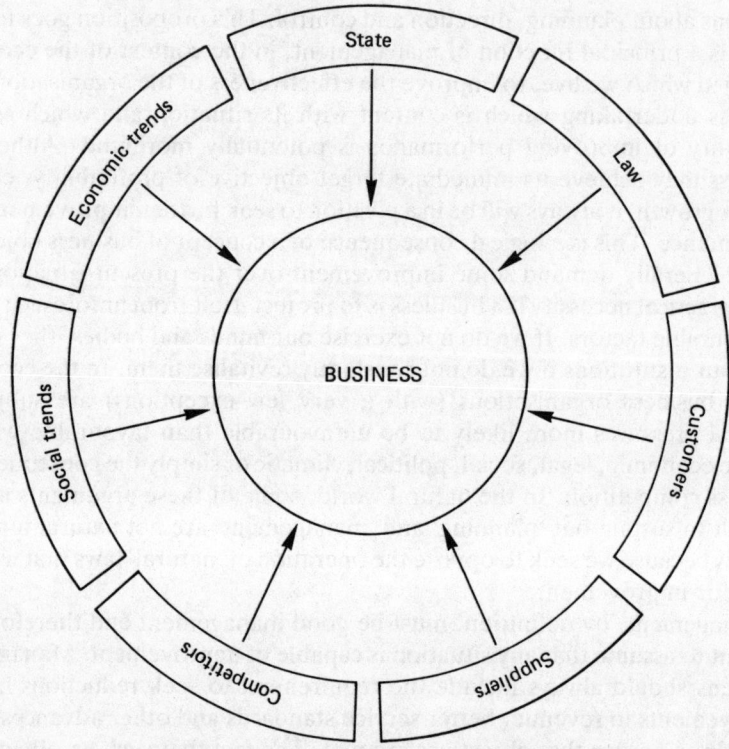

Figure 5   The business environment

by leaders of fashion. Price and quality themselves are not solely within the influence of suppliers. Price may be influenced by taxation or by external influences on cost of manufacture; quality may be influenced by these and by constraints related to health or other matters of public interest.

As with all business decisions, it is not enough to react to such external factors when they arise; management attention must be directed constantly towards the environmental relationship. Marketing and Public Relations functions are created to improve and strengthen links with customers; solicitors and other professional advisers are employed to provide protection against legal and social hazards. Management responsibility in relation to the environment is not simply to create an appropriate interface; it is concerned also with the vital question of information. The business needs to know what is happening outside, so that it can protect itself from and adapt to any environmental changes which may have bearing on its objectives.

Strategic Decisions

The management responsibility for these four key functions is essentially fulfilled through the making of decisions. Necessarily those decisions closest to the prime objectives of the business — the strategic decisions which will have significant effects on the resources and goals — are the most important and are likely to be taken at the highest levels of management. To create new production facilities, to launch new products or services, or to change the objectives of the business itself are significant in terms of the ultimate effect on business activities and of the time span. This is so both in the sense that major planning decisions may take a long time before coming to fruition and in that the consequences of such decisions are felt long after they have been implemented.

The installation of a computer system provides an example of both aspects. Planning for a major new installation of computer facilities may take considerable time to progress through the stages of feasibility study, system design and implementation. Such a prolonged planning process, combined with the disruptive effect where the new systems and procedures are materially different from the old, argues for a reasonably long life for the new system. This is so that the effect of change can be absorbed and the new system reach its full potential, and because further change within a short period might well be too difficult to accept.

Major business decisions such as the removal to a new location or substantial change in marketing strategy cannot be undertaken lightly because they also have lasting impact. Whatever may be the theoretical logic of business mergers or reorganisation of public authorities, the reality is often that it takes a very long time indeed before the new (larger) whole has become more efficient than the (smaller) separate parts. (The effects of change in business organisation and systems are discussed in more detail in chapter 7.)

The strategic decisions are important not only in themselves but also because of the many associated major and minor decisions which will be involved — the build-up of planning processes and the break-down of policy decisions to the subsequent 'action' decisions at various management levels (figure 6). It is no part of this thesis that major planning decisions may be accepted as a result of entrepreneurial flair or may be treated more lightheartedly than projected 'bicycle sheds' because they are more difficult to understand. No business decision, and least of all major strategic decisions, should be seen solely as the actions of individuals; on the contrary, a substantial proportion of the typical business organisation structure, of the external services on which it draws, and of the information systems it creates may be concerned wholly with supporting the making of these decisions.

Tactical Decisions

In the sequence of decision-making, planning obviously comes first and then, from the policy decisions, subsequent action decisions are made, working their way down through the management and operational structure to create the ability to comply with policy and put it into effect. In their relevant context, management action decisions concern what to buy, to make, to stock and to

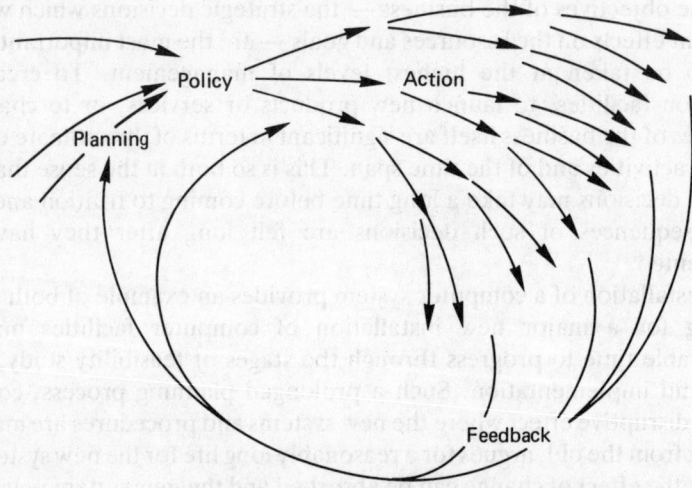

Figure 6   Information flows

sell. Allied to these are 'qualitative' decisions about how much to pay and how much to charge, when to take action and where. The enabling decisions also include those determining what systems and methods to use to carry through the other decisions, bringing in the functions of direction and control of resources and also those aims to improve the effectiveness of the organisation.

Decision-making, however, is not simply a sequence of planning, policy-making and on through various stages of operating decision to action. That would be so if everything went 'according to plan' and there were no external influences, imponderables or unexpected events on the way. The reality, of course, is quite different and much of the management process is concerned also with reactive decisions. These may relate to matters which could not have been dealt with at earlier planning stages because insufficient was known at the time, or because an unexpected event has meant that previous decisions can no longer be implemented. In many businesses, and at many management levels, resolution of immediate problems can become the dominant activity, depending on the nature and importance of such problems, and may itself make special demands upon the organisational structure and activities of the business.

Throughout this examination of information systems and the application of business machines we have come back to one familiar proposition: that management of business activities always concerns people, and therefore must take account of human behaviour. Although we may look forward to reaching total reliability and efficiency in machine elements of many business systems, we cannot entertain the same expectation of people because human behaviour must always, in some respect, remain unpredictable. Some management decisions, therefore, will be in reaction to unexpected events. Naturally, to the extent that planning decisions and the operating decisions which arise directly from them are well founded, the number of reaction decisions will be fewer but the well-run business will still plan for contingencies so that there are ready-made solutions to a range of possible problems.

Decision Processes

It is a common and quite false assumption of those awaiting anxiously the outcome of business decisions that they can be self-fulfilling or always followed by immediate implementation. It is often also assumed that business decisions are usually personal, associated with direct instructions. Some decisions may be described in this way but most will be part of the framework of rules and procedures within which the business operates. Some decisions may be conditional upon others, some may be taken as a matter of course — except where an explicit, countermanding decision is made. Much of what occurs in a business undertaking is a matter of routine because most business activities involve specialisation in a particular field and consequently some element of repetition.

Delegation

The logic of attempting to improve business effectiveness will lead to creating a framework of routine activity within which the organisation can work, and to the delegation of responsibility for lower tiers of decision. Such delegation may be quite substantial — as, for example, with the subsidiary companies of a financial holding group. Such subsidiaries may operate as if they were independent organisations, constrained only by some overall financial objectives. Even within tightly organised business structures it is usual to delegate responsibility for decisions to the point at which appropriate information is available and resulting action can be taken. It can be a serious impediment to the achievement of objectives if responsibility for decision-making is retained at too high a level. Substantial delegation of decision authority or complete freedom within very broad limits is not necessarily always desirable or beneficial, but there is no doubt that concentration of decision-making above and apart from operating levels can lead to substantial loss of flexibility and efficiency.

Operating Decisions

Making decisions which determine the success of a business in achieving its objectives is an essential characteristic of management activity, but decision-making is not confined to management. Every job or process can be seen as a series of decisions and even at the lowest levels of skill and experience decisions are being made constantly. They may be circumscribed by limits imposed at higher management levels in the form of rules and procedures, or of direct instructions, but there is no situation involving human labour which does not also involve some operating decisions. Driving a vehicle, controlling a machine, typing a letter, answering a telephone — all these involve a range of operating decisions between the basic decisions to start and to stop. The significant elements for consideration are that there is a choice, and that the requirement and opportunity for decision-making in exercising that choice at the operating level creates also the opportunity for error, for misunderstanding, or for some other cause of system deficiency or failure. This sense of choosing between different courses of action with certain knowledge and certain constraints is a description applicable to both operating and management decisions, and the difference between them is really somewhat blurred.

Perhaps the characteristics which most clearly distinguish the management-decision function are the greater consequences of the decisions and the higher ratio of decision-making to action. However, that is really not quite enough. The decisions by the airline pilot and the railway signalman, in carrying out their own duties, can have disastrous consequences, but we would not regard them as having managerial functions. On the other hand, the supervisor of cabin stewards or of railway booking clerks would certainly be seen in that light. The supervisor of only one or two people holds managerial responsibilities because he is concerned with direction and control of some part of the organisation's resources. The operating decision does not involve going beyond previous decisions; the signalman, for example, is not allowed to decide to bring in extra help or to use more material resources than those provided with the job. The clerical supervisor may be empowered to do so.

In looking at the 'planning' and 'improving' functions of management, the distinction between management and operating decisions is much more clear cut. The operator may have some limited scope to plan his own work and may elect to seek means of improving his own performance, but only if these clearly have some impact on the activities of others could they be classed as managerial in any sense.

A particular characteristic of the operating decision which will distinguish it from most management decisions is its timing: it will usually immediately precede the action. In contrast, the majority of decisions under the four management function headings will be separated clearly in time from the actions which flow from them.

Check List 3

To achieve objectives which have been identified as necessary to its purpose, business managers must make decisions. The activities of every employee can be expressed in terms of decision; at the highest level of management these will be strategic planning decisions related directly to the principal objectives of the business.

The Functions of Management
    Direction of control of resources
    Planning future activities
    Improving effectiveness of the business   }   Making decisions.
    Linking the business with its environment

Management Decisions
    What to buy, make, stock, sell.
    How much to pay, to charge.
    What systems and methods to use.
    What resources to acquire, dispose, use.
    Resolving problems.

Further Reading

Appleby, R., *Modern Business Administration*, Pitman, 1981.
Arnold, J. and Hope, T., *Accounting for Management Decisions*, Prentice-Hall, 1983.
Clifford, J., *Decision Making in Organizations*, Longman, 1977.
Cooke, S. and Slack, N., *Making Management Decisions*, Prentice-Hall, 1984.

4 Organisation

Organisational Theory

The term 'organisation' implies an ordered structure. The starting point for examining this aspect of business management is that the achievement of objectives is much more likely where there is definition of tasks, allocation of responsibilities for decision and action, combined with effective communication to provide a flow of information between the decision/action points. Because a business undertaking usually finds itself involved in repetitive activities, it will discover that it can benefit from making use of knowledge, experience and skill to further its objectives. The disorderly mob is rarely likely to achieve a constructive result because without organisation there is no clear understanding of responsibilities, no ordered flow of information and no leadership. If there is no continuity or consistency of purpose or action, there is no accumulation of the kind of knowledge and skill which can improve effectiveness in use of resources. In carrying out the management function of optimising this use of resources, therefore, a first step must be to devise an organisation structure which will make possible a formalised relationship between decisions, action and information flow.

The organisational structure of a business obviously will be influenced by its purpose and its objectives, as well as by external constraints such as the legal framework, social conditions and conventions, and its relationship with other businesses in the 'market place'. However, there are similarities in principle between organisational structures which apply regardless of their purpose and objectives. The smallest organisational unit — the 'one man business' — may have no definable organisational structure but will, or should, have some organisation of activity. There should be some ordered division of work periods into segments, in each of which there is concentration on a particular task to produce ordered and disciplined use of time, and to gain the benefits of repetition.

A business which has several employees will tend to allocate its work so that each person assumes a different responsibility: the larger the business the further break-down of the organisational structure will be found desirable. This subdivision usually will be by function to exploit the benefits of specialisation: the use of skill, experience, work simplification and mechanisation to make more effective use of the resources available.

From the organisational viewpoint, this concentration into functional subdivisions is also advantageous because a limited range of activities in each section facilitates easier control and communication, fitting conveniently and logically the principal functions of management. As an organisation grows larger it tends to develop an 'inverted tree' or hierarchical structure as each functional subdivision splits at successively lower management levels into smaller units embracing the different functions (figure 7). In charting this tree structure one can visualise the grouping of activities and the management decision-making and information flow chains down through the hierarchical structure from the highest management level to the lowest.

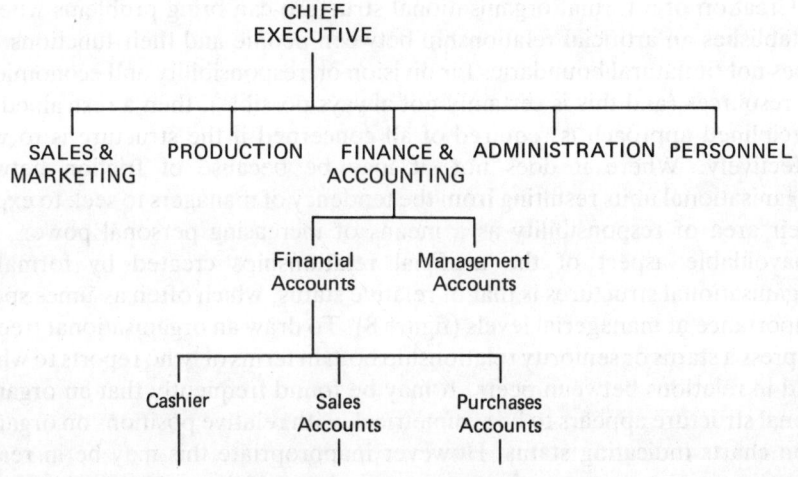

Figure 7   Organisation tree

To determine organisational structure simply by bringing like tasks together is not enough to ensure efficiency, effective control or good communication. Too many tiers lengthen the management chain and bring inefficiencies through communication failures. Too few may weaken management control. There needs to be a balanced relationship between the number of 'chiefs' and 'indians'. At the highest level of the typical management hierarchy there will be a Chief Executive to whom a number of senior managers of different functions reports directly (for example, Accounting, Production, Personnel, Sales and Marketing). Given that one of the principal functions of a Chief Executive is to control the activities of subordinates, the number of those subordinates will itself be significant. If there are too many, there will be no possibility that the Chief Executive can pay proper attention to their activities; if there are too few, then there might be so much attention given that the subordinates could not work effectively.

The organisation structure must also place the point of decision at the right level. However appropriate an organisation may appear in theory, it will not work in practice unless it balances the relationship between decision and action. Thus, allocating responsibility for direction and control of resources within a given departmental unit will be pointless unless the manager also has been given the authority necessary to carry out those functions. The manager who has not been given authority to spend money cannot be given the responsibility for saving it; similarly, the manager who does not have authority to appoint his own staff cannot be held responsible for recruitment failures. It is not only a question that the authority given should be commensurate with the responsibilities but also that those concerned should be aware of both; the 'job description' is always necessary not just for contractual reasons but so that people can understand their place in the organisational structure.

Creation of a formal organisational structure can bring problems where it establishes an artificial relationship between people and their functions. If it does not fit natural boundaries for division on responsibility and economic use of resources (and this is certainly not always possible), then a restrained and disciplined approach is required of all concerned if the structure is to work effectively. Where it does not, it may be because of friction between organisational units resulting from the tendency of managers to seek to expand their area of responsibility as a means of increasing personal power. One unavoidable aspect of the artificial relationships created by formalised organisational structures is that of relative status, which often assumes special importance at managerial levels (figure 8). To draw an organisational tree can express a status or seniority relationship both in terms of 'who reports to whom' and in relations between peers. It may be found frequently that an organisational structure appears to be symmetrical, with relative positions on organisation charts indicating status. However inappropriate this may be in reality, there is often also pressure for symmetry in terms of the numbers of employees grouped at various reporting levels (the larger the department, the larger the responsibility). It is necessary to take account of attitudes, to make sure that individuals are satisfied that they have the authority they need and that the boundaries of that authority are set appropriately. Everyone expects to be treated equitably in relation to others, although this should not mean ignoring sensible rules for organisation structures for the sake of some hierarchical symmetry which panders to vanity at the cost of efficient decision-making.

It is also necessary, as a matter of common sense, to ensure that the organisational structure is appropriate to the business objectives, which may not be wholly compatible with the operating efficiency of individual units. It is most unlikely that all parts of an organisation can be at optimum efficiency at any one time. There must be a balance so that the organisation as a whole runs most effectively even though this means that the condition of individual sections varies.

An aspect of human behaviour which should be taken into account in determining organisation structure is the nature and quality of people concerned with management: this is a question of adaptation to make the most effective use of that prime business resource. Change in management or other

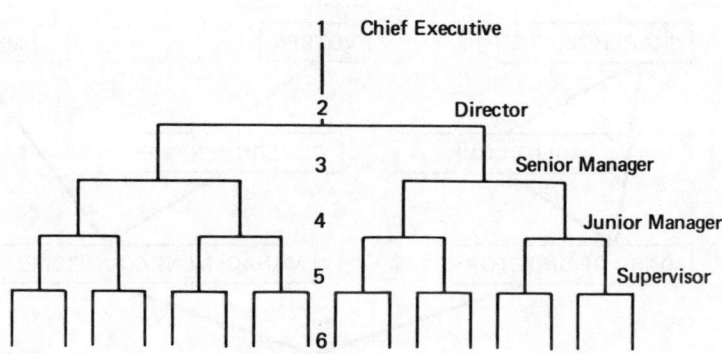

Figure 8   Organisational symmetry and status levels

key positions in an organisational structure should rarely result in dramatic change in organisational grouping but could well be followed by more subtle shifts to exploit differing strengths of different individuals. In reality, an organisational structure which at first sight appears to contravene some of the basic rules of organisation may yet have evolved effectively because of the particular attitudes and skills of those responsible for its management. Such organisations will be vulnerable to undesirable effects of changes of personnel.

Management and Control

So far, management responsibility for control of resources has been examined within the context of the organisation structure. It is necessary also to look at external influences and to recognise that responsibility for the exercise of management functions in any business will be found to be divided between the owners and the managers they have employed. Their relative influence will depend on the constitution of the business and the personal influence of individuals. Where ownership is concentrated in few hands, the distinction between the two may be blurred or disappear; where ownership is widespread, formal management structures will operate, with effective control being exercised closer to the organisation. The entrepreneurial organisation, created, developed and managed by its owner, may be contrasted with the State-controlled business where the ultimate owners (the voters) and managers are separated by the legislature and the departments of Government.

Organisation structures for such different kinds of business may not necessarily be greatly different from one another. The usual pattern is to have a committee or Board providing a link between owners and managers (figure 9). The Board will communicate with the owners through such formal channels as shareholders' meetings, and with the management of the business either

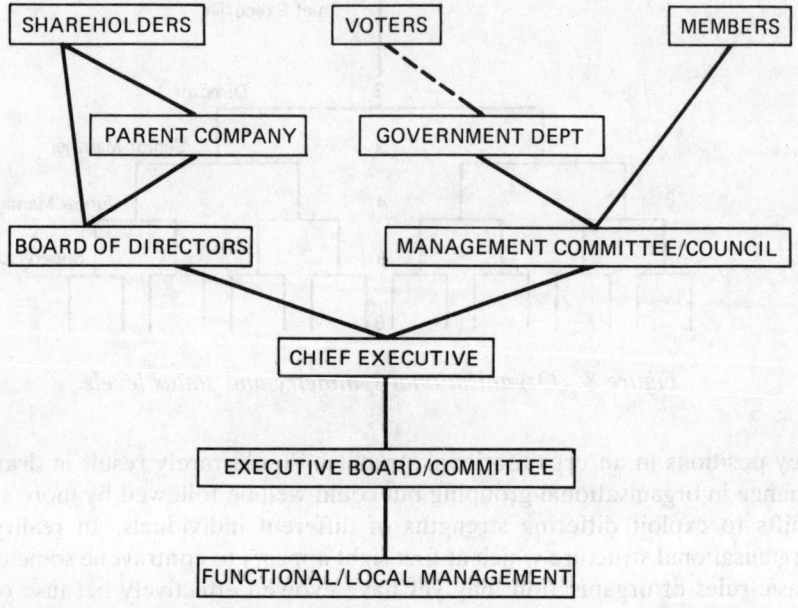

Figure 9   The chain of management

through appointment and supervision of executive officers or directly as executives themselves.

In a public limited company there will be a Board of Directors responsible to the shareholders, whose key exercise of control is the power to appoint this senior-most level of management. In a State-owned organisation, the equivalent of the Board of Directors may be a policy committee or council which is responsible to the appropriate public service authority and which has reporting to it a management board for the organisation. The influence of ownership over the typical (large) business may, therefore, be indirect and intermittent but it is nonetheless important because of the very great influence in most business undertakings of those appointed to the highest levels of executive management. It is quite usual for the most senior executive — the Chairman, Managing Director or Chief Executive — to have such influence as to be able to dominate personally the objectives, decisions and structure of the organisation and, effectively, to assume many of the rights of ownership itself. Whether this characteristic of 'personal leadership' (which is apparent in State-owned industries and in political management functions as much as in private institutions) is to the benefit of the organisation or not it is a reality to be taken into account by those seeking to understand management and information systems. The quality of personal leadership is as much an aspect of personality as is the behaviour of individuals in their relationship with organisations, and is of far greater importance in its consequences.

Management Hierarchy

Typically, management structures are hierarchical and pyramid-shaped, having the owner's representatives at the apex and, below, tiers of management spreading down to the lowest levels of authority (figure 10). Sizes of organisational units are most often described in numbers of employees (influencing the less desirable aims for symmetry in numbers which have been mentioned earlier) but, whether one looks at the structure in terms of people, of importance of decisions, or of total resources controlled, the pyramid shape is usually logical and inevitable because decision-making and supervision are most effective in a 'one-to-many' situation.

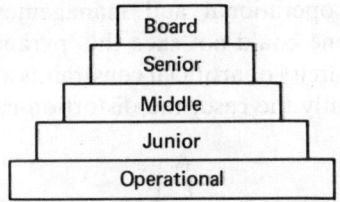

Figure 10   Management hierarchy

There is difficulty when concentration of power in the hands of individuals is misused to produce quixotic or otherwise mistaken decisions but a clear line of authority right through the management tiers and the allocation of defined authority to individuals at appropriate management levels are necessities for decisive action in any organisation. One probable reason for sluggish and indecisive behaviour of many public bodies is that the executive management structure is often overlapped by committee tiers. When formal responsibilities are allocated to committees (which, by their nature, must be indecisive), individual managers can achieve effective and prompt action only if they can find means of bypassing the proper committee channels.

Levels of Authority

The ordered symmetry of the typical business organisation structure may result in part from attitudes to status and other aspects of human relations which are not true reflections of business need, but there are also logical reasons for structures which contain balanced hierarchies operating through defined levels of authority. The one-to-many relationship of supervision, fulfilling the management function of direction and control, inevitably forms a pyramid with intermediate control levels between the highest policy and lowest operating points of the structure.

The argument for symmetry in terms of numbers of people supervised is not valid in an economy where personal skill and machine support have such an important bearing upon labour 'productivity', but there is an argument for symmetry in terms of those measures which reflect importance of decisions and complexity of tasks. The relationship between supervisor and supervised must take account of the reasonable limit of size of responsibility within which competent performance can be assured. In other words, the manager should have the right degree of responsibility, working to the sustainable maximum of ability and physical capacity (as should anyone in employment).

The view of management levels in the organisational pyramid illustrated in figure 10 is certainly inappropriate if one uses the criterion of 'value to the business' in determining relative status. Where remuneration does properly reflect value there are ample valid reasons for someone with managerial responsibilities receiving lower remuneration than someone without them, and if one illustrated the operational and management tiers in a business organisation structure one could not slice the 'pyramid' horizontally (figure 11). Where economic scarcity or artificial constraints affect relative remuneration levels, as is frequently the case, the distortion can be even greater.

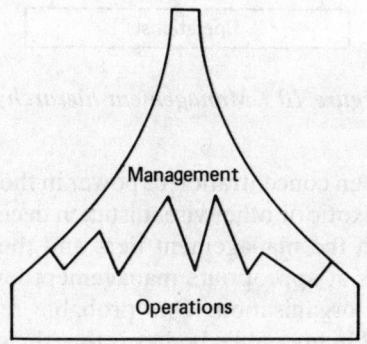

Figure 11　Remuneration hierarchy

Nevertheless there is administrative convenience in attaching status and price labels to people, placing them in categories. It may help to reduce risk of friction through envy although this can, surprisingly, be contained, as shown by the absurd disparities of remuneration often found within the same industry. A more telling reason for equality is the facility of communication between separate departmental and functional units. Where responsibility for decision-making is partly allocated to committees, as in many public and private non-profit-making bodies, inequality in status and authority between committee members radically increases the difficulty of effective committee operation. Similarly in business situations where agreement and co-operation between managers of different functions is likely to be the most effective way of achieving results, it is often found desirable that the managers concerned meet on 'level terms'. An even-handed relationship between supervisor and those directly supervised also has advantages. Given the organisational principle that there is a limited number of people who can be controlled effectively by a single manager, there is also an implication that the manager's time will be spread equally between those individuals, whose status is equal because their responsibilities are also more or less equal.

One can find practical examples where this is not so, yet where the organisation still works effectively; but, as a generalisation, this balance does make it easier for management to function effectively because people can fit into a structure which they are able to understand.

One of the most important principles of business organisation is that it should not be dependent upon personal relationships; the behaviour of a business must not be influenced by personal bias if danger of distorted judgements is to be avoided. It is perfectly possible to work in harmony with someone for whom one would have, socially, a distinct dislike provided that organisational rules do not generate friction and are observed by everyone concerned. Formal servility and social equality must be compatible if business organisation is to work.

Organisation and Information Flow

Organisational structure has been discussed principally in terms of decision/action relationships and the grouping of business activities into homogeneous or compatible units for greater effect. It must also be seen as a means of providing for information flow for decision-making. Progress from decision to action involves a flow of information (usually) down through the organisation structure to successive management and operating levels; information must also flow to the decision points to provide a means of making those decisions. This involves a feedback of information up through the organisation structure, from the external environment and, laterally, from other management and operating units. In principle, there is no reason why one should not be able to see an effective flow of information from and to any location where it is necessary.

If such information flow is interrupted or if the information itself is not satisfactory, there is something more to be considered than questions of logistics or procedures. The manager, being given authority over his own 'department', should be able to make sure that decisions made within that department are put into effect and that any information required is provided. If information is needed from other departments, and if these other departments fail to provide it, the only channel through which a remedy may be sought is back through the management hierarchy to the point where the lines of command from both departments meet. This may be right at the apex. Obviously, the most satisfactory organisation is one in which all units work in harmony because they are properly organised and enjoy an established and effective working relationship. Even so, a business organisation structure has to provide for the possibility of some breakdown in information flow or in co-operation, whether this occurs for technical reasons or for reasons of personality. A substantial proportion of time at higher management levels may be devoted to resolving these kinds of problem.

Communication

Problems of communication and relationships can be resolved or contained in the efficiently designed organisation by means of a careful definition of responsibilities, and this becomes essential where physical location of operating units is incompatible with a homogeneous functional structure. At one location it may be easy to divide an organisation into functional units such as Production, Accounting, and Personnel. Where the organisation is spread geographically, as is typical with large business undertakings, the functions may themselves become fragmented because there is a necessity to have similar functional elements at each location. For example, the manufacturing business with a number of plants may find it necessary to have production, accounting and personnel sections at each plant location. The multiple retail business will have similar organisational requirements at each branch.

One approach to branch organisational problems is to give each location a substantial measure of autonomy; this is the solution often favoured by large businesses which are an agglomeration of a number of different activities. Instead of operating through a head office and subordinate branches, such a business may operate instead through a holding company, exercising financial control over a number of subsidiaries each one of which has its own management and organisational structure. In effect, the holding company behaves as the owner.

Where there is necessarily a close relationship between various operating locations and where there are important advantages in having all parts of the organisation behave in the same way, some measure of central control and an effective structure for internal communication become very important. The Government department with public offices throughout the country, the department store group or the multi-location manufacturer will find neither the centrally controlled functional organisation nor the decentralised autonomous operating unit concepts satisfactory, because of the spread of functions over various locations and the problem of communication between the centre and the periphery. At the branch location it would not be appropriate to have representatives of each business function reporting separately to functional superiors at higher levels. Such an organisation would gain nothing from specialisation and would find its inter-functional problems having to be resolved at the level of the Chief Executive.

The alternative of ensuring effective management control at each location by bringing all functions under one local manager resolves these problems, but brings the possibility that the functions at branch locations will not all operate in the same way. For one part of the same organisation to treat its customers or employees in a different way from another, or to use different administrative procedures, would remove the advantages of having all the operating units identified as part of the same business. The solution has to establish a balance between central control and autonomy, and to provide functional communication links to complement the main command structure.

'Line' and 'Function'

The 'functional' link is necessary to ensure that there will be proper communication between functional specialists, where the organisation has separated them departmentally, and between those specialists and others outside the function who depend on them for policy and guidance. It should be the responsibility of the head of a particular function to determine policy, procedures, training and operating standards and to provide information, guidance and control, whether or not the employees concerned are also directly within a functional management structure. A Chief Accountant and a Head of Personnel would have functional responsibility for methods of handling cash and for employee-recruiting procedures respectively where these activities occurred in departments not directly reporting to them. Employees of other departments engaged in these activities would be expected to conform to standards and procedures laid down by the functional heads, and to provide a feedback of information to ensure that procedures and standards were being maintained. However, it would not be appropriate for the functional head to issue instructions directly to such employees; where instructions were necessary, these should be channelled through the line management. The important distinction between line and function is that the functional communication link might be direct for information, but the link for control must be exercised only through the line management chain. Thus, in a distributive organisation operating through a branch structure one might find the highest level of management (the Board of Directors) largely composed of functional specialists (such as the Chief Accountant and Personnel Director) but with the probable addition of one or more senior managers to whom had been allocated general management responsibility for the branch organisation. Functional specialists at the senior level might have very small departments reporting directly to them, their influence being through the relationship with appropriate people at branch level.

This does not dispose of all the problems of divided organisations. To the customers, a business is the retail shop or sales office with which they have dealings and not the Head Office which has no meaning for them. If a shop or sales office manager is able to meet the customers' requirements within the rules and objectives laid down from the Head Office, there are no problems of communication; if he is not, the local branch may see autonomy as the only means of giving satisfaction to the customer. The centre may see this leading to the undermining of corporate policies, and to the subsequent creation of difficulties through the setting of precedents. It is a natural consequence of separation that those at the periphery should seek to move away and those at the centre to strengthen their control and influence.

Organisation theory does not give a wholly satisfactory answer to this kind of problem because the influence of people and their personalities in these situations become so important. The definition of relative responsibilities must be drawn with great care but, even so, the result must be a compromise because there are losses and gains to be balanced. Perhaps the most telling contribution to effective organisation of scattered units is efficient communication (figure 12). If distance imposes no delay in communication, reference back to the centre is not the problem it would be where one must wait for authority to act. Computer systems have eased communication problems for dispersed organisations by making it possible for them to operate, for information purposes, as if all parts were at one location. The development of communication-based information systems in recent years has had a profound effect upon organisational structures — notably those of multi-national companies which had found their optimum size of production or distribution unit greater than that of any individual national market. Where before they might have treated each national subsidiary as an autonomous unit, they now find it economic to spread manufacture and assembly of products between a number of plants in different countries. They no longer suffer penalties in transfer of information and the economies of scale of manufacture have outweighed disadvantages of greater movement of materials across frontiers.

The ability to move information easily is probably the most important factor in organisational efficiency. It is essential to effective working of any action/ decision unit and makes it easier to overcome deficiencies resulting from an inappropriate organisation structure. If any enquiry has to be referred through

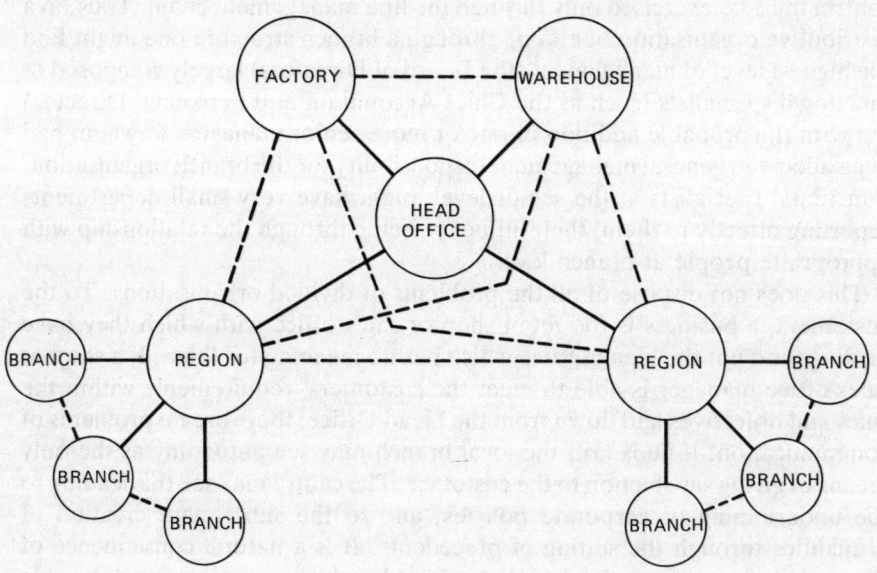

Figure 12   Communication 'lifelines'

another location, or if wrong information has been provided, a means of ready communication can quickly rectify or prevent any problems resulting from such deficiency.

External Services

One other aspect of organisational structure is worth further reference — the considerations which may lead one organisation to contain some functions within its organisation and others to buy those services from outside. One business may have its own legal department, its own transport facility, and its own management consultants; another may employ none of these except on a contractual basis from external, independent specialist organisations. Optimum size for economic operation is one consideration; the relevance of skill and experience or the economies of scale in providing an economic and effective service will influence decisions on whether or not it is profitable to buy-in such services from specialist suppliers, or employ appropriately qualified people within the business. The larger the scale of operations, the greater the proportion of business functions will it become advantageous to bring in.

There is also an argument about acceptability, a factor which influences many business decisions. On the economic side it may be a question of price or quality — will the internal department produce a result at greater or lesser cost than would an outside contractor, and is it able to produce the quality of product that the external supplier can offer?

Types of Business

It is usual to illustrate organisational structure of business undertakings by reference to manufacturing and trading concerns, which have essential functions described under such headings as Sales, Marketing, Production and Administration, as well as supporting services of various kinds. This is convenient because buying/making/selling concepts are relatively easy to explain and because this part of the economy is the most important, comprising all the essential wealth-creation activities. It is also appropriate because this sector provides examples of every kind of business system and technique, including the overwhelming majority of examples of innovation in information systems management.

However it is advisable to remember that this 'productive' category is not synonomous with privately owned business. Much of industry in most countries is in the hands of the State, including a large proportion of heavy industry, energy and transport — the prime industrial activities. These industries, which dominated the economies of the industrialised countries in the 19th and early

20th Centuries have declined relatively in importance as new industries and occupations have grown. Advanced industrial societies now contain a large and still growing proportion of supporting services which includes many of the largest employers. Much of this area of business activity is also under State control. Where the 'service' and 'information' industries differ from the 'productive', they can offer valid example and lessons to the student of business systems, and the development of information system techniques owes as much to Government administrative departments, defence establishments and social services as it does to manufacture and retail distribution.

It is really most appropriate to see all business activities initially as containing a number of common elements which are applicable to all, and then to examine the implications of the detailed differences in organisation and information requirements which result from their special characteristics (as publicly owned, large, non-profit-making etc.) which distinguish the particular from the general.

Government Services

Government services are broadly those services and facilities, financed largely through taxation, which are provided by various branches of Central and Local Government. Central Government services are managed through functional departments which are grouped together at senior management level for administrative and political convenience and, within each branch, are divided into specialist units dealing with particular geographical areas or activities. Such organisations have a 'Head Office' for central administrative and political control, providing some common services centrally or on an inter-departmental basis.

Organisational structures and allocation of responsibilities in Government services may be found to be more strictly defined than in most other undertakings, but Government Departments tend to acquire a reputation for sluggishness and inefficiency, implying an inability to effect decisions promptly and deficiencies in two of the four main categories of management functions: improving the use of resources and relationship with the environment. There can be no doubt that where there is absence of competitive pressure and no need to operate profitably to survive, the urge to improve must be weaker. But the bureaucratic structure associated with Government — the organisation of business undertakings into units with carefully prescribed limits of authority, highly centralised control and essential policy-making removed from the organisation itself — is there more because of the nature of the 'market' than because the organisation is a branch of the State. Wherever a State organisation is considered to have behaved unpredictably or inequitably it immediately comes under very great pressure; the organisation then develops a greater concern to protect itself from criticism than to provide the best possible service. Nonetheless, many Government departments do try to follow closely the principles of good organisation practice: notably, in such activities as Defence where constraints imposed by sensitivity to public reaction are not quite so great.

A prominent feature of Government Service which gives it one of its particular organisational characteristics is the preponderance of 'information processing' in many departmental activities. Such activities as social security, taxation and supporting services for agriculture, trade and industry are essentially concerned with information collection, analysis and presentations. These operations are also necessarily on a large scale because, unlike manufacturing and trading concerns, the 'customers' of many Government services are the entire population. Maintenance of social security records is a data-processing operation of a massive size. Before the recent advances in business machines, such organisations would have been essentially clerical with many information-handling elements, in contrast to the more easily defined sequence of production activities in a typical manufacturing or distributive business undertaking. Although still 'labour intensive', these kinds of Governmental information service activity are potentially suitable for extensive application of Information Technology.

The significance of decision-making is also different in Government from the 'private sector'. Apart from the elements of bureaucracy there are different priorities and consequences of decisions. Such considerations as seizing opportunities, avoiding delays and appraising returns on investment really seem to have less meaning in a non-commercial information service environment. While it may be acceptable for a Government report on a matter of national consequence to be produced years after the event, it is difficult to conceive a commercial situation in which such a leisured digestion of past events would have any place.

Many Central Government activities have close affinity with commercial business undertakings but it is at Local Government level that trading concepts are much more often to be found. Although Local Government activities are usually 'non-profit-making' services financed through taxation, such as the provision of libraries, parks, highways, police and fire services, they are all likely to have elements of conventional business organisation structures. They have functional divisions of accounting, production, personnel and business services because they do all 'produce' some kinds of goods or services and these involve many of the aspects of planning and control decisions, as well as the general need to improve effectiveness in use of resources that will be expected of the commercial concern.

Large Corporations

A tendency to bureaucracy is by no means only a characteristic of the Government Service; it is also a function of size. In a large organisation the length of communication chains often brings fear that independent action at remote points may bring unacceptable deviation from corporate policy. Bureaucracy has been a typical feature of large trading organisations as well as of Government Departments — noticeably, the very large public and private corporations which have operated in monopoly situations without the normal pressures towards greater efficiency. This is a situation which is probably tending to change as new solutions to communication problems are provided by computer-based systems and as the increasing burden of labour costs makes the traditional clerical bureaucracy no longer sustainable.

With due regard to such considerations as size and monopoly position, State-owned industries are often very close to privately owned business in their structures. The statutory basis under which they are constituted affects such matters as the scope and purpose of the organisation and the relationship between owners and managers, as it does in different ways for privately owned business undertakings which also have a recognised legal status. Generally speaking, the state-owned business will have less freedom but greater financial security and (for the monopolies) market protection.

There are many state-owned businesses operating as subsidiaries of major State corporations which are very difficult to distinguish from privately owned businesses, either by their behaviour or by their organisation, simply because they operate under very similar conditions. Even the large State corporations seem to approach organisational matters in a similar way to their private counterparts. One may have 'officers' and the other 'managers', but the difference is likely to be more in job and departmental title than in function. Most large businesses have boards of management whether they be called 'Councils', 'Boards of Directors' or 'Committees', and most organisations have a Chief Executive whether under that title or as 'Chief General Manager', 'Managing Director' or 'Principal'. All organisations have financial departments containing the functions of cash management, book-keeping and financial information. Some element of production will be found whether it is extraction of minerals, manufacture of machines or consumable products, provision of transport capacity, supplying professional services or arrangement of social or political events.

Some obvious characteristics of large corporations are direct consequences of size: large numbers of transactions, many employees, more significant revenue and expenditure decisions. These will be associated with larger and more complex management and organisational structures. Unit sizes of departmental subdivisions will be large; there will be many more functions retained within the organisation than would be found in the small business. The large corporation will employ many of its own specialists instead of buying in their services when required; it will also find it economic to introduce special expertise in situations which, for the small organisation, would be ignored or assumed to be part of some more general management responsibility. Organisational concepts such as corporate planning and internal audit to provide special expertise in planning and control matters are essentially large corporation functions. The organisation chart of the large corporation will be very different from the simple concept of sales, production and personnel; functions like sales will branch into specialised areas of sales services, planning, support, administration and so on, often to the extent that the ratio of planning and information services to essential production functions can be proportionally higher than in a smaller business. Up to a point this may produce net benefits in measured productivity, but can also indicate an organisation which has grown beyond its optimum size and is becoming increasingly difficult and costly to manage effectively.

Small Businesses

We have to look at the smaller business to see more sharply defined differences between state and privately owned business undertakings, and between different kinds of business activity. Within the general principles of organisation and the common frameworks of necessary functions, the privately owned business undertaking may be found to have greater flexibility in its approach to organisational matters because its lesser subjection to political constraints gives greater freedom to its management in adapting organisation structure to the needs of business. The greater significance of survival and profitability objectives will also bring a readiness to modify organisation structure to ensure that it does provide an optimum solution. This may be seen both in the form of a rapid pace of evolution and in the more dramatic moments of major reconstruction. Whereas the large business is likely to be the first to introduce a new organisational concept — such as the 'data processing department' or the 'information centre' (see chapters 10 and 12) — it is the small organisation that is more likely to be found adopting an unconventional approach like grouping nominally separate functions such as accounting and sales because it appears to suit the particular needs of the business.

The small business may also seem prepared to breach the soundest of organisation theories without apparent harm because communications problems, by definition, are easier to manage and because the influence of individual personalities and attitudes is relatively greater. The idiosyncratic owner–manager of a small business may be successful where the conventional manager of the large corporation simply could not hope to succeed. One must therefore look more carefully at the small organisation to evaluate the significance of individual attitudes and the kind of historical and industry-related factors which may be particularly influential.

Associations and Charities

There is a tendency to think of membership organisations generally as small businesses. Many of them are: the local sports and social clubs, societies and political organisations are mostly small in terms of income and resources. But some are extremely large, and we cannot truly generalise about this category of business in terms of size. Some membership organisations which exist to support particular causes or interests have huge membership and are very substantial businesses by any standard. We have to consider such organisations as Trade Unions and associations of car owners. The element all these organisations have in common is that (on the whole) they exist for the benefit of their owners, not so much in the sense that any 'profits' will belong to them but that the owners are also the customers for whom the services of the organisation are performed. This should provide a much closer link between organisation and customer than would apply with a private trading organisation or with the Government Service.

Identification of the owners' interest with that of the customers will have some effect on objectives and also on organisation; the authority of employees relative to that of owners is likely to be much less than in the kind of business with which ownership has a more remote relationship. However, larger membership organisations do develop some of the characteristics of other large businesses. Very large membership organisations have been described as 'self perpetuating oligarchies' because the membership, being very large and physically remote from the centre of operation of the business, and being only affected in a very modest way by its actions, is likely to attempt to exercise ownership control only in exceptional circumstances. In this respect, it operates in much the same way as do the many small shareholders who make up the ownership of very large public companies. Sometimes, restriction on control is deliberate with the membership being allowed only 'associate' status; in these organisations one can detect the greater influence of employees, with more concern for their interests and less for such matters as improving the effectiveness of the organisation.

Profit-making and Non-profit-making Businesses

To a large extent a distinction between 'profit' and 'non-profit' is likely to be meaningless or positively misleading when looking at different types of business organisation. A public utility in private or State hands would not necessarily show any sharp difference in its organisation structure or in its policy. A much greater distinction would be found between a business which has to struggle to survive and one which is accustomed to easy profits; a rigorous attitude toward costs and revenue is much more likely if profits are hard to come by. Since a non-profit organisation must generate a sufficient surplus of revenue over expenditure to service its loans and fund its fresh capital requirements, we may be talking about only a relatively modest difference in net revenue between that situation and one where a true net surplus is generated.

In parts of the communication industries, where increasing revenue is more important than reducing costs in achieving profitability, often little regard is paid to economy. A similar lack of attention to cost may be found in some organisations which finance their activities out of the surplus after their costs have been covered. Perhaps the most significant influence of the non-profit-making status is likely to be the restriction imposed on business behaviour by the legal framework of that status; it may be less easy to alter organisation, purposes or objectives. The trading concern could alter itself radically to reflect market changes and ensure its survival; a charitable organisation might find itself obliged to remain the same until the purpose of the charity was fulfilled, when it would be likely to cease existence.

Monopoly, Oligopoly and Cartel

The concept of monopoly is associated with the ability to influence success in the market place because of the large proportion of the market supplied. A true monopoly has all the market to itself with no competition of any kind. Between that and the business in a totally free market of which it has only a very small share, there are various degrees of monopoly power such as the quasi-monopoly of being the sole supplier of a unique product which people do not necessarily have to buy, and the market leadership of the most important supplier of an essential product in a competitive market. Thus supply of gas and electricity is in the hands of monopoly suppliers of their respective products, but these are not monopoly suppliers in the energy industry because they compete with each other. In the commercial world, the device of branding is an attempt to acquire a unique reputation which will reduce the impact of competition.

Monopoly in the true sense is only likely to be found where there is patent protection for a limited number of years, and there are few examples applying to products which could be regarded as so important economically that the supplier could exercise the monopoly power of generating exceptional profits. This is partly because monopolies are either exercised by the State, when generating excess profits is unlikely to be the prime objective and because, in the general industrial and commercial sectors, constraints are often imposed which make it difficult for one organisation to achieve a dominant position. It is, therefore, difficult to single out the monopoly element as having any major impact on organisation; we really have to see it as a tendency shown in objectives of expansion rather than in the normal business structure.

Oligopoly is probably a more significant feature of business organisation because it is less easy to restrain than monopoly, and because of the tendency of organisations within many industries to prefer moving in harmony. The term 'oligopoly' is used in economics to describe the state of limited competition which exists when a few large producers or suppliers dominate an industry or market. Typical examples of oligopoly in operation are where competing organisations limit their price competition so that the customer sees differences only in marginal areas, or where the (major) organisations share the market, accepting voluntary constraint and preferring to secure rather than expand market share. This can be found in a range of industries including petrol retailing, banking and finance, and in the distribution of many kinds of consumer product. Such agreements affect environmental relationships between organisations and often the size and locations of the organisations themselves.

A more formalised and extreme form of restraint on competition by nominally independent suppliers sharing a market is the cartel. A cartel operates to influence the selling price by agreed restriction of output, often with that output being distributed under the control of a selling organisation set up for the purpose. Marketing Boards for agricultural products are typical examples of cartel operations, as is the international grouping of primary producers in the oil industry.

Integration and Conglomeration

When looking at theoretical concepts of business organisation, we see the organisation firstly in two aspects: the internal organisation and the relationship with the environment. The former divides itself up into detailed structures with decision, action and information relationships between them. The latter comprises a wide variety of influences and information links related to customers and users of business services, suppliers of resources used in the business, the owners of the business and the general environment of legal, social, political and economic factors.

We often tend to think of owners having a direct and sole relationship with a business, but most are also owners of other businesses. Clearly this applies to the State-owned undertakings which form a very substantial part of modern economies although the link with and, consequently, influence of the owners is often a little remote. It also applies to a large portion of the private sector in which most businesses (as a proportion of the sector) are owned by other businesses.

To achieve objectives of survival, profit or expansion, the path of integration or conglomeration is often chosen. Integration is an attempt either to increase market share by expanding horizontally to absorb like or complementary businesses in the same market, or to secure essential supplies or market outlets by expanding vertically to absorb functions of former suppliers and customers. It may also be done in either direction to achieve economies of scale, or to eliminate intermediate activities so as to improve the economics of the business as a whole.

Conglomeration might be the result of attempts to achieve similar ultimate objectives by different means. It might be a question of reducing the risks associated with having all eggs in one basket, or to join a 'cash-hungry' business to one which is 'cash-rich'. It might also be attempted as a means of using surplus resources available for manufacture, distribution or management; it might be the result of essentially financial objectives where different businesses are grouped together purely because they seem individually to be sound investments.

It is essential to understand this multiple ownership relationship in order to understand a business. Objectives may be different from those of an independent organisation because the business is seen in the context of a much wider range of activities. This might have the contrary effects of either an apparently viable business being closed or another which is clearly insolvent being kept alive. In either case the explanation could be found only by looking at the objectives of the larger whole.

Organisation and the Impact of Business Activity

The Nature of the Business Activity

The nominal organisational structure, with its various departmental sub-divisions, may appear to be similar when one makes a theoretical comparison of two business undertakings. A closer examination of the businesses in operation may show that there are substantial differences in size and relative importance of functions which reflect differing needs arising from the business activities. Thus businesses which are predominantly concerned with extractive, manufacturing, distributive or service activity might appear to have broadly similar management functions, but the resources which they control and the decision/action processes which they represent will reflect the particular nature of the industry. A business in an extractive industry such as oil production or mining essentially comprises substantial material assets in the form of a natural resource and extractive plant. Primary influences will be the minimum size for viable operation, the fixed location of the extractive activities and their relationship with the market.

In contrast, a commodity brokerage organisation might be (physically) extremely small in relation to its turnover, with virtually no assets, and might not even see the commodity in which it deals. A direct selling organisation might be largely composed of sales functions, and a public service would have a very small selling function (largely under the heading of 'Public Relations').

Where a business is geographically spread, various functions may be subdivided in regional organisational structures. The size of units will depend upon the balance between such factors as economies of scale for particular processes or activities, cost of communications and transport between these activities, and constraints restricting location or size at source of supply or at the point of distribution to the market. There will also be factors arising from the nature of the product or service itself, such as the influence of perishability, of fashion, or of legal restrictions such as licensing and public safety regulations.

Custom and Practice

We should not be too ready to assume that organisations are always a true reflection of business needs. That would be the same as assuming that all business decisions are sound and all business objectives clearly understood. If one compares business practice in different countries, for example, one can find that such industries as Law, Banking, Insurance and Retail Distribution, which in theory could have similar objectives and organisational needs are, in reality, considerably different because they reflect the influence of different social environments.

The good business practice of fitting into local conditions (essential for the prospective exporter) is only finely distinguished from the cautious adoption of conformity. Much of what is done in the name of good business practice can more properly be attributed to fear of unconformity or breach of tradition. Organisational structures are more likely to retain unnecessary relics than to introduce new elements in advance of needs because the virtue of tradition is often prized above those of innovation or objectivity. In the same vein, competing businesses will be found to mimic each other's behaviour in the market, presumably because of a paradoxical belief that the competitor is superior in judgement. This is particularly to be noted in competitive situations in retail markets where, if one supplier takes the bold step of innovation, there is an immediate move by competitors to align themselves with closely similar products; this even applies to the actual style of marketing. More remarkably, one may find this kind of timid conformity being applied within business organisations where one cannot employ any kind of valid marketing argument. Thus labels attached to management functions, details of organisation structures and attitudes towards information systems may find close parallels between organisations in the same industry, often in sharp contrast to other industries and much beyond that which true differences in business needs might appear to demand. It is as if each industry forms a club within which particular conventions hold.

One can find logical explanations related to such matters as flows of information between units within an industry and movement of people between similar firms, but one can also detect some lack of confidence, implying a deficiency in management quality or in information available which might, if rectified, lead to different approaches in more enterprising organisations. Appointment and promotion to business management is not necessarily a consequence of merit, so one can ascribe inappropriate organisation and decisions to management incompetence; but it is also true that a powerful and general contributor to such deficiencies is inadequacy of information systems, whether they provide good managers with bad information, or fail to reveal the cause and effect of bad management.

Convention and fashion in organisational structure are not constant; adherence to tradition and 'staying with the crowd' do not prevent change any more than do fashion and language remain the same. One notable area of change in the 20th Century has been the proliferation of management functions, including a growing proportion of 'support' in relation to 'production' activities. Change in economic fundamentals such as growth in population and in wealth have led, through increases in size of markets and new ranges of products and services, to increases in size of business units. These have brought new complications in organisational needs for management planning and control of the larger business units. There is also an effect of the greater intrusion of Government into business activity which is to be found in most developed countries. Regulations which affect relationships with employees, working environments, conduct of business activities and collection and recording of information have moulded organisation structures, requiring the introduction of new functions and information flows.

The Need for Organised Information Services

The increasing importance of information and the consequent need to provide for it in the organisation structure is one area of change affecting business which is of particular interest in this study. The discovery and application of 'information' as a vital element in effective business operation today is the result of changes in the nature and the needs of business management. When management of business undertaking ceased to be the preserve of the entrepreneur or the inheritor of such directly acquired wealth, the function of professional management began to emerge. With this grew an understanding of business management needs and techniques, with lessening dependence on subjective decisions and pragmatic approaches to business problems, and much greater concern for the theoretical and practical factors influencing effective business operation.

The growth of professional management may be partly a consequence of social changes but it is also a result of the greater complexity of business. The professional business manager has been able to recognise the importance of information, but the growth of information services as part of business organisation is also a necessary outcome of a combination of changing technology and economic, social and political structures which have added complications to business decisions. These have brought a need for new organisational structures to support decisions and to provide information, as it has become recognised that this is the key to effective decision and action. Most of the new organisational elements in business introduced in recent years have been to provide information — auditing, market research, operational research and work study, corporate planning, business consultancy and data processing. Business machines may have been introduced in the first place to make more effective use of people in handling of traditional business records; they have long since become the essential means of providing information for management and communication between the source of that information and the decision point where it is needed. In the next chapter the nature of business information is explored further. We are concerned not simply to examine the provision and use of information but to pursue the proposition that information has become the most important resource of all.

Check List 4

The term 'organisation' implies an ordered structure. Achievement of objectives is much more likely where there is definition of tasks, allocation of responsibilities and effective communication. An organisation which is created for a particular purpose will usually be involved in repetitive activity where knowledge, experience and skill become significant factors in the achievement of objectives.

Organisational Theory
Effectiveness of management: managed ratios.
Allocation of points of decision to the right level.
Balancing authority and responsibility.
Compatibility of functional and organisational relationships.

Management and Control
Ownership.
Management hierarchies.
Levels of authority.
Line and function.

Type of Business
Government services.
Large corporations.
Small businesses.
Associations and charities.
Profit/non-profit.
Monopoly and cartel.
Integration and conglomeration.
Holding companies.

Further Reading

Appleby, R. C., *Modern Business Administration*, Pitman, 1981.
Cooke, S. and Slack, N., *Making Management Decisions*, Prentice-Hall, 1984.
Hiner, O. S., *Business Administration — An Introductory Study*, Longman, 1978.

5 Management Information

To make decisions needed to achieve objectives, an organisation structure must be created within which points of responsibility for decision-making are allocated. Those responsible for making decisions must be provided with information about resources and activities, and with the means of acquiring, processing and distributing this information.

The Business Problem

However, provision of information without regard to its use serves no purpose. Information is not useful for its own sake: it must be relevant to the needs of the business and must answer the right questions. It may appear simple enough to establish a theoretical link between the objective, the decision and the information required to make that decision possible but, in relating any theoretical concept to reality, account must be taken of practical questions: we must have in mind how the economic world works. Thus, we may say that if we have to decide how to get to a particular destination, we need a map; for the business destination we need to know more — is that really where we wish to be, what are the alternative methods of getting there, what may happen on the way?

In a primitive economic environment, business activity might be just a matter of 'travelling hopefully' and the entire edifice of objectives, organisation and information would be superfluous. In modern society where no business can operate in isolation it is the norm for business decisions, organisation, and the information requirement supporting them to be relatively complex regardless of business size. Only rarely will there be one possible outcome of any business decision and equally rarely only one method of implementing that decision. Between plan and implementation there will be all kinds of hazard, including many which are unpredictable: a business plan can never be formulated free of any constraint because there are always likely to be legal, social or economic factors affecting every aspect of business decisions.

To reach the business destination, it is also necessary to know the starting point. Some business undertakings, while nominally aiming towards an original objective, may be so affected by external and internal influences that they lose sight of the essential business purpose. It may seem odd to suggest that those responsible for the management of a business undertaking could not know its purpose. If they do not, there is no way that they can be sure of making the right decisions, but there is often no other satisfactory explanation for business behaviour. Diversification, as a movement away from concentration on existing activities, is often regarded as a prudent and necessary adaptation; it can also imply a loss of understanding of the true nature of the business. Pursuit of expansion through agglomeration may set in train the ultimate collapse of the expanded organisation. Producing a better product is not necessarily the appropriate response to competition; it may be the type of product itself that is the problem. (Making a better steam engine was no defence against the diesel and electric locomotive, although that was the response of the steam locomotive engineers.)

Identifying the Business Purpose

A satisfactory answer to the question — "what kind of business are we in?" — is the probable starting point for successful management of any business undertaking. Understanding the nature of the business is more than a matter of defining the industry, product or service. A firm engaged in the distribution of building materials, for example, must decide if this activity should also include manufacture and if it should sell to 'trade' or 'retail' customers, or both. It must decide what it means by 'building materials'; should this include garden tools and domestic electrical equipment as well as sand and timber?

This is not to say that a business undertaking is required to specialise or even to fit itself into any conventional classification of business activity. Vertical integration — to absorb successive stages of production and distribution of a specific range of products or services — or horizontal integration — to increase marketing strength by widening ranges of products and outlets — are both valid strategies in the right context. The important consideration in arriving at the business identity is to recognise the distinction between what a business does, or makes, or sells and the economic needs it satisfies. The manager must understand what the business is actually doing, and how its performance relates to its success or failure. The business problem must be defined. In information terms this means that the successful organisation will have accessible, usable information about its activities, sufficient to be able to compare its performance with its targets and to identify its strengths and weaknesses.

It must also be able to evaluate the possible consequences of future events. Planning, which has been identified as one of the key responsibilities of management, brings with it a necessity to look ahead and to forecast the possible effects of current policies and trends, and to evaluate the further consequences of changes in policy.

For each of the four prime functions of management there is, therefore, a clear link with information needs: for planning the business needs information to help look towards the future; for direction and control it needs to know what it is doing; for improving effectiveness of the organisation it needs to understand what its problems are; and for linking with the environment it needs to have the means of collecting and analysing information which will help to understand it.

Viewing the Business Problems

The unsuccessful organisation is usually one which has failed either to provide for future change, or to identify and correct current problems likely to affect future performance. The question — "what kind of business are we in?" — must also be asked in terms of — "what kind of business are we going to be in?" The question — "are we profitable?" — must also be asked as — "will we be profitable?" Information needed for business success is also a matter of understanding the past. Factors identified in looking at a current problem are incomplete if they do not explain why the present position was reached. Historical data is often a more important source of information than current data in making decisions which involve interpretation. In many situations the question — "what shall we do?" — may not be answered until the question — "what did we do last time?" — has been answered. At the very least, the fact that there is knowledge of the outcome of comparable past situations brings an element of caution, and helps towards a more careful analysis of current situations and thus to a better use of all the information available.

Analysis and interpretation is more than a matter of applying human judgement to factual data. It must be part of the definition of 'information' that it be understandable and usable; any information which provides facts but begs further questions is of little practical value. One might certainly wish to know, for example, that a business is running at a loss, but to make use of that information one needs to know also where this loss is occurring and why. The total information available must provide an overall picture, together with a breakdown of that picture, across the organisation structure and through the decision/action chain, so as to enable management to draw valid conclusions about causes and likely effects.

Business Information

Information for Control

The immediate and most pressing need a manager has for information is usually to assist the control and direction of the business. This requires knowledge of the resources available, how they are deployed and what are they producing. A manufacturing organisation needs information about labour, machine capacity, raw material stocks and consumption, and work-in-progress, and about what has been bought to provide future capacity and what has been sold to absorb current and future output. In a wholesale or retail organisation, machine capacity, raw materials and work-in-progress may be replaced by information about such things as vehicle capacity, stocks for sale and selling space. The categories of information most important to a business depend upon its nature and its objectives; for example, most activities of an Electricity Distribution Board derive ultimately from consumption of electricity, so that consumption figures might be the key information source; an airline might be interested primarily in its sales of passenger and cargo space. Sales or commitments are usually the trigger for an organisation's other activities; information about what has been sold, with what has been consumed and produced, and what resources are available, together with supporting information necessary to decide upon the use of those available resources, comprise the core of information needs to control current activities, with one important qualification — performance must be evaluated.

Information for Measuring Performance

To control business activities effectively, there must be interpretation of information about these activities so that performance can be measured. It is not enough to know that there is vehicle capacity in a transport undertaking so that a consignment can be despatched; there must be some means of knowing that capacity has been used in the most effective way, and also that such capacity is appropriate to the transport needs.

Sales information provides another example. Information about sales is incomplete without an analysis showing comparative information, whenever a comparison is relevant (as, for example, between sales representatives, products, territories or competitors). Such information is likely to be needed both comparatively within the current sales period and between periods, as in a comparison with the equivalent time for the previous year. Any business will wish to have some measure of the way each of its organisational units has performed, and, as a whole, it needs to know how it has made use of all the resources available to it. Information must be labelled in some way (such as by area, department, employee, product, etc.) and evaluated in relation to a target or standard so as to establish some measure of performance.

Information for Recording

Business information is primarily a matter of keeping records; facts about current events are not enough. Automatic responses and *ad hoc* decisions arising from unexpected situations may draw only on current information but the great majority of management decisions rely on information which has been accumulating for a period. If balanced judgements are to be taken there is usually a need for some means of comparison. Historical information is necessary wherever appropriate reaction to new transactions or occurrences depends on knowledge of past situations, or wherever an analysis of past activities can contribute to the resolution of business problems. Detection of crime, action by social caseworkers, diagnosis of causes of machine failure and resolution of many other problems found in business will be influenced greatly by answers to the question — "has it happened before?" Performance figures may have little meaning unless there is a bench mark, a standard or a previous record against which comparison can be made.

The need for records to support decisions does not just relate to internal records. If a business is considering launching a new product or service, it will first examine information related to the market; from this it will expect to derive forecasts about future market trends. Having launched the product it will then wish to keep records from which it can compare results with plans over a period and decide whether or not the project achieved its objectives.

Records are also a general necessity for orderly conduct of business. It has long been fashionable among those who have no understanding of business management, or who do not have responsibility for taking business decisions, to affirm that record-keeping in general is a menial task, largely an unnecessary expense and an indication of a pedestrian approach, inimical to efficiency. The reverse is true: methods of keeping records may not always deserve admiration but record-keeping is inescapable in a well-ordered business. Failure to keep good accounting records is a quick and certain way to the destruction of a business, however innovative and dynamic it may have been in its approach to the market.

All the extensive mechanisation of business administration and the development of sophisticated communication techniques over the last thirty years have not yet brought the 'paperless' society in which the office memorandum is no longer required. When we reach that ultimate development of office technology, there must be an electronic substitute for the memorandum because any organisation which depends on the current knowledge and memory of its employees (even on such a simple matter as communication between two people) will find human memory a dangerously fallible method of recording.

Over a fair range of record-keeping activities the business organisation has little choice, of course. Maintenance of some form of accounting record is mandatory for tax assessment and to meet statutory auditing requirements. In any civil proceeding related to law of contract — the most likely form of litigation in which a business organisation may be involved — records of such transactions relating to them will be the heart of the matter. Some records may be kept simply as a protection against such an event.

Information for Forecasting

Planning depends heavily on historical records but keeping of records is not sufficient in itself to provide useful information, any more than would any 'raw' facts be adequate for judgement about performance or for resolution of immediate business problems. Interpretation of historical information — taking raw data and turning it into useful information — is an essential part of resolving business problems. To produce useful information for forecasting usually involves mathematical interpretation of past records: extrapolation to indicate trends, probability calculation, or extension of factual information under various hypotheses to answer the question — "what if?"

The forecast is a usual starting point for management information — the material from which the business plan is constructed and against which subsequent performance will be measured. The kind of major business investment project which looks ahead to a commitment many years in advance may demand much more time in its planning and forecasting phase than in its construction and implementation. The development of some of the first computer-based systems for passenger seat reservations by the large airlines was in this category, involving extensive use of scientific method to resolve immensely difficult problems about transaction patterns and peaks on which the economic and physical viability of the systems depended. The project for a tunnel across the English Channel was delayed rather by politics than by economics or logistics, but the collection and interpretation of information leading to accurate forecasts about costs and revenues for such a project must be fully as important as the skills to resolve the many technical problems.

Such examples also illustrate the point that forward planning does not depend only on information available from within the business. Information from external sources may be of paramount importance because environmental factors play such a key part in the objectives, decisions and operation of almost any business activity. Sales forecasts for example, depend not only on examination and interpretation of past sales figures but also on an understanding of the market. In any organisation, understanding the behaviour and requirements of customers is essential as is knowledge of competitors, suppliers and of social, economic and political influences in general.

Business Information Needs

In chapter 3 the concept of information flow was introduced in relation to the link between decision and action, and in chapter 4 this was extended further to bring in the idea of organisation structures being designed to ensure that information is provided to the right decision point. In this examination of business information we have now to consider in more detail the kinds of information flow which will be relevant to business needs.

Much management activity can be seen as a process starting with identification of a problem or opportunity, proceeding through evaluation of alternative courses of action, to selection of the most suitable solution, putting that solution into effect, and ending with an assessment of the resulting performance and feedback of information to review the management decision (figure 13). In this context, management use of information should not be seen as selection and interpretation of facts at a particular time for a particular purpose, but as a need for a continual supply of information of various kinds: facts related to the existing situation, forecasts, analysis of alternative courses,

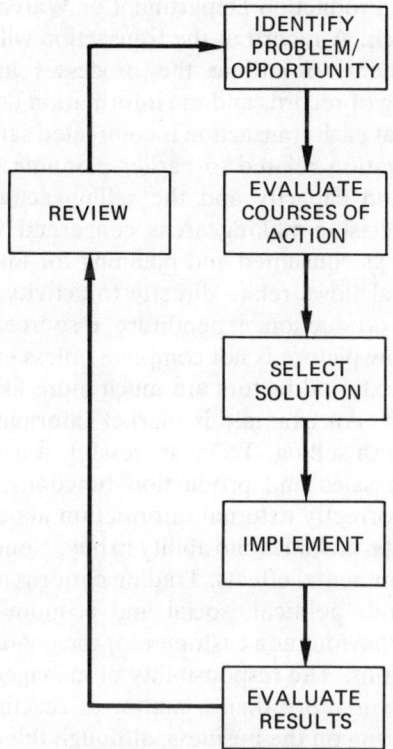

Figure 13   The management process

instructions and procedures, and communication of results. These information needs are usually supplied in the form of an information flow — from operating points towards management for information about performance or constraints affecting future decisions, and from management for advice and instructions which determine the action elements of the business.

At the 'action' level, therefore, there are two elements of activity: the action itself to implement the decision, and the keeping of records or collection and supply of specific items of information on demand, from both of which the feedback to management will come. This continuous two-way flow of information represents the main stream of internal communication. But it would be a gross over-simplification to see this as only a vertical movement. In volume, there is likely to be much more information flowing 'horizontally' through the organisation structure between different departments. The events or transactions which give rise to series of processes in business operation involve keeping records and transmission of information as each transaction is completed and the repercussions of events are absorbed. In a typical trading situation, for example, activity by a Sales Department generates orders which will be received by an Order Office for checking and formal acceptance, and then transmitted to a Production Department or Warehouse for completion, and finally to Despatch. A record of the transaction will be transferred to an Accounting Department to initiate the processes involved in collecting payment. The keeping of records and the information flows from them will be intended to ensure that each transaction is completed satisfactorily, to provide a feedback of information related to earlier planning decisions which have created the production capacity and the selling activity, and also a feed 'forward' to other decision-making areas concerned with such matters as replenishment of stocks consumed and planning for future activities.

While these internal flows relate directly to activity of people within the organisation — sales, production, expenditure, resource utilisation, etc. — the whole information flow picture is not complete unless external information is taken into account. External factors are much more likely to be beyond the organisation's control. An example is market information for any business which is concerned with selling. To be successful, it cannot rely only on the efficiency of its own sales and production functions; it must also understand and interpret correctly external information about competition, about customer requirements, attitudes and ability to buy. None of these influences is itself free from environmental effects. Trading patterns may be affected by the wide range of general, political, social and economic factors as will the organisation's own behaviour as a customer for the goods and services it needs to conduct its operations. The responsibility of management for dealing with environmental factors is more than a matter of reacting to external events which have some bearing on the business; although this clearly must be done, to treat all external events as 'Acts of God' is not likely to ensure survival. As with internal information, external information flows will be continuous and will require record-keeping, analysis, interpretation and judgement (for example, collation of information about competitor sales to complete a market picture, or initiation of market research to discover information which cannot be obtained through ordinary market experience). Estimating the probable occurrence of real 'Acts of God' is not just a necessary function for the insurance world (which depends for its survival on the accuracy of its forecasts); the business world in general must also make its own appraisal of such external risks and prepare appropriate contingency plans.

The Information Machine

We now have a fourth model, or aspect of business. Just as one can describe a business in terms of networks of objectives and decisions, and of organisational structures containing related jobs and responsibilities, so we can also describe it in patterns of information flows linking various decisions and actions.

The means by which information is provided consists of a series of activities collating original data about transactions with records of past events, with processing requirements and various rules and factors which will influence the processing, and then transmission, editing, selection and other manipulation of this data to provide information where it is required in suitable form. It can be seen as a manufacturing process with its own version of such elements as raw materials, production control and output. Data is input, transmitted, stored, processed and output.

At this point we are moving closer to an understanding of the importance of computers to business, because the computer is an information machine. It has developed in its present form as a means of providing information to points of decision, replacing other methods because of its superiority of speed, cost, accuracy and relevance. In its early days, distinctions were made between a computer as a scientific calculating machine and as a data processing machine for business purposes. The data processing concepts are still valid, being related to keeping business transaction records, and their analysis and presentation for further action or decision. Today the use of computers is very much wider and new types of computer application have been given new labels such as 'information retrieval', 'telemetry' and 'decision support' (see chapter 10). These are still concerned with recording, processing, transmission and presentation of information, and the computer is still essentially an information machine but the term 'computing' with its connotations of calculation is being superseded by the wider concept of 'information technology'.

Data and Information

Reference to 'data processing' as an appropriate description for much of business information activity offers a suitable point to introduce the term 'data' in its information system context. In computer technology, data is defined as 'that which is given': raw, unprocessed facts which require editing, analysis, summarising or other processing before they become usable. When 'data' is of use it becomes 'information'. 'Data' in effect is original data and 'information' is information which is usable; this provides a convenient terminology to distinguish between the input and output functions of information systems.

One question has been begged in this preliminary examination of business information requirements. How can we be sure that we really have 'information' — that we do not simply have 'data' which is superfluous or misleading? We cannot say with the philosopher that all knowledge is useful. There is a cost to acquiring knowledge and, since we start with a proposition that business activity must be relevant to objectives, then the expense of collecting and analysing information which serves no useful purpose would be incompatible with any likely objectives. As with all things, there is some limit to be observed. Acceptance of the fundamental importance of information systems must always carry with it the qualification that they conform to the opening propositions: relevance to the needs of the business and providing answers to the right questions.

As with objectives and decisions, we can identify information requirements by working down through the organisation structure: information requirements will be determined by the decisions that need to be taken and from this should be derived the requirements for recording, information flow and presentation. Although in reality it may be found quite often that a business looks at its information for management solely in terms of making better use of basic records, that would be no more than a matter of making the best of things rather than taking an objective view of what is truly required. Some records may be kept for no other reason than to meet a statutory requirement, or may be an essential part of the routine processing of day-to-day business transactions, but the important information — that which is to feed the major decisions — is likely to aid those decisions properly only if the information flows and records have been designed 'from the top down' (figure 14). To make such objective assessments requires management ability; it requires other information about what may be available and what may be achieved, and it requires a fuller understanding of business processes and the part that information plays in them. It is noteworthy that a 'top down' view of information systems is of relatively recent significance. Most system improvements have been and still are aimed at lower levels, and the production of information for management as a primary objective of business systems has only gained general acceptance since the computer became established as a business machine.

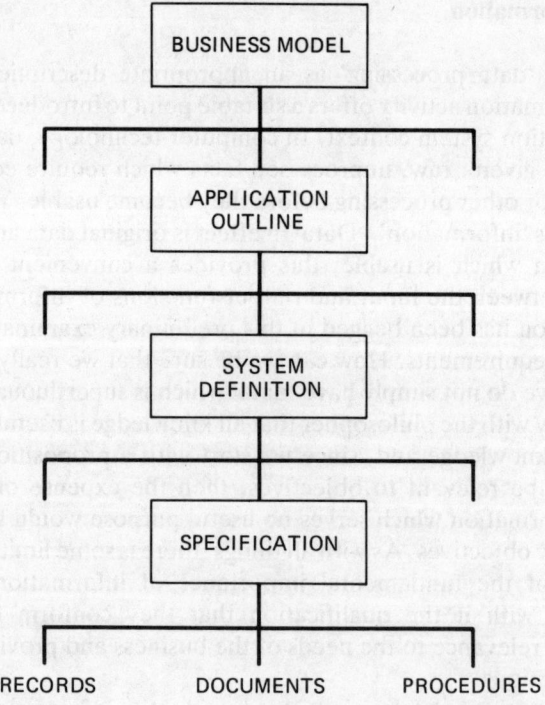

Figure 14 'Top down' system development

One important qualification to the definitions of data and information is that data does not necessarily have to be altered to become useful; it may simply be a matter of making it available at the right time and place. Much of the business problem is one of communication because data recording and processing do not always take place at the point where the information and output is required. The means of transmitting data — in practical terms, post, telephone and electronic data transmission — are essential parts of information systems. As is explained later, it is the bringing together of these communication techniques with computers that has so changed the scope and importance of machine information systems in the last few years.

Financial Accounting

Money as the measure of control, performance, cost and profitability is the most important element of business information; every kind of business undertaking has a financial function, keeps accounting records and depends on financial information for most of its major decisions. Understanding of financial terms and concepts is necessary for any business manager and this is an appropriate starting point for a closer examination of business information.

Capital

When a new business organisation is to be created, the first action is to decide what the business will do; the second is to obtain the financial resources required to set it up. Initial finance may be obtained from private sources (shareholders or membership) from the money market (banks or other finance houses), or from Government or Government agencies. It may be in the form of permanent investment, of long or short term borrowing, or of outright State grants. Even at such an early stage, before the business is little more than a legal entity, the management processes of planning will have begun; there will be objectives and there will be the need for information.

Initial funds will be used as 'capital' to acquire assets essential to the business — premises, machines, vehicles and other material resources which will provide facilities that the business needs before its operations can start. Capital will also be required to finance provision of initial stocks of goods or materials and a labour force to set the business going. Once in operation, further 'working' capital will be needed to maintain the business; to meet all day-to-day expenses until productive activities have generated sufficient income to match expenditure.

The kind of business project that involves heavy capital investment and a long delay before a return is received, such as planting a forest or sinking a mine, or speculative construction of a new warehouse or office building, is likely to require very substantial working capital. It may be a long time before such a business builds up its 'production' and income to the point where there is a net financial benefit.

Cash Flow

If expenditure is not met by taxation, then funds must come from one of three sources: from further borrowing, from payments received from customers, or from credit allowed by suppliers through delay between receipt of goods and the payment for them. If the organisation is to be viable (that is, not continually operating at a deficit which has to be met by taxpayers or membership subvention) this flow of funds must provide sufficient income to meet all business expenditure on production activities, and cover the costs of replacing those machines and other fixed assets which were acquired initially. It must also provide payment for the use of any money which has been borrowed — payment of interest on money borrowed is an expense just like any other. If one looks at the use and movement of funds in a business (in financial reporting, often called the 'source' and the 'application' of funds) one can see it in terms of a flow of cash into and out of the business, with a balance of cash held to provide for immediate expenses. (figure 15).

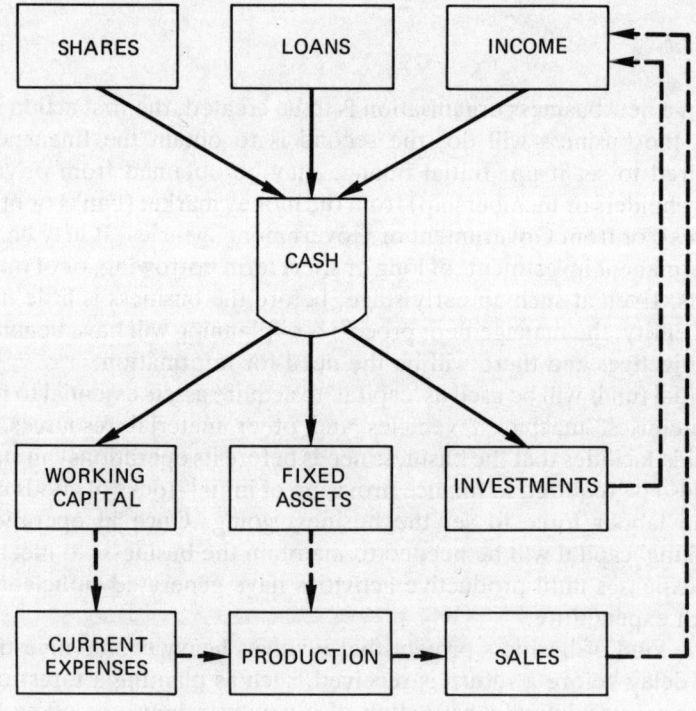

Figure 15   Cash flow

This concept of 'cash flow' is, in the short term, more important than profitability in any business undertaking. If a business does not have a sufficient inflow of funds to match its committed outgoings, and is unable to borrow to cover the difference, it will go out of business whether or not its accounts show it to be profitable.

This can happen, paradoxically, as a result of business expansion when the future might be regarded with some optimism. In commercial transactions it is usual to allow customers some weeks of credit before they pay for the goods they have purchased, and the achievement of expanding sales successfully might cause a business to be short of cash simply because of the time-lag between increased expenditure on higher production and compensating increases in receipts from sales.

This brings us to two essential features of financial information. It is necessary for a business to know the 'source' and 'application' of its funds, and to be able to produce a 'Balance Sheet' (see later) which shows the 'liabilities' and 'assets'. It is even more important (in the short run) to have information which will enable the business to map expected cash outgoings and receipts from given courses of action, so that it knows that it will have sufficient cash to do what it intends or will have enough time to make the necessary arrangements. The Cash Flow Forecast, showing period by period in advance the effect of the business's commitments and expectations in terms of inflow and outflow of cash, is an essential record for financial management (figure 16).

CASH FLOW STATEMENT (Extract)
(£000)

This month			Next month
Actual	Variance from budget		
1304	+ 27	Operating Receipts	1560
(833)	−119	*Less* Payments	(945)
471	+ 92	Operating Surplus/ Deficiency	615
—	—	Capital Expenditure	(550)
(42)	+ 42	Other Receipts/ Payments	—
429	+ 50	Net Surplus/Deficit	65
(533)		Balance/Overdraft B/F	(104)
(104)		Balance/Overdraft C/F	(39)

Figure 16   Cash Flow Forecast

Financial Data

The data sources from which information showing the general financial condition of a business is obtained, and from which financial forecasts can be derived, are the basic business transactions — income/receipts and expenditure/payments, related to all sales and purchase items which make up the activities of the business. Recording of these transactions in two forms relates to the movements of cash — receipts and payments — and to the effects on profitability — income and expenditure. The differences between monies received and expended, and values receivable or payable are, in essence, matters of timing.

Keeping a record of financial transactions is more than a means of gauging overall financial conditions. It provides invaluable information sources for action to control the processing of transactions through which these financial records are related, for initiating further action (as, for example, when Sales Despatch triggers Sales Accounting action to collect the resulting debt) and for ensuring that resources are being properly used.

Ledger Accounting

Every undertaking keeps records of its business transactions in the form of financial accounts. Such accounts are needed to provide evidence to meet statutory requirements governing the conduct of business affairs, as well as to inform owners and management of the state of the business and thence to enable them to make decisions about the future, as mentioned above.

There are many different ways in which financial information may be used and presented to assist decisions, and there are conventions about keeping basic accounting records derived from legal requirements, business customs and standards adopted by the accounting professions, all of which vary from country to country. The underlying concept of 'ledger accounting' is, however, generally accepted. This provides for maintaining detailed records of income and expenditure under complementary account headings, reflecting the two aspects of any transaction: the item bought or sold (the 'nominal account' entry) and the business or person to whom it was sold or from whom it was bought (the 'personal account' entry).

This concept of 'double entry', with its objective of achieving an overall balancing of all debits and credits in ledger accounts, and the associated use of summary accounts to control accuracy of recording and to provide usable information, was sensibly evolved originally to meet the practical necessities of manual accounting methods. With the introduction of machine systems these conventions have been modified; modern methods of recording and presenting financial information may be difficult to reconcile with traditional account-ancy, but the general principles remain. It is essential for anyone concerned with business management to have some understanding of business account-ing; this is also desirable for anyone who wishes to acquire a good understand-ing of business information systems.

Such concepts might appear simple enough when related to easily identifiable transactions such as payment of employees' salaries or billing to customers for value of goods sold to them but, in the realities of business activity, accounting is not simple or straightforward. The first business computers were gladly exploited by employers grappling with problems of manually calculating employee pay, which might be made up of as many as 60 different elements, but these tiresome calculations are relatively straightforward compared with decisions about allocating costs of an item of capital equipment over its working life, or making provision for future tax liability.

It is because business accounting records can become extremely complex and inaccurate, and because they must satisfy interested parties outside the organisation itself (the owners and the Government bodies having some claim for tax or other impost), that it is mandatory for all private and public organisations of any consequence to employ external auditors to inspect financial records and certify that proper books of accounts have been kept.

Final Accounts

One important part of this certification, and an aspect of business accounts which may be all that the outside observer is likely to see, is the final accounts: the summary of ledger accounts which is prepared at the end of each (annual) cycle of business activity. In the United Kingdom there are customarily two principal forms of report in the final accounts: the Profit and Loss account and the Balance Sheet which summarise respectively income and expenditure over the accounting period, and the financial position of the organisation at the end of that period.

The Profit and Loss account shows totals of expenditure on labour, materials and other purchases, and provisions such as 'depreciation' to take account of the declining value of machines and other capital assets. Against this is set income from sales and other sources, the difference between the two sides (income and expenditure) representing a surplus or deficit of income for the period (figure 17).

Profit and Loss Account for year ended

	£millions
Sales/Turnover	3486.7
Operating Expenses	(3148.6)
Operating Profit	338.1
Investment Income	16.0
Finance Costs	(69.9)
Profit before tax	284.2
Taxation	83.9
Profit after tax	200.3
Dividends	98.0
Retained Profit	102.3

Figure 17   Profit and Loss Account

The Balance Sheet summarises the assets — property, machines, stocks, cash, and the debts owing to the business — and the liabilities — to trade creditors and to those who have provided funds (figure 18). The difference between the value of all the assets and of the liabilities represents the true value or the 'net worth' of the business to the owners. To be understood properly, Balance Sheets require careful qualification as well as knowledge of the underlying accounting structure. As with the detailed accounts, they are not always easy reading. Nevertheless, they and other elements of final accounts are extremely useful in providing some appreciation of the main elements of business activity and the essentials for prosperous survival. Comprising a summary of all the financial records, they are one of the main end-products of any business information system.

Balance Sheet as at

£m

CAPITAL EMPLOYED

Tangible Assets	733.2
Investments	167.4
	900.6
Inventories/Stocks	565.4
Accounts Receivable/Debtors	670.5
Cash	119.6
	1355.5
Accounts Payable/Creditors due within one year	(920.9)
Net Current Assets	434.6
Total Assets less Current Liabilities	1335.2
Accounts Payable/Creditors due after one year	419.6
Provision for Liabilities	30.3
	885.3

FINANCED BY

Share Capital	132.7
Reserves	752.5
	885.3

Figure 18   Balance Sheet

One further useful observation can be made about financial information. Although there may be wide difference in the type and number of transactions between one business organisation and another, there will be found a substantial element of similarity between all financial accounting systems. One can break down the financial recording of business activities to common groups of elements such that (with some relatively modest exceptions dealing with special circumstances in individual industries) common accounting systems may be applied in which differences are confined to account 'labels' and to the volumes and values of the transactions recorded.

As has been shown by the popularity of 'packaged' computer applications, many business needs for financial information can be met from standard system modules with little adjustment. Where differences between businesses may become sharper is in the use that is made of basic information for management purposes, and that is an aspect which is discussed later.

Financial Measurement

Finance and accountancy uses a number of terms which are related to aspects of financial measurement

- Profitability: aspects of the relationship between income and expenditure
- Return on investment: ratio of income or benefit received to a given value of investment
- Stockturn: sales revenue as a ratio to stock value
- Liquidity: availability of cash.

These and other terms will be found in varying guises as essential measures of financial performance and condition.

When using financial information to judge business performance, even at the overall level, it is not sufficient to establish that a surplus has been made or that the business has sufficient cash to meet its immediate obligations. To acknowledge that business objectives have been achieved implies that the nature of the return on investment or other benefit derived has met the criteria for fully effective business operation. It should also be implicit that the return is at least as great as could be obtained from using the same resources elsewhere. If we have money to lend, our choice of borrower will depend on risk, the period of the loan and the interest or other return we receive. Risks and accessibility being equal, we will choose the higher interest. From the borrower viewpoint it must be expected that the 'market rate' will be paid; therefore, the purpose for which the loan is required should be such as to generate a return commensurate with that payment of market rate of interest. Admittedly, with intangible or indirectly connected returns from such State-funded projects as roads and social services, estimation and comparison of rates of return may be extremely difficult but the principle remains valid.

The argument follows through to the general question of business profitability. If a private business is not generating a return from all the capital invested in it equivalent to the return that capital could have received if invested elsewhere, then the business will have no hope of attracting further funds should it need them. A business must be 'credit worthy'; for this to be achieved, it must have appropriate financial objectives, leading to an acceptable credit status. There must be information which helps managers to exercise proper financial control over the business activities and which allows those wishing to assess its credit status to make informed judgements. Financial information, therefore, goes beyond recording and analysing data about business activities; it must include also information specifically for financial management.

Management Accounting

Balance Sheets and Profit and Loss statements, and other aspects of final accounts and key measures of performance, are needed to provide owners and senior management with information about the general state of the business, to support major policy and investment decisions and to provide summary information in compliance with statutory requirements. However, the use of financial information for management purposes is much greater than this and extends right through the organisation structure.

The term 'Management Accounting' is relatively recent in business, as is the general concept of management information. Previously 'Cost Accounting' was used because interpretation of accounting information for management usually related to costs. The growing importance of financial information for effective control of business over the last forty years has led to the recognition of Management Accounting as a major functional and organisational element of normal business structures. It has become established as at least equal to, and sometimes more important than, the 'financial accounting' and 'treasury' functions of maintaining accounting records and supervising funding which have always been accepted as essential aspects of business financial management.

Management Accounting is an information function. It does not have to be carried out in the sense that it does not arise directly from the basic activities of the business and, if the Management Accountant ceased to work for a period, the business would not immediately come to a halt. Without this function, however, there would be inadequate understanding of the business. There would be no means of identifying significant elements of income and expenditure and no means of assessing and comparing performance in the use of business resources without the two prime, associated elements of management accounting — Costing and Budgetary Control.

Costing

It is not possible to know if a business undertaking, as a whole or in respect of any of its activities or products, is profitable or financially viable without knowledge of its costs. The objective of survival therefore depends on such knowledge. It would be equally impossible to achieve other types of business objective because they all imply an understanding of costs. To improve profitability means either reducing costs or improving revenue, or both. Improving revenue, whether for profitability alone or as part of an objective of expansion can only be achieved successfully with an understanding of the cost side of that expansion. To expand sales through launching a new product makes sense only if the selling price of that product is greater than its cost.

An aim to reduce costs, whether or not this is the over-riding consideration, will feature in most business plans. Successful implementation of such plans requires information about how costs are made up and how they have occurred. That is the theory, and that is the practice in well-managed undertakings, but it does not always occur. The process of controlling costs is often cruder.

A practice much favoured by Government bodies is to set overall spending limits, exerting pressure to reduce costs by setting those limits lower than the declared need of the organisations or departments subjected to financial control. Whether this method is chosen because there is insufficient information about costs or because the allocation of responsibilities within the organisation is badly conceived, there is no doubt that such a simplistic method does not work very well. Spending departments react by providing inflated forecasts of their financial needs, by always spending up to authorised limits whether resources are needed or not and, where forced to achieve economies, by excising selected essential activities sufficient to create general alarm and exert counter-pressure on spending limits. Whatever the merits of the original cost-reduction objectives, such situations demonstrate a lack of good cost information, and of good management.

Cost Centres

There are two aspects of costs to be considered: the relationship between cost and return — whether an action is likely to be worthwhile in financial terms — and 'unit-cost reduction': producing a given result with fewer resources by improving productivity. Savings can be achieved by cutting out activities which are not financially justified and by becoming more efficient. Both of these things bring us directly into the sphere of information systems and of computers.

The basic principle of costing as an accounting technique is to attach cost labels to business activities so that information about accounting transactions (recorded in ledger accounts) can be analysed to provide a picture of cost make-up and origin. Where this information does not derive directly from records created for other routine accounting purposes, special records may be set up — as, for example, in connection with estimating cost of future activities which are to be brought into planning. Cost labels are broadly of two kinds, one related to 'cost centres' — analysing expenditure between organisational departments — and the other related to unit costs — showing the make-up of total product cost in terms of proportions of resources that have gone into the production process.

One of the main objectives of subdividing a business organisation depart-mentally is delegation of financial responsibility and, as one would expect, identification of cost centres usually follows the organisational structure. Conventional financial accounting records provide a breakdown of total expenditure over the various 'nominal' headings: pay, accommodation costs, fuel, etc. These two ways of looking at expenditure — cost centre and nominal account — can be brought together to provide a further breakdown. From this, a comparison can be made and significant items of expenditure can be distinguished from minor ones.

A distinction can be made between the main 'production' activities and those which support them (including provision of management information). Support service costs can be allocated proportionately against production so that a clearer picture is obtained of the consequences of resource decisions, such as to take on one extra employee. The direct cost of an employee is the salary and any pension, insurance or taxation elements which follow from the employment. These last items may add an additional 20 per cent or more to the salary cost, but that total still may represent only a minor part of the total cost of employment. Provision of the 'work station': space, furniture, equipment etc., and of the services that the employee will use — personnel, training, communications, transport, stationery and other materials — add to the total financial commitment. In some industries it can mean that the true cost of an extra employee is several times the money actually paid as salary.

Information about such matters as 'hidden' labour costs offer an important lesson to management. If the implications of employment decisions are viewed in terms of the total contractual commitment, they can be found to represent a substantial investment for each person, even at low skill levels. At the very least it is desirable to have a clear understanding of possible consequences, both direct and indirect, of such a decision at the time it is made, and it is an indication of the inadequacy of many business information systems that employment of people has tended to be treated much more lightly than employment of other resources. In business, it has always been easier to employ a typist than to buy a typewriter.

Unit Costs

In any 'trading' situation it is desirable to identify the unit cost of products or services. Whether or not the selling price is directly related to the cost (for example, by a percentage 'mark-up'), it is advantageous to know where the profit (or loss) is earned. Establishing unit costs is rarely a simple matter, nor is such information always readily obtainable from basic accounting records. Even for a 'single product' business, unit costing is more than a question of apportioning total expenditure over the number of units produced. Allowance needs to be made for the proportion of total capacity used and the probable effect if volume of output changes. To allocate cost to individual processes or stages of production, or to allow for any variation in the end product, it is necessary to decide on some method of apportioning expenditure so that costs will be reflected fairly against each process or product.

One notable effect of the increased attention paid to costing in the last 40 years has been a dramatic reduction in the range of choice for the consumer. Manufacturers and distributors have discovered the cost of 'small selling lines' and have concentrated their efforts on production of limited ranges from which economies of scale can be derived, and which can be supported economically with appropriate marketing expenditure. Whether or not such decisions always have been entirely sound is another matter, and is itself an indication that information about costs and other internal aspects do not represent all the information that is needed to make fully balanced and objective business decisions. Nonetheless, there is no question that it is desirable to take proper account of all the elements of cost of using resources, and relate them to the productive activity of a business.

Fixed and Variable Costs

In building up cost information, a general distinction is made between fixed and variable costs. In any business, certain minimum costs are incurred whether the organisation is active or not; a factory which is producing nothing or a shop which is empty will still bear the same costs related to acquiring the resources to create production facilities (accommodation, machines, equipment etc.) as it would if it were in productive operation. There will be costs which, although necessary to running the business, will not vary directly with the amounts produced, such as the provision of administrative and decision support services to maintain production facilities and to provide information for management. These 'overhead' expenses include many of the activities of personnel and accounting functions, cleaning and maintenance of accommodation and equipment, and many of the costs of marketing and selling. There will also be costs which are directly related to production, such as raw materials, fuel and labour engaged in production processes (figure 19).

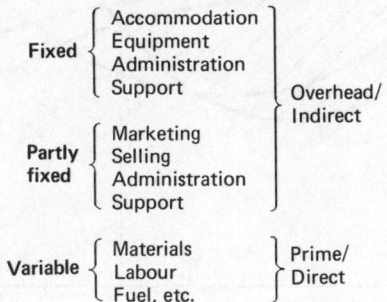

Figure 19   Fixed and variable costs

The relationship between fixed and variable costs is important to understanding factors affecting profitability. The effect of an increase in output on unit costs usually will be different for each extra unit produced, because fixed costs will remain virtually unchanged until capacity is filled whereas variable costs will change in differing degrees as output rises. Starting with a very high cost for the first unit (depending on the size of the fixed cost element), the unit (average) cost at increased output levels will fall because the marginal cost (the addition to total costs through adding one more unit of production) will include only the variable elements.

In classical economics, marginal cost is a key indicator at two points in the scale of production: where it equals average cost at the lowest cost per unit and where marginal cost equals marginal revenue (the net addition to total revenue from selling one more unit) to show the maximum profit. Easily demonstrated in theory, but much more difficult to identify in practice, reliable information about marginal cost and its relationship with marginal revenue would clearly be of great value to any business-making decisions about expansion and profitability (figure 20).

One reason why practice is more difficult than economic theory is that few businesses have one product for which revenue and cost can be plotted in smooth curves. Although it is true that we can look for falling marginal cost as overheads are spread more thinly over expanded production and as greater efficiency in use of resources is achieved, there are limits to this process. When

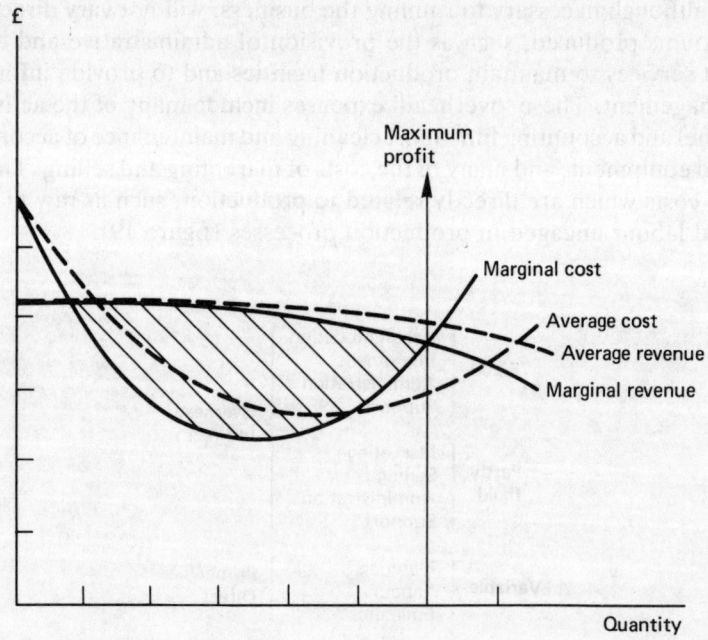

Figure 20   Economic theory: significance of the margin

the physical capacity of a factory, warehouse, shop, hospital ward or passenger bus is filled, there must then be a sharp increase in the fixed cost element to provide a further unit of capacity. Fixed costs, therefore, will increase in steps. Semi-variable costs — the indirect costs of supporting services — will increase in smaller steps, but these are still greater usually than those related to increases in production itself.

Optimum Size

Economies of scale are limited and even direct costs will not remain the same per unit for unlimited expansion. In other words, there is an optimum size for any kind of business activity. This may be determined by limitations of technology or of the economic environment as, for example, with means of transport. It may be a consequence of physical limitations of human energy or skill, of the size and location of sources of raw material, or of markets; it may be concerned with the complexity of handling excessive volumes of information; or it may be through limitations of management ability.

Technological change and the development of more effective information and management systems have permitted sustained growth of very large organisational units, catering for (in many cases) world markets, but it is also notable that it is usually large organisations which have labour problems; they become too big for the effective management of people. This illustrates another important consideration in the approach to questions of management information. Costs do not rise (or fall) evenly with changes in the size of the business because the optimum size for any individual process, activity or organisational unit will not be the same throughout. At any one time an organisation may be at its peak of efficiency in one respect and very inefficient in another; the overall optimum position represents a compromise. Cost information systems must be able to identify these different optima or, at least, those which are most significant so that correct decisions can be made at critical junctures.

Cost Allocation

Much of cost analysis, whether by cost centre or by unit of production, is a question of allocating expenditure in appropriate proportions. With departmental costs one has to consider how to allocate the cost of supporting services; with unit costs one has to deal with fixed and semi-variable costs. This means that it is necessary to determine the costs of using fixed assets and other resources employed in the business (such as cost per machine hour, per vehicle mile, per labour hour, per square metre of accommodation). Cost of accommodation is vital to the economics of many business undertakings (as, for example, with High Street shops or city centre offices) and it would be imprudent to charge accommodation cost as a general overhead without considering which functions are using the space. An appropriate basis for allocating costs must be determined (for accommodation, it might be in proportion to the space occupied); it is usually difficult to decide what that cost should be since it will be made up of different elements including rent, maintenance of the fabric, heating, lighting, cleaning and property taxes.

To produce useful information about costs involves four major elements

- Basic records of all relevant aspects of expenditure
- Identification of cost headings to be applied to each cost centre and production unit
- Establishment of appropriate criteria for cost allocation
- Extraction, calculation and accumulation of cost figures under appropriate headings.

There is one further consideration: if cost calculations are based on expenditure data, one is necessarily applying (at least in part) historical data to a current situation. This may be satisfactory if the wish is to know what the actual costs have been, but if the intention is to apply cost estimates to future activities (as in Budgetary Control — see the next section), then historical records will be inappropriate because future cost of resources may change and because the actual production situation itself may also be different. Whereas some costs may be predicted with accuracy, others may not be known at the time that cost calculations are made.

It is usually necessary to introduce some element of estimation into information systems as, for example, by the creation of 'standards' set from a basis of historical data adjusted for future expectations. The quality of such information will have direct bearing on the quality of decisions which use it and, since the use of some form of estimation is moving cost information away from the firm base of certified accounting records, these kinds of information system need additional elements of control.

Budgetary Control

So far, costing has been examined as a means of providing information from which essential decisions can be made: information for planning new activities, for identification of business problems leading to more effective use of resources, and for better understanding of profitability in the interests of ensuring viability for the business. It is also relevant to day-to-day management matters, including preparation of short-term plans and monitoring and control of normal business operations. There is a general business need for projection and allocation of expenditure and revenue, to give a detailed financial picture of the next activity period as a prelude to operational decisions, and then to relate actual results to those projections in order to maintain control over the fulfilment of short-term plans.

The general concept of Budgetary Control is that detailed estimates of future expenditure and revenue are prepared for each cost and revenue heading under which information is to be accumulated; estimates are usually broken down over each month of the next (financial) year. These figures are derived from the physical targets (amount and nature of planned output, and resources required for its production) to which estimated prices are applied. The targets will be derived from quantitative and financial projections which it has been decided must be met if the business as a whole is to achieve (expansion or other) objectives set for the next year. The resulting financial plan becomes a fundamental part of the information systems, linking primary objectives and decisions with operating functions.

When approved by those responsible for direction of the business, the financial plan becomes a budget against which actual expenditure and revenue will be compared month by month so that variances from the plan can be identified and, if necessary, action can be taken. Variances may be caused by failure to adhere to original intentions, by unexpected events, or by deficiencies in the plans themselves. The importance to business managers of budgetary control is in making it possible either to know that everything is going according to plan or, if not, to be able to identify where and why actual results deviate from plans.

Preparation of budgets is usually supervised by financial officers with the participation of all the operating and service functions; the financial department will be responsible also for the provision of comparative budget and actual figures which involve setting up information systems in parallel to basic accounting records. For many businesses these budgetary accounts supply key management information for both departmental and corporate management levels. Revenue and Expenditure summaries, together with Cash Flow Forecasts will be found as essential elements of control of business operations for Boards of Management; these are more important in reality than the (historical) annual summaries provided by the end of the year Profit and Loss accounts and Balance Sheet (figures16, 17, 18 and 21). Periodic Revenue and Expenditure summaries for management must be produced and examined close to the events to which they relate so that effective action can be taken; final accounts will do no more than present a considered and audited view of the previous year's performance of the business, well into the following year.

COMPANY OPERATING STATEMENT — MONTH £000

Budget	Actual		Year-to-date	Budget±
−26.7	553,3	Orders Processed	2397.3	+307.7
−0.3	(86.2)	Sales Expenses	(411.1)	+30.3
−26.4	467.1	Net Sales Contribution	1986.2	+277.4
−10.0	(376.5)	Operating Expenses	(1510.5)	+236.2
−5.5	(47.8)	Provisions	(209.2)	−10.9
−10.9	42.8	Trading Profit	266.5	+52.1

Figure 21   Revenue and Expenditure summaries

Management accounting, in all its various aspects of analysis and presentation of cost and revenue information, can be used to illustrate some of the particular benefits that have come from machine accounting and computer-based information systems for financial management.

Preparing management accounting information involves adding to basic book-keeping systems additional layers of calculation and analysis which, if done by hand, could require as much work again as is required to produce the essential accounting records. With machine systems, the marginal cost of such extra work usually is relatively small; in consequence, better management information has proved to be one of the most substantial benefits of computer systems, often more valuable than economies in handling the repetitive routines of basic record-keeping. The increasing sophistication of computer systems, creating the ability to introduce more and more complex elements of machine decision, has also made possible easy access to selective information. The concept of 'management by objectives' — formalising relationships between decision and action responsibility and linking them clearly to detailed strategic and tactical plans — requires information systems which will readily provide effective support at every decision level. The easier it is to provide such information cheaply, quickly and accurately, and in a form in which it can be understood, the more likely it is that business management theory will be matched by practice. It is not surprising that anyone concerned with decision-making in business, when offered the choice, will opt for information systems which will respond to questions by providing the answer when it is needed rather than present a haystack of figures in which to search.

Quantitative Information

Financial information is not sufficient for all purposes; the calculations for financial plans need quantitative data first. In the preparation of a budget, the primary targets, which might be framed in financial terms (such as sales value) would give rise to quantitative budgets (such as sales and raw material quantities), which in turn would be evaluated to arrive at the detailed financial budget.

There are also many situations in which financial measures of performance are inappropriate or give only a broad indication of problem areas. To provide fully useful management information, financial and quantitative data must complement each other. Although money is an essential measure in business, it is unsuitable or impossible to use in many management information systems without qualification: for example, in a situation where the value of money is declining (a normal condition in much of present-day economic society). When prices of goods and services are rising, it can be misleading to use cost of labour and machines, or value of sales, as comparative measures between different accounting periods. A business aiming for a 5 per cent expansion will not have achieved its objective if the value of sales increased by 5 per cent in a year in which inflation was 6 per cent. For true comparison, allowance has to be made for changes in wage rates, in capital and maintenance costs of machines, and in market selling prices; like must be compared with like and it is desirable to use measures which are stable, such as working hours or numbers of units sold.

Quantitative data can be made available as readily as can financial data; at every stage of business activity such data should be generated to provide a picture of the work situation. For direction and control of resources there needs to be data showing how these resources have been allocated and used for different tasks. In manufacturing, for example, the production process may start with schedules of resources to be used at planned times (materials, machines and labour) for given quantities. In the day-to-day control and subsequent analysis of production performance, work-in-progress at each stage will be measured. From this information the business will know what it plans to do, what its work situation is at any given time, and what it has done in a given period. This quantitative information shows a different, complementary aspect of business activity to financial information, as well as providing basic data for the financial picture which is painted in costing, budgeting and financial period-end accounting.

Stock Control

An aspect of quantitative information which is important in any kind of business undertaking is the recording of stocks. Whether the business is manufacturing, trading in wholesale or retail markets, or is providing a professional or public service, some part of its resources will be in the form of stocks. Stocks of raw materials or finished goods are information sources of obvious significance in trading concerns; equally important to a transport undertaking are stocks of vehicle spares and stocks of books to a library. Stocks represent value 'tied up' in the business: working capital which has to be provided in anticipation of future activity. The size of stock poses a dilemma; an excessively large stock means higher operating costs because it represents money which otherwise could be used productively elsewhere; too small a stock means a business cannot meet its commitments and other resources will be in enforced idleness. From the financial management viewpoint, cost of holding stocks is seen as a burden on the business; from the production and sales viewpoints, ready availability of particular items of stocks are seen as essential to meet production or selling commitments. The understandable and unavoidable 'conflict of interest' between financial, production and sales management which is typical of business activity usually involves a compromise; if this is not to be arbitrary and unsatisfactory, it must be based on a firm understanding of the situation both from the financial and quantitative aspects.

As with other kinds of management information, it is not sufficient to have a static or historic view of the stock situation. Management information must be dynamic; it must help managers to take objective decisions about the future —

to anticipate shortages, or to prevent over-stocking by correlating information about stock 'movement' and 'balances' with data about likely future consumption and replenishment.

That most useful of economic dicta — the 'Pareto principle', or the '80:20 proposition' that 80 per cent of stock items represents 20 per cent of stock or sales value, and vice versa — has its place in management information. A 'Pareto distribution' refers to situations where data values are not spread evenly, so that data categories do not have the same significance. The 'Pareto principle' has been identified with typical business transactions where a minority of stock items or transactions represents a majority of values or significant events. The concept of 'value engineering' as an essential management tool is really an extension from the common-sense observation that Pareto's principle or something akin to it does seem to operate. In any mass of stock items or business transactions some will be more important than others, and it is on these important items that the financial health of the business will depend. The business that engineers its control systems and the efficiency of its operations to take particular account of expenditure or revenue items which represent the greatest value is likely to achieve the best results. Computers have made it very easy to undertake value analysis and it is this ability to focus quickly on matters of importance that has led to marketing policies which eliminate uneconomic 'small selling lines', and to production policies involving rationalisation of parts content and processes. To turn common-sense theories into practice, however, requires the application of effective means of collecting, analysing and presenting information so that the business can know what is important to it.

Management Reports

The variety of management reporting can be summarised under the following headings

- Key financial control — monitoring critical performance points against plans
- Support of long-range and project planning
- Location and diagnosis of business problems
- Facilitation of the day-to-day business
- Exception reporting.

In the earlier examination of management information needs, mention is made of some essential reports for overall financial management, including final accounts and cash flow forecasts. In a business of any substance these financial reports will be complemented and supported by many other reports aimed at resource planning and control, showing how resources such as materials, machines and labour are being used and the commitments for their future use. 'Corporate planning' may be identified as a specific responsibility — planning and information services which are concerned with the longer term (say, 3 to 5 years ahead). Any organisation which intends to be in business for more than a year must concern itself with long-range planning in some sense, and certainly must do so wherever significant capital expenditure is involved or there is a material difference in time between a decision and its ultimate effect. Long-range forecasting is essential to proper management control; a computer project itself provides an obvious example of a business activity which requires long-term information about use of resources and possible effects on decisions and action.

However, information about the future can only be factual about committed events such as contracts for construction of plant or delivery of machines; even these contain some uncertainty because cost of construction may rise and delivery may be delayed. Much forward planning is speculative, notably in forecasts related to revenue. Sales forecasts might be based on extrapolation from past trends, on analysis of market research information or derived from sales representatives' reports. With a continuing operation involving no significant change from one period to the next, desirable results are often obtained from extrapolation of historical data but, where there are new activities or a large number of variables likely to affect the end result, more sophisticated techniques of management reporting may be required. The use of scientific method for the construction of mathematical models or evaluation of probabilities if properly conducted, is much more likely to provide reliable indications of the range of possible consequences of management decisions than are subjective views and opinions.

Management reporting needs to be seen as going beyond the preparation of regular report summaries, whether extracted from routine recording systems or specifically designed for management information.

Ad hoc information gathering is an appropriate method of providing support to business decisions in many situations; simulation to test hypotheses before being committed firmly to a plan of action, or sample analysis of current activities or historical data to locate and measure business problems are examples. Random checking is well established where quality control is needed as a means of measuring performance against standards without undue expense. Information systems do not have to be constructed by taking every piece of raw data and distilling from it every drop of essential information; it should be an accepted management function to make use of whatever techniques are appropriate for the production of usable information, bearing in mind always that the information must be worth more than it costs to produce.

Check List 5

To make decisions, an organisation must have information about its resources and activities. Information is not useful for its own sake; it must be relevant to the needs of the business and must answer the right questions. Finance is the most important element of business information, and understanding of financial terms and concepts is necessary for any business management.

Financial information is not sufficient for all purposes; there is also a need for quantitative information and physical measures of performance where financial measures are inappropriate.

Defining the Business Problem
What kind of business are we in?

Management Information Needs
Controlling activities.
Measuring performance.
Keeping records.
Forecasting.
Environmental information.

Financial Terms
Capital: equity, loan, working.
Source and application of funds.
Cash flow.
Final accounts.
Revenue and expenditure.

Financial Measurement
Profitability.
Turnover.
Return on investment.
Liquidity.
Net worth.

Management Accounting
Costs: unit, fixed, variable, marginal.
Budgetary control.

Quantitative Information
Scheduling and work-in-progress.
Stock recording.
Utilisation of resources.
Sales analysis.
Forecasting.

Further Reading

Arnold, J. and Hope, T., *Accounting for Management Decisions*, Prentice-Hall, 1983.

Cooke, S. and Slack, N., *Making Management Decisions*, Prentice-Hall, 1984.
Hindmarch, A., *Accounting — An Introduction*, Macmillan, 1977.
Hitching, C. and Stone, D., *Understanding Accounting*, Pitman, 1985.
Lucey, J., *Management Accounting*, DP Publications, 1983.
Savage, G. and Small, J.R., *Introduction to Managerial Economics*, Hutchinson, 1967.

6 Systems

The examination of business management topics so far has progressed from concepts of business objectives to the decisions necessary to achieve those objectives, the organisation structures which identify the decision/action relationships and the information required to support the business decisions. This chapter is concerned with the systems which must be created to provide the information.

System Theory

Definition of a System

As a starting point for an explanation of basic system concepts it is desirable to offer some definitions. Most attempts to present a clear, memorable and succinct definition of a 'system' usually leave the impression that they do not quite provide a satisfactory explanation. Easy agreement on a definition is not helped by the lax way the term 'system' has been appropriated to computer jargon. In the world of computing one finds it used to mean both the particular use to which the computer has been applied and the computer equipment itself. The 'System Analyst' is concerned with that application whereas the 'Systems Programmer' is concerned with the technical facilities provided with the computer. Although open to some confusion, neither of these uses of the term is incorrect because a system can be a physical system (as in a machine) or it can be an information system (as in the business use to which the machine is put). Some care is needed to avoid misunderstanding and it is fortunate that a neat and apt definition is less important than a general appreciation of the elements which make up a business system, and which must be remembered by managers when considering the development of new systems.

A definition which takes account of all the basic system elements is that a system is a group or pattern of associated activities which will usually contain all of the following

- A common purpose
- An identifiable objective

- An established sequence of procedures and data flows including varying numbers of elements of input, movement, action, storage and output (figure 22)
- Feedback of information about and control over the system
- A definable boundary enclosing the system activities
- Dependence on specific data.

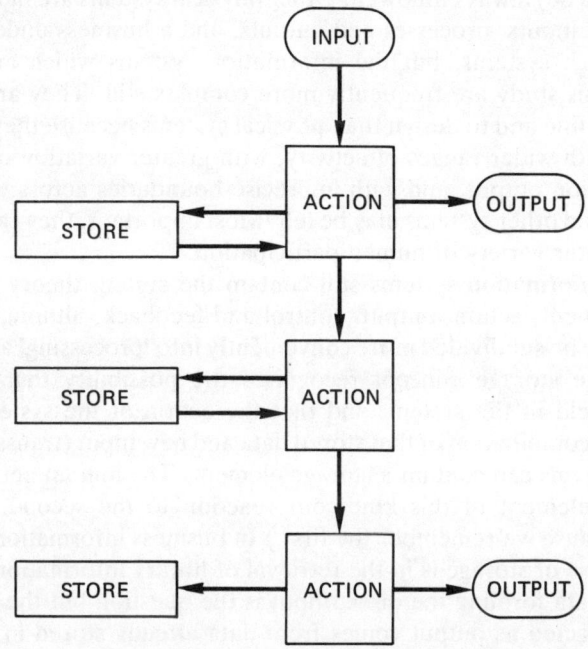

Figure 22   Basic system elements

Physical Systems and Information Systems

The system concept is most easily illustrated by reference to mechanical or other physical systems: vehicle brake, fuel or electrical systems, blood circulation or nervous systems in the human body, railway and road traffic signalling systems, commercial and industrial heating, and lighting and communication systems. Any of these could be readily defined in system terms. A vehicle braking system, for example, is intended to restrict the speed of movement of the vehicle through the application of braking pressures. Input to the system might be (say) manual pressure on a foot pedal, to be sent through the system to produce an output in the form of other pressure which causes moving wheels to be retarded. Information would be fed back as indications of changed speed, and control might be exercised by increasing or decreasing brake pedal pressure, dependent upon whether the result of the original pressure had been too little or too great. The boundary of the system would be the physical extent of all the items of equipment concerned with the whole process of braking. The data on which the system depended would be the pressure on the brake pedal.

Although a vehicle braking system may have a substantial degree of engineering sophistication, it is usually a fairly simple system concept with one kind of input data, one kind of output, and one simple set of procedures which are (or should be) always followed. Other physical systems are more complex, with multiple inputs, processes and outputs, and a business undertaking will use many such systems, but the information systems which are the main concern of this study are frequently more complex still. They are also more difficult to define and to design than physical systems because they are usually concerned with wider ranges of activity, with greater variation of data input and information output, and with imprecise boundaries across which strong influences from other systems may be felt. Most important, they can be subject to much greater variety of human participation.

Business information systems still contain the system theory elements of input, movement, action, output, control and feedback, although the action elements may be subdivided more conveniently into 'processing' and 'filing' or 'storage'. The storage concept recognises the possibility that data might already be held in the system, and that the action of the system might be affected by a combination of that stored data and new input (transaction) data. (Physical systems can contain a storage element. The human nervous system contains an element of this kind: our reaction to the second pin-prick is different because we remember the first.) In business information systems an example of use of storage is in the retrieval of library information, where the transaction data forming the direct input is the question but the information which is extracted as output comes from data already stored in the system. Necessarily, such a system will also have facilities for input of the stored data; provided the system retains the common purpose and identifiable objective, there is no reason why it should not have different processing, storage and output elements related to differing inputs, including distinct phases of operation and facilities for handling a number of transactions or activities at the same time.

System Boundaries

A general characteristic of information systems which needs to be examined in more detail is the boundary concept. The boundary should not be seen simply as enclosing one system but as separating two or more systems which meet at the points of input and output — the 'interface' between systems. Thus, a typical business administration system concerned with processing customer orders would be linked at the point of input with customers' order preparation systems (the order being the output of one and the input to the other) and, at the point of output with systems for customer accounting, stock replenishment and order despatch. A business undertaking can be seen as composed of a number of such interlocking information systems representing all the main business activities — order processing, stock control, sales accounting, and so on (figure 23).

Since the location of boundaries is dependent on the purpose and objectives with which the system is identified, it can be seen that the size and scope of a business information system (or of a physical system, for that matter) is not pre-determined in any sense. There can be systems within systems — larger systems made up of a number of sub-systems. The United Kingdom economy as a whole can be considered as a system composed of 1 500 000 businesses, each of which is composed of various administrative and other information sub-systems (just as a human body may be described as a complete system made up of separate physical, interlocked sub-systems).

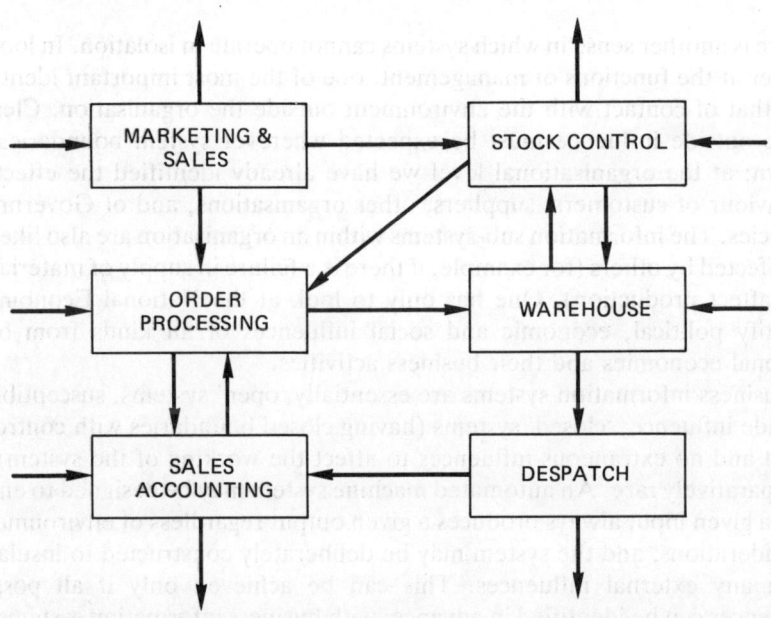

Figure 23   Interlocking information systems

Systems within businesses often coincide with organisational divisions because they usually represent the same managerial areas of responsibility. For a system to operate effectively it would be logical to have it under unified control so that all its parts and processes can work in harmony and its objectives remain clear. However, we must be a little cautious in accepting generalisations about business information systems because one of the special elements of computer-based systems is that they make it possible to escape from the restraints of manual systems and to extend information flows across organisational boundaries.

It may be inferred from the concept of a system as working within a defined boundary according to an established sequence of procedures that these procedures will all be designed to meet the purposes of that system. While this is true in general it needs qualification in two respects. The first is in relation to the input and output interfaces. At these points of contact with other systems there is common data which must be in a common form; in some way, therefore, each system must adapt to the other so that information can flow between them. If not imposing an actual restriction on the working of one or both systems, this must mean that neither can be designed or operate in isolation.

Closed and Open Systems

There is another sense in which systems cannot operate in isolation. In looking earlier at the functions of management, one of the most important identified was that of contact with the environment outside the organisation. Clearly, some outside influence must be expected wherever system boundaries are drawn; at the organisational level we have already identified the effects of behaviour of customers, suppliers, other organisations, and of Government agencies. The information sub-systems within an organisation are also likely to be affected by others (for example, if there is a failure in supply of materials, it will affect production). One has only to look at the National Economy to identify political, economic and social influences of all kinds from other national economies and their business activities.

Business information systems are essentially 'open' systems, susceptible to outside influence; 'closed' systems (having closed boundaries with controlled input and no extraneous influences to affect the working of the system) are comparatively rare. An automated machine system may be designed to ensure that a given input always produces a given output regardless of environmental considerations, and the system may be deliberately constructed to insulate it from any external influences. This can be achieved only if all possible influences can be identified in advance; with business information systems this is extremely difficult because so much external influence is the result of human behaviour which cannot be controlled from within the system.

To protect open systems from the unwanted effects of external influences, the system design must make provision for adequate means of feedback and control. It is desirable that a system be able to adapt itself to environmental change, or to correct any malfunction resulting from influences against which it has been unable to protect itself. When it cannot do either, the system must be changed or superseded by another, and it is in the nature of business activity that most organisations find themselves constantly having to adapt to change. In the current economic and social climate the rate of change is very rapid indeed, a reason why business today needs much better information systems than were ever necessary before.

Sub-system Interdependence

The idea of a business organisation as a system composed of a number of sub-systems linked by controlled flows of operational data and reacting to various kinds of controlled influences from other systems is still necessarily a gross simplification of the reality. Within an organisation, the functional and administrative divisions created to provide effective management will themselves be shaped by the need to divide the total business system into sub-systems containing common elements. In many cases these elements will share information and will most certainly be interdependent. The system boundary often will be a compromise and may be changed if one of the factors influencing the shape and scope of a particular sub-system is changed (for example, a change of management, of location or of data volumes). Of particular relevance is a change in method of achieving systems objectives brought about, perhaps, by the introduction of computer techniques in place of other methods. There is often an aim in the development of computer-based information systems towards an integrated structure as a means of bringing together all common functions and activities in a way which would not be economically viable with manual systems.

In the development of any business system (or of a business organisation itself) careful specification of each basic element is essential, but none is more important than the boundary. Identification of the interfaces with other systems is vital because the boundary will reflect declared systems objectives and identify the area within which action and decision elements may be changed and new procedures developed. Because one is never able to create a new system in isolation from others, the 'interface' with those other systems (which may themselves remain unchanged) can often be a major constraint in system design.

The scope of a business information system is most easily identified by grouping together all processes having a common source of prime data, which will flow through a series of linked operations until all information and action deriving from that data is completed. However, when one looks at business information systems, this concept frequently proves to be an over-simplification. While it might be true generally for a business as a total system, the sub-systems within it will not necessarily divide neatly into activities using separate data. For example, in a trading organisation, sales might be the prime data source for the business as a whole but would also act as one of the main data sources for the separate sales, production and accounting information systems within the total business.

Nevertheless, common data is the material which provides the flow that links associated activities in an information system, and the main system structure will usually be developed on the basis of one or more prime data sources. This is notably true of computer-based business data processing systems, which are usually constructed to handle substantial quantities of data related to a specific business application.

Types of Business Information System

In this section, business information systems are described in categories related to the principal business activities; in chapters 10 and 11, which are concerned with computer-based information systems, types of system are considered in slightly different terms, being categorised by reference to technical characteristics. In neither approach can systems always be labelled neatly under specific headings. All business systems are necessarily subject to the variations implicit in any activities relating to human behaviour. Systems may change, overlap, be continuous or intermittent, and perform precisely or unpredictably. Some systems may be found which do not fit easily under any heading; others would appear to embrace some or all of the categories.

Accepting the limitations of such categorisation, for the purposes of this examination six headings are identified

- Administrative
- Production
- Measurement and Analysis
- Monitoring and Control
- Library
- Communication

Administrative Systems

The administration category refers generally to the supporting services which are essential to the conduct of the main productive functions of a business. Usually the most important administrative systems in their relationship with the principal activities of business and in their use of resources are those concerned primarily with processing large volumes of repetitive data to maintain basic records about financial and quantitative aspects of business transactions, such as those for Sales, Purchases and Payroll.

With the typical Sales Accounting system, the main input transaction data will be sales charges (invoices) and cash receipts which are processed to update customer personal account files. From these customer accounting records, edited detail and summaries will be produced on demand or at regular intervals to provide such outputs as statements to customers showing their debt position, and reports and analyses for management. Purchases Accounting and Payroll can be described in comparable terms of stored and transaction data with sorting, editing, accumulating and other processes for production of output reports to meet *ad hoc* or regular demands for information.

The boundaries of such systems can be drawn with reference to homogeneous groups of output information, to central files related to conventional accounting, and to specified types of input transaction. Such system boundaries might well (and with manually operated systems usually would) coincide with organisational sub-divisions; for example, running the systems mentioned above possibly would be the responsibility of Sales Accounting, Purchasing and Pay sections of an Accounts Department.

Another notable characteristic of administrative systems is the repetitive nature of the processing of generally similar transactions. Calculations and other processes often may be relatively simple, but neither this nor the routine nature should in any way lead to the conclusion that administrative systems are of no great consequence. Effective administration is essential to the well-being of any business undertaking, and the collection and recording of administrative data also provides the foundation for many other important business information systems.

One other typical characteristic of the Administrative System is that it may be buffered from the main productive activities in the sense that a (short) delay in processing administrative data is not necessarily of vital consequence to the business. Thus an interruption or delay in posting of accounts may well have a cost and implications for the quality of some business decisions but will not immediately bring the business to a halt; this is one reason why administrative systems are sometimes considered as of lesser importance.

Production Systems

In contrast, business systems described under the 'production' heading have a more direct impact because they are concerned with essential business activities such as processing orders or scheduling manufacturing activities. Production systems may be similar to administrative systems in being concerned with processing large volumes of transaction data but have the distinction that system output is more likely to lead to immediate action involving employment of business resources. A typical example of a production system in a trading concern would be Order Processing. Order Processing systems are concerned with the actions following receipt of a customer's order — ensuring that the order is understood, that the customer is in good standing, that the goods ordered can be supplied, and then fulfilment of the order by providing instructions for action through linked Production or Despatch systems. Very little delay will be acceptable in the operation of such a system and, if the flow of orders is interrupted, the associated systems will also cease to operate after a very short time.

For trading businesses, the core of organisational links and systems relates to the key activities of selling, production and distribution. Whatever the product or service, production system data flows will be linked together in a sequence of events or processes which can be seen usually as starting with a 'sales plan' or 'order transaction'. For industry and commerce in general the starting point will be with the customer, for the professional business or social service the client, for the school the pupil, and so on. Productive systems carry transactions through to the satisfaction of the order, supported by administrative systems which help to provide the necessary resources and ensure that the productive processes can be carried out.

Measurement and Analysis Systems

While the two Administration and Production categories might loosely enclose the routine, continuing activities, they will not provide for all management information needs. To give effective support to management decision-making functions, a business must expect to create information systems appropriate to these purposes. These 'Decision Support' systems are essentially concerned with measurement and analysis, related to such matters as performance and planning projections.

To carry out the functions of Costing and Budgetary Control described in chapter 5, businesses instal systems to provide financial information for management; these systems (as with many others for measurement and analysis) combine special recording with analysis of data already held in the basic administrative systems. Administrative accounting systems are often used as a source of information for management decisions in addition to their main function of processing data about day-to-day business transactions. A Budgetary Control system providing comparative information to departmental and senior management about sales income, for example, would draw on Sales Accounting for much of its data; similarly, a system for analysing unit production costs would draw on Payroll for part of its data about the labour contribution to those costs.

One can find other relevant examples from the non-financial or quantative areas of management information. Most departments and functions in business undertakings use information systems to measure and analyse performance — labour and machine utilisation, vehicle usage, wastage of raw materials, etc. Of these systems, some may be departmental, concerned with transactions within a specific organisational unit, some may be functions, involving input of data from a large number of separated systems with outputs going to other parts of the organisation. As a further generalisation, these Decision Support systems will tend to be associated with vertical (upward) flows of information to appropriate decision levels, in contrast to the Administrative and Production systems in which the primary information flow is horizontal.

Systems which exist to support planning decisions can be included also under the heading of Measurement and Analysis. To some extent this support will be provided as a byproduct of systems designed primarily for dealing with current activities but, in general, systems to support planning decisions involve an extra dimension of analysis or creation of fresh data input. For example, analysis of historical data accumulated previously in administrative systems will contribute to planning, and much of the data brought in from the external environment is obtained to support future plans. Systems created for planning purposes may be *ad hoc* (for example, a specially commissioned market survey) or may be part of the business routine (for example, collection and further analysis of statistical data published by Government). Internally, special systems may be set up to examine courses of action, through the use of scientific method for simulation or preparation of alternative projections. It is easier to show a relationship between these kinds of system by reference to the use of their output rather than to their content. They can make quite substantial demands on resources directly employed or provided as a 'bought-in' service from another business organisation. A business which depends for its livelihood on market information (such as a commodity broker or currency trader) will see this kind of management information as its first requirement.

Monitoring and Control Systems

Measurement and Analysis systems tend to be separated (however marginally) from the past or future events to which they relate, and much of their output will be in the form of advisory reports and recommendations. The overlap with Monitoring and Control is obvious, but the latter may be generally distinguished by their closer proximity to events and by their tendency to be concerned rather with 'physical' system elements than 'paperwork'.

It is a temptation when exploring the subject of business information systems to concentrate on those which, until the advent of computers, would have been appropriately described as 'paperwork systems'. On the whole, those systems which produce a considerable measure of detailed and complex information and which have varied data inputs do tend to be complex and, because of the substantial element of human interpretation and decision required in handling outputs, use paper still for a substantial proportion of output despite the rapid advance of machine systems.

However, there are many other aspects of business activities which need to be identified in a survey of business information systems, and which tend to receive less attention because they are predominantly physical systems using machine elements for automatic operation. If we take some of these systems for granted because they have a relatively small human element, it brings a necessary reminder that our view of systems is so conditioned because we are looking at a particular point in time. If we look forward it should be possible to see that many of the present 'paperwork' systems (including those which contain significant human-decision elements) will become highly automated; if we look back only a short way we can see that many current monitoring and control systems now using machines were largely manual. The differences indicated by the manual/machine/automatic/paperwork/physical system labels are in the way that the systems are put together and in the location of their boundaries. Automated control systems contain all the elements identified in systems theory and are still concerned with data flows. Thus, automatic systems for control of electric power distribution, or for managing road traffic through signalling systems, have input data in the form of keyed operating instructions, sensor readings and other signals; the systems process this transaction data by reference to other stored data to produce such outputs as signals to control the operation of switches as well as (still) some visual outputs for human monitoring and intervention.

Library Systems

A library is a collection of files, records, reports or other information which is available for access when required, and a Library system comprises the processes and data flows necessary to make that service usable. Provision of library information can be the primary function of a business undertaking (of which public lending libraries are only one specialised example), but every business has some need of library systems and, within nearly every kind of business system, there will be some library functions associated with storage of data. The special characteristic of the Library system is that stored data is likely to be the most important feature, and may be very large in relation to the transaction data (the request for information).

Library systems are essentially support systems, providing information needed as part of an analysis or planning activity, or supporting decisions directly at any operating or management level. A sales representative needs access to library information about products, prices and delivery, an enquiry clerk needs information about the services the business provides, an engineer needs technical data, and a barrister needs law reports. In these systems one can make clear distinctions between the permanently stored or 'fixed' data (the price list, timetable, or the book) and the transaction or 'variable' data (the request for information). In the later examination of computer systems it is argued that the balance between transaction and stored data does have a marked effect upon system characteristics. Library systems can span the whole size range of business organisations; one may contrast systems existing solely to support decisions of individuals within a single job (which today provides one of the most effective uses for the personal microcomputer), and the systems such as those for telephone directory enquiries or for social security records which call on huge files of data.

Communication Systems

In an era which has begun to recognise the true importance of information as an essential business resource, it is necessary to regard communication — the presentation of information at the appropriate time and location — as being the one essential element of all business activity. Public telecommunication and postal service networks offer prime examples of major business systems for providing general communication facilities, and comparable private systems can be identified within business organisations in the form of internal telecommunications and inter-office main services.

The dominant element in such systems is data flow and they are designed for the transfer of data from origin to destination without processing or storing elements of any consequence. Much of business activity is concerned with communication; finding the most effective means of transmitting decisions, facts or other items of information to their proper destination is as much the secret of business efficiency as is to decide what information is needed in the first place.

Interaction of Business Systems

It will be obvious from this brief outline of types of business system that the distinctions between them may not be clear; they may be closely interwoven and change character with their design and with the movement of their boundaries. Stock control, one of the prime subjects for business information systems, provides an illustration. It concerns recording stock movements of raw materials, components, finished goods etc. from warehouses and stock-rooms, replenishment of those stocks and various information outputs to other systems. Routine recording of stock movements and balances is an administrative function; information for replenishment action is a production system function; value analysis of stock holdings or the application of exponential smoothing techniques to material-consumption forecasting are measurement and analysis functions intended to support management decisions. If the handling and movement of goods in a store is controlled by machine (as in an 'automatic warehouse' — computer-controlled machine facilities for the physical storage, location and handling of goods in a warehouse, usually linked to information systems for stock management and associated with the use of pallets and tiered racking systems, and automatically controlled vehicles) there will be a monitoring and control element. Interrogation of records to discover stock availability or answer general questions about stock items is a minor form of Library system. Thus, although we can use Administration, Measurement, Control and other labels to make broad distinctions between types of information system to be found in business, it is probably better to look at these labels as sub-system modules contained within business systems, and which may vary in relation to each other. If one wishes to examine a system in detail or to design a new system, then the differences as they affect output, storage, system interfaces and so forth become more important.

In such an examination there is also a need to recognise special elements which support the system itself. In any kind of system there will always be some control element which is there simply to protect the system output. The basic system concepts of feedback and control themselves involve some kinds of data flow, processes and outputs. Thus some output information displayed or printed for use by a system operator may be provided solely as a means of feedback from which control adjustments or other changes can be made, to rectify system faults or counter effects of input degradation. Much of management reporting is of this kind — the functions of the accounting auditor and of the production supervisor involve analysing system performance to detect deficiencies. In computer-based systems and, particularly, in open systems which are especially vulnerable to external influences or which require precision in output, the feedback and control elements will be proportionately large; in some cases they may form a dominant part of the system. Data validation, customer service and quality control functions in business are all largely concerned with feedback and control of the system they support.

A map of business systems will appear as 'groups' and 'layers' of activity. To unravel the systems in an existing organisation it is necessary to build up from each detailed system element to find the structures and interconnections and, ultimately, the primary data flows and objectives which present a coherent view of the essential business purposes. In developing new systems, the process is reversed, starting from the top, identifying these main flows and objectives in a business model, and then breaking down the system to further levels of detail until a precise definition of each basic element is possible (see figure 14).

System content

With many physical control systems (such as those for vehicle braking or fuel supply or, on a larger scale, for traffic control) it is usually possible to see tangible evidence of their existence and extent. One may or may not know how the system works but neither the evidence of its existence nor the knowledge of its physical processes has any useful meaning without an understanding of what the system produces, what is its purpose, and how it is used. Familiar objects such as motor cars and telephones can be used effectively with this knowledge; understanding how they work and how they have been constructed is not of any great importance to the user. One must know all these things to design and build systems, but also that design and construction is not the end in itself. In the context of computer-based systems it is worth reiterating one of the original propositions: that it is what the computer produces which should be of interest, not the 'machine'. The machine is a (physical) system in itself but the information system is the data and the processes that make use of such resources as machines, equipment and people. One may describe a business information system, in physical terms, as comprising documents, files, records and reports, items of machinery and equipment, communication facilities, accommodation, and also as employing people with various skills. To make sense of a system, it is necessary to explain the use of those resources: what is contained in the documents and files, what data and processes are handled by the machines, and what decisions and actions are taken by the people involved in the system. There needs to be a description of the system in terms of the procedures, data and other elements which make up the system content. If one wished to describe a system with sufficient clarity to enable someone else to participate in its use, it might be enough to provide a general description supported by instructions explaining each task in terms of 'what to do', 'what not to do', and 'what to do when something goes wrong'. To understand a system well enough to be able to change it, or to define a new system in terms suitable for someone intending to construct and use it, there must be much more technical knowledge of detail, describing the constituent elements and factors which may affect them. A report or manual prepared to provide such a description or system must certainly include the following elements

- System objectives and requirements
- Data definitions

- Data flows
- Data volumes and patterns
- Input form and content
- File structures, format and content
- Ouput form and content
- Operating and Control procedures and processes
- Timing and frequency of operation.

System Objectives and Requirements

Where it is considered desirable to label a business information system, the logical means of deciding what the label should be is to look at what happens with the system output and from there, to discern the distinctive make-up of the system elements. For this, we really need to look at two other aspects of systems: the objectives and the requirements. System objectives identify the results which the system is expected to achieve — the consequences of decisions and actions influenced by information produced from the system. Requirements are the characteristics which the system must have in order to achieve those outputs.

These objectives and requirements should be determined in the first instance by fitting the proposed system outline into a business model which will show the proper relationship with the overall objectives of the business. Within that, more detailed objectives of the functional area in which the system is located must be defined. To specify the requirements it is then necessary to look at links with other systems — the interfaces which will exercise some influence over system inputs and outputs, and other external factors which will affect system performance. From these can be identified various factors which will impose limits on the scope, structure and operaton of the system. To specify the system requirements firmly, we then have to look at these factors and see how they affect such considerations as cost, capacity and time. This is done in the next chapter.

Data: Definition, Quality and Flow

Data must be defined in a business information system. There must be a label for each kind of data so that it can be recognised; it must conform to a specified format and content wherever it is used so that procedures for processing it can operate. It must be identified in terms of volume and pattern because these affect system capacity and the way it is organised. If two business systems have the same identity 'label' but one processes a hundred times the transactions of the other, the two systems in practice will be very different indeed. Again, if data volumes are the same but for one system all transactions are concentrated within a very short time-scale and for the other are spread evenly throughout the working period, the systems will need different characteristics to meet these distinct requirements.

Data may enter a system in one form and then be changed as it is processed and stored; this may be because the physical medium by which it is transmitted changes (as, for example, when an input of physical pressure or noise is turned to electrical impulses) or because a different form is needed for convenience of access. The system processes may involve manipulation of data: combination with other data, calculation to generate new information, or simple rearrangement to provide output in a more convenient form. All these changes need to be identified so that data flows can be traced.

Transaction data presented to a system may not be received at the point of interface in a form immediately suitable for input. Data for an order processing system, for example, might come from the interfacing (customer) systems in various forms and then be translated into standard format for use within the system. At the point of output similar problems of reconciliation with other systems may arise; output information may have to be tailored specially for each of the other systems for which it forms an input. It is not enough to offer a general description of this data. It must be defined so that all types of data are taken into account. We accept readily the necessity for such precise specification of data with computer systems but the principles apply generally, whatever techniques are used; a manual information system might appear to accept data in a wide range of formats whereas a computer system would only accept data specifically tailored for it, but the manual system would still be unable to operate effectively if the required data content were not present.

Input

The term 'data' was distinguished earlier from information to identify the 'raw', unprocessed facts which a system takes (from other systems) and from which usable information for decision and action (in other system areas) eventually emerges. In most business information systems the 'transaction' is usually the primary data source which triggers the system action. Transactions may be random or constant in pattern, regular or sporadic in flow, and constitute a trickle in volume or a flood, but they will usually form the key ingredient which determines the structure of the system.

However, transaction data is unlikely to be the only data required by the system. To process the main source data, a business system will also need reference to its own 'fixed' data sources. This fixed data will include that necessary to determine the rules to be followed in carrying out all the processes in the system; it will also include qualitative information which will affect how those processes are performed. The concepts of 'variable' data relating to the transactions which are processed through the system, and 'fixed' data relating to the constant information stored within the system, are applicable to most business information systems. A sales information system, for example, needs new data relating to sales transactions and stored data relating to prices, customers and products; a monitoring system controlling telecommunications message traffic or factory heating needs transaction data signalling events occurring at operating locations, and stored data giving the criteria for consequent action.

Files

Fixed and variable data are not necessarily coincident with stored and transaction data. Where stored data is used as a library source for retrieval on demand, or for collation or comparison with new transaction data, a business system really has two parts: the creation and updating of the library record which is triggered by receipt of new source data, and the release of that data as useful information in response to any enquiry or instruction. Such a library of stored data may be for use in one system, or may itself be a common data source which is required for a number of systems.

This brings us to another concept, specially related to business information systems — that of the 'file'. A file may be described as an ordered set of records, labelled and held in a way to provide convenient access data for retrieval or alteration as required. The primary data 'entities' contained in the file records are labelled for identification and access, and will have additional definition of attributes and of relationships with other entities. In a file of hospital patients records, for example, data related to each patient (entity) might be labelled with the patient's name to which would be linked personal details (attributes) and cross-references to ward and medical attendance (relationships to other entities).

The structure of a file may be seen in two ways — 'logical' and 'physical'. The logical structure comprises the labels, indices and cross-references for access and identification, and the physical structure the location of all related items of data and the medium on which they are held.

These formalised concepts of data and files are essential features of professional system design and management, notably in computer information systems where precision in data definition and file structures is mandatory. However, even in a general consideration of system theory it should be realised that a disciplined approach to these system elements is essential given the acceptance that information is a vital resource.

Output

Reference has been made to input (data) as the trigger for action and as the apparent determinant of the structure and scope of a system which may seem to give it the primary importance. However, if we look at the purpose for which a system is designed it can be argued that the first matter for consideration is the output. Output from a business system is usually conceived in terms of information for action or for decision: instructions for direct or indirect operation of machinery, printed information for management decision support or data in any appropriate form as input to another system. Typical examples are control impulses to machine tools, summary analyses of production activities as management information, and invoices notifying customers of charges for goods despatched to them.

The medium, format and content of output from a system will depend upon the next stage of use, which may not necessarily be immediate nor involve direct human activity. Presenting output information in a usable form can be a simple matter of making it available when it is required. Convenience may be further served by sorting, analysis, selection and interpretation to provide relevant information in a digestible form.

Four broad categories of output are identifiable

- Informing
- Reporting
- Interpreting
- Instructing.

For each of these categories there will have been some implicit or explicit element of decision-making in the system, whether or not the immediate consequence of the output is itself a decision. It would be wrong to assume that the point of decision always lies between systems, or that we can map all business activity as a combination of multiples of three linked elements — information systems, decisions, action (or physical) systems. All elements are interlaced: an information system may contain decision elements such as those necessary to overcome problems inherent in using data in its raw state. It may also contain action elements which follow automatically when data conforms to acceptable criteria, and from which the output or decision relates only to those transactions which do not conform.

Processes

Data elements are related and changed to information through the action of processing functions, which can be defined as procedures such as sorting, editing, calculation, selection and other manipulation of data to change it from raw material to finished product. Formal procedures should specify what is to be done with given data in given situations, including the alternative courses of action where a choice is necessary.

They will be expected to show also what must not be done, and what happens when procedures cannot be followed because data is absent or inaccurate. The procedures should include both the operating elements to deal with all routine matters and the control elements to protect the system, or to enable it to adapt or otherwise deal with any exceptional condition however caused. Specification of control is equal in importance to other aspects when one is developing new procedures, even though it may not be essential for understanding an existing system.

System Operating Characteristics

While data volumes and patterns are an essential part of system requirements, they do not themselves give an indication of the timing of processing or output functions. Part of the specification of a system must be the time it is scheduled to take in processing a transaction or completing a cycle. Frequency and timing of output information must be defined absolutely and in relation to the related data input. It must be possible to answer questions such as — "does the system operate continuously or at planned times?", and "how long does it take to process a given number of records, or to produce an output result following a given input?" For example, there is a contrast between the routine accounting administrative system in which daily transactions are processed to produce weekly, monthly, or other output at planned times in relation to the period of the transactions to which they refer, and the automatic control system which is required to produce an immediate response to each data input. Apart from helping to complete the understanding of the relationship between one system and another, such information is also needed for a clear view of the resources required or used by the system.

Check List 6

A system may be defined as a group of associated activities with identifiable boundaries capable of definition and operating under sets of prescribed rules. An organisation requires systems with rules and procedures to provide the information necessary for decisions to be made, so that objectives can be achieved.

A business system comprises a set of procedures which use the organisation's resources to process inputs to produce defined results. Business systems are essentially information systems for processing data and maintaining records, for controlling the use of resources and for directing activities. Whatever the purpose or detailed nature of a system, certain elements and concepts which form the basis of system theory and practice are common to all.

Elements of Information Systems
    Input, processing and output.
    Movement and storage.
    Control.
    Feedback.
    Boundaries: closed and open.
    Data dependence.

Types of Business Information System
    Administrative.
    Production.

Measurement and analysis.
Monitoring and control.
Library.
Communications.

Further Reading

Awad, E., *Introduction to Computers*, Prentice-Hall, 1983.
Hiner, O. S., *Business Administration*, Longman, 1978.
Kilgannon, P., *Business Data Processing and Systems Analysis*, Arnold, 1980.
Kroeber, D. and Watson, H., *Computer-Based Information Systems*, Collier
    Macmillan, 2nd edn, 1986.

7 Changing Systems

System Design Factors

As with most human associations, perfection in business systems is beyond normal expectation; it is easier to find systems which work badly. If perfection is too much to expect, however, a reasonable standard certainly is not and where a system is inadequate it may well reflect a deficiency in management because achieving more effective use of resources (which must come from better systems) is a management function. Many business systems have grown, evolving and adapting without conscious thought about system needs and characteristics. The 'pressures to improve', which are identified in the first chapter as a fundamental feature of modern business, can be accommodated only if improvement of systems (and the resources allocated to that improvement) has a high priority in management thinking. It is no coincidence that business undertakings which perform well devote substantial resources to system development (as they do also to development of their products and services, and the renewal of their capital assets) but, however good the quality of management and however high the priority given to system development, designing systems for efficiency is not an easy matter.

The primary objective in this chapter is to examine some of the factors which influence system design and which must be understood if optimum solutions to system problems are to be found. An efficient system, whether developed by evolution or by deliberate design, must balance a number of complementary or competing factors which limit design freedom in some ways. It must also be robust, flexible, easy to operate and, above all, suited to its purpose.

Objectives of System Change

'Being suited to its purpose' means that a system meets its design objectives. When a new system is being developed these objectives should be clearly understood and agreed at the outset, and should be capable of measurement so that the system in operation can be judged against them. When looking at a system already in existence, there is a need to understand the objectives to evaluate the effectiveness of the system.

The range of possible objectives of a system change is extremely wide, but it is probable that the following headings will cover most reasons for embarking on a system investigation

- Cost reduction
- Maintaining a competitive position
- Meeting external change
- Expanding capacity
- Changing the range of business activities.

A completely new system is comparatively rare in business, (except when a new business is created); usually, the question is one of changing an existing system and the most frequently declared objective is to achieve a cost reduction. The impetus towards such a change may come from a planned scrutiny of the business activities, from some external pressure, or as an indirect result of some arbitrary reduction in available resources. It may be decided, prudently, that a system deserves review because it has been running for some time and that there must now be a better way. It may be considered advisable to look at its systems again because planning forecasts have shown that they will not meet future needs. A system review may be a reaction to an increase in costs caused by external factors such as increases in the price of 'bought-in' items, in labour costs or in taxes. On a less thoughtful level, a weak management, finding its costs growing out of control, may attempt to constrain them by imposing a total limit on expenditure to force subordinate levels of management to find more economical ways of carrying out their functions, so causing them to seek economies in better systems.

There is no reason why the desire for change should not come from an awareness and anticipation of future influences or from a basic philosophy that improvement is always possible, but there is no doubt that most system change is a reaction of some kind to external pressure. Competition from other trading businesses is one pressure which particularly affects industry. New materials, products, manufacturing and distributing techniques, or aggressive marketing by competitors, may adversely affect the market for a company's products. If it is to stay in business it must respond by changing itself, either to secure improvement matching that of the competition or to adapt in other ways to ease competitive pressures. In such situations, the system design objective may be related specifically to the competitive situation.

Change in the operating environment is becoming more and more a key factor in design objectives, as freedom of decision and freedom of action in business become less and less. Legal requirements concerning health and safety, changes in taxation, or industrial disruption caused by strikes and political disorders in which it is not directly involved are typical examples of external pressures which may oblige a business to take some measures to counter unfavourable effects. Thus it may become necessary to introduce new record systems as a result of new legislation, or to find different materials or services because those previously used are no longer available or have become unreliable. Such defensive changes may cause a chain reaction of modifications to products, processes and systems until equilibrium is restored. Changes affecting cost and availability of labour are probably the most commonplace in current economic society. The continuing rise in the minimum acceptable level of living standards and the associated rise in personal expectations about the nature and conditions of work are as much the cause as the consequence of system (and technological) change. Where business organisations cannot change their systems and techniques, their products and services may soon disappear in an advanced economic society in which change in systems has become the normal rather than the exceptional state.

Although the emphasis so far has been on design objectives relating to survival or restoration of equlibrium as a reaction to external factors, design objectives equally may be aggressive in intention. When the intention is to expand and to lead by improving competitive position, the prime objective may be to increase productive capacity or otherwise create the ability to do something which was not previously possible.

The 'real-time' airline seat reservation system (possibly the most influential development in computer applications in the 1960s) was not aimed at reducing the cost of seat reservation, nor was it initially a reaction to external pressures. Its principal aim was to allow airlines to expand at a time when existing manual or electro-mechanical systems could operate effectively only up to a transaction limit well below the projected expansion of passenger traffic. Without such changes the optimum size of individual airlines would have remained much smaller. (Subsequently, smaller airlines were forced to adopt similar systems to defend their competitive position, because of the benefits offered to travellers by the computer seat-booking systems.)

To meet overall design objectives a system must be designed round certain specified requirements. These may have the effect of ruling out some alternative solution, or of introducing some general constraints to the specification of the preferred solution. System requirements set the framework within which the system designer must operate, and there will always be some constraints even in situations where, in theory, no constraints at all should be found. This refers back to the proposition made at the beginning of the chapter that there is a number of design factors which will need to be balanced. It is not realistic to visualise the design of a system for business information totally freed from constraints, because many of the factors which have to be taken into account are incompatible at their extremes. There is a 'trade-off', and the optimum system solution always must be a compromise giving a balance between these various factors which are examined further under the following headings

- Cost
- Time
- Capacity

- Accuracy
- Acceptability
- Compatibility.

Cost

Cost is usually considered to be the most influential design factor because reduction in cost is often the principal objective in the design of a new business system. Any system change, whether mainly involving use of machines or more concerned with people at work, is still essentially an investment decision; resources are to be used to bring about a change which will produce some benefit in return. This return should be partially or wholly quantifiable; if it is not and if there appears no likelihood of any tangible advantage arising from the change, then the system change may become pointless or, at best, a gamble because there will be one certainty — that the change itself will involve some cost. If there are machines, equipment or other productive facilities to be provided, they will have initial (capital) and running costs which will be represented by an outflow of cash in some form or other. Any new consumable materials, or new people involved in running the system, will also bring additional cost; all goods and services will have to be paid for. In addition, there will be the costs of the investigation leading to the design and implementation of the system changes. This last aspect deserves to be stressed because it is often the most important cost element.

To set against these costs may be savings from discarding other systems — savings in labour, in machine costs, and in space or consumable materials. There may be other less tangible (and, consequently, less easily measured) benefits, such as those which make it possible to expand at lower marginal cost, or to look optimistically for larger sales because the system change improves market prospects.

At the time system change is contemplated, the estimate of costs may well be more certain than the estimate of benefits (although the costs themselves could include many intangible items). Nevertheless, the extent of potential benefits is likely to impose a primary constraint and, except in circumstances where some other advantage is so important that a negative return will be acceptable, we may assume that a new system will not be allowed to cost more than it earns.

If the amount of capital expenditure is the limiting factor, then the specific cause for concern is finding ways of funding the project but, if (as is usual) total expenditure over the life of the system is the key consideration, there will be limits to the choice of solution because of cost considerations throughout the development of the new system. Cost of the planning activity itself, capacity of equipment, limits on running costs — all these impose constraints on the theoretical design of the system, and on other design factors which must be traded off against cost savings. Careful account must also be taken of the effect of cost constraints on potential benefits; the price of a more economical solution may itself be a lower return.

Time

Time must be considered in three aspects. Two are related to operation of the system: time to complete the cycles of processing, and the ability to produce results at the time they are required. The third aspect is the time required to complete development of the new system. All of these must be estimated at the outset, and may have some bearing on other factors as well as having direct impact on the nature of the system and the way its design is carried out.

One consideration is that any system must be capable, on average, of processing all transactions put into it within a designated period, otherwise arrears will accumulate progressively to a point, ultimately, where the system must collapse. Where effectiveness of the system depends on producing output information at a precise point in time (as in the airline seat reservation system example given previously), such a system must be able to operate reliably to a given response standard, so ensuring an output within a fixed time of the transaction input however many transactions arise. These 'peak load' and 'response time' factors are vital elements in the design of systems which operate in 'real time'; that is, systems which must operate to these precise standards because other surrounding activities depend upon them. With the contrasting 'batch' type of business information system (where data is accumulated on a 'batch' basis and various stages of processing are buffered from each other before the final output is produced) design constraints may be less severe but still extremely important. In a financial accounting system such as Invoicing or Monthly Expenditure analysis, for example, no batch processing arrangement would be tolerable which did not produce results within a short specified time after the period of related transactions; generally speaking, where business information is used in direction and control of business activities, its value deteriorates as it becomes further away in time from the event from which it originates.

Even with system planning activities, the expected time between the first stage of a feasibility study and implementation of a new system may be a factor determining whether or not the system change is attempted. One of the major criticisms which circulated in earlier days of computer information systems was that the time spent in designing and programming could be so long that system requirements would have changed again by the time the computer programs were ready. The solution to problems of planning time may be found by designing flexible systems or allowing substantial modification during planning (as with complex machine systems like aircraft), and by setting firm completion dates for planning and deploying resources sufficient to meet that deadline.

Capacity

Just as a system must be designed within planned limits of cost and time, so it must also be designed for a given capacity. The basic proposition should be that capacity will be sufficient (or can be varied without unacceptable penalty) to meet both requirements at the inception of the system and future changes within the total planned life. This may be extremely difficult to determine accurately if there are many factors likely to influence volumes and patterns of data to be handled by the system; if the planning period itself is lengthy, current information about expected system requirements and volumes may be unreliable because estimates are being made so far ahead. A system which starts its design stage today may operate (say) from a year hence, for several years. To provide for an expanding business, planned systems must be capable of adaptation to very substantially increased volumes of data, which may impose complex design problems, or a cost dilemma, or both. To provide sufficient capacity at the beginning so that the system can accept expansion without change implies greater initial expenditure; generally speaking, cost and capacity are variables which must be reconciled through some form of trade-off: the greater the capacity, the greater the cost.

Capacity is not simply a question of being able to handle the gross number of input transactions. A business information system may be required to handle many types of transaction and stored data, and must provide capacity for this variety and for the total 'stored' volume of data as well as the 'throughput'. Where a system is designed to provide a library of information, storage capacity may have to be extremely large relative to the capacity to process day-to-day transactions.

There is another variable which will affect consideration of capacity. When estimating sizes of files or throughput of data, changes in sizes of those files and variation in rates of flow of data must also be considered. Where these are variable, capacity may at one time be adequate and at others excessive or insufficient. Where the data flow can be controlled, the designer may consider how far fluctuations may be smoothed to provide even demand, and how much the impact on time for throughput may be varied. For systems which are conditioned by their environment, the impact of transactions may be outside the control of the system designer. This is obviously so with transaction-based systems which are required to operate whenever data is presented. Variations in delivery for many goods and services may (up to a point) be acceptable to customers but for many other business activities, including types of public service, booking and enquiry systems and much of the retail trade, design capacity may be the peak load and, if this is the paramount consideration, providing peak load capacity might well outweigh consideratons of cost.

Accuracy

Only a theoretical system always receives wholly accurate data and always carries through its processes with complete accuracy. In the real world one must take account of design deficiencies in systems, or defects or consequences of wear in physical elements, of the vagaries of human behaviour in the use of systems and of changes in environmental factors which invalidate original system design criteria. One cannot afford to design a system which depends on absolute accuracy, because it will never work, nor to allow systems output to be corrupted as a result of inability to intercept or control inaccurate input data. It is an essential element of system design that some form of control be introduced to ensure that acceptable performance can be sustained indefinitely. The design must provide for operation to a given standard of accuracy, with proper disposal of the error margin.

Errors and failures also may be caused by factors other than through the input of inaccurate data and, if not able to prevent their occurrence, a system must at least provide some form of feedback so that subsequent corrective action may be taken.

The significant task for the system designer, from a recognition that errors are probable, is to set and achieve a standard of accuracy which will meet all system requirements and design criteria. This may involve the introduction of special controls to reduce or eliminate particular kinds of error, to measure standards of accuracy achieved and to enable the system to maintain an agreed standard of reliability and performance in every aspect. Controlling reliability of systems may involve duplication of checks or of processing, or the provision of reserve capacity to reduce or eliminate effects of partial system failure. These considerations clearly bring the system designer back again to the 'trade-off' relationship with cost and capacity. To provide accuracy, protection and control, a system must become more complex, larger, more costly and, probably, take more processing time. The higher the standard at which the system is to operate, the greater proportion of capacity must be devoted to accuracy controls. If speed or cost are essential, then it may be necessary to accept a higher risk of failure; if failure is unacceptable, then some degree of slower operation or higher cost may be unavoidable.

It may be noted that the question of accuracy, although it may not appear to arise at the outline or modelling stage of developing a system (in that we tend to describe systems in quantitative rather than qualitative terms of inputs and outputs), certainly must be part of system requirements and will represent a significant proportion of the actual design work; in the extreme case it may absorb a greater proportion of planning capacity than the objective design itself. If one looks at business information systems in operation, one can usually find special statistical and accounting routines which provide checks and balances and produce control totals from which users of the systems can monitor their action and report on unacceptable discrepancies. In computer systems, the usual first stage of any operation is validation of entry data. Output from most business systems includes some control data from which instructions can be fed back for trimming and correction of the system in operation or, in uncontrollable situations, can cause intervention to prevent unacceptable damage. Control information may also be produced as an input to adjacent systems designed to examine and act upon it. Thus, as support to a routine data processing system, there may be auditing, query and error-correction functions to handle corrupted or rejected data as well as maintenance, repair and recovery facilities. For the system which is vulnerable to environmental influences, which processes data largely generated by human action, or which contains a significant proportion of manual processes, accuracy may be the dominant design factor.

Acceptability

As with most human associations, there can be a substantial difference between theory and practice in business information systems. A system designed to resolve business problems and meet user objectives can only be shown to be effective when it is used as intended. To reach this stage, it is implicit that the change from the old system be carried through successfully, and that the new system be brought into operation to the standards set in its design. For this, the first essentials are that the design be compatible with the environment in which the system will work and be accepted by all those who have some influence upon its success. If precise account is taken of all requirements and objectives in the specification of a system, it is tested over the full range of data it will encounter, and all necessary controls are provided, it may still not meet objectives if it does not fit into its working environment from the outset.

To consider acceptability in its full sense we must consider criteria going beyond evaluation of quantitative data (data types, volumes and patterns, processing algorithms or economic factors) to more subjective matters such as attitudes. These are of fundamental importance both to effective operation of any system and to the feasibility of changing to new systems. It may well be possible in appropriate economic and social conditions to impose and sustain systems which do not have the ready acceptance of those involved, but this will be a rare circumstance, and one in which it is unlikely that a high standard of operating efficiency can be achieved. Design of any system must take account of its acceptability to the 'user', who is represented in two ways — by those responsible for management of the functions affected by the system, and by those involved in its actual operation. Development and supervision of business systems being a management function, the first stage of acceptance must lie with the managers who determine system objectives and requirements. There will be a point or points of management decision at each stage of system development — setting the framework within which the system review will take place, approval of proposed changes in outline and as a formal investment proposal, and final acceptance of the new system before it is introduced.

It is not sufficient that any proposals submitted meet all requirements in the view of the system designers; they must also be acceptable to those responsible for making the decisions to introduce the new system. There may be situations where that responsibility is not discharged soundly; there may be some resistance to change of any kind or there may be a firm management view of the direction to be taken in the system development. Whatever the motives or attitudes of managers, the system designer will be obliged to look for wholehearted acceptance of system proposals, and much of the process of developing business systems is aimed at ensuring support of those who will use the system, before any irrevocable commitment is made.

The most satisfactory planning situation would seem to be one in which the business policy and user management judgements are soundly based and in which the design of the new system has been carried out with meticulous care and skill, but this is still not enough to ensure that a new system will be effective if there has been no comparable acceptance at operating level. There may be some natural resistance to change or other objection to be overcome; it is certain that it will be desirable to ensure that the new system, by its ease and convenience of use and demonstrable benefits, can be understood and its operating procedures learned quickly, and that it be compatible with the skills of those responsible for its operations. Furthermore, the period of acclimatisation to the new system must not be too long nor the 'learning curve' too steep and, when a plateau of operating efficiency is reached, the system must then be capable of running in harmony with user needs and ability. If it proves impossible to reconcile incompatible views or to achieve acceptance of a solution which is most satisfactory by all other criteria, then the question of acceptability will impose a severe limitation on design freedom. There are always enough examples from contemporary events to demonstrate that system problems can be intractable; inefficient use of resources may be tolerated, new machines remain idle, and potentially flourishing businesses may even be destroyed because problems of system acceptability cannot be resolved. These are not simply emotional matters; attitudes may be the result of (undesirable) external influences but they may also come from historical factors arising within the business, or be a symptom of some underlying physical or technical problems. The framework of technical limitations in which engineering industries must work and which they accept (often without question) applies in appropriate ways to any business system design. There are physical limitations affecting all resources whether they be organic, inorganic or climatic; these become particularly severe when a system is being designed to operate close to any absolute physical limit. Since the concept of developing business systems includes trying to improve something that already exists, system design is as likely to be extending the limits of existing methods or technology as to be attempting something which involves completely new techniques or moves in a new direction.

Compatability

Acceptability criteria do not apply just to those people and resources within new system boundaries; they apply also to interfacing systems. Compatibility at the point of interface is likely to be one of the more severe constraints on the design of a new system because the interfacing systems may not be susceptible to change. If, to make a new system cost-effective, it is desirable that the interfaces be changed, the impact of such changes on peripheral systems must be judged carefully. It is self-defeating to improve one system at the cost of lowering the performance of another. This problem of the impact on surrounding systems may be a question of changing the way data is handled, of altering the number of transactions or otherwise changing conditions under which the adjoining systems operate.

The consequences of a system change may extend far beyond its boundaries. The purpose of introducing a new information system might be to contribute towards better management decisions, and these may have some impact on a whole range of other business systems within and outside the organisation. For example, a proposal to introduce a Budgetary Control system could have an implied effect on every part of a business. It would have to provide for new information to every organisational unit, and would require new or changed system modules at each point for assembling data and for examination of budget variances.

In making sure of compatibility in system design, we have to look beyond the links with other information systems to all the environmental factors which have some influence on system operation. Any proposed change must comply with the law, and with the policy and general procedures of the business undertaking. It must be physically possible to achieve the changes — to take account of available resources, of climatic conditions or of any other factor which could have some bearing on the feasibility or economic performance of the system proposed. Under this heading of compatibility will be many of the factors which create difficulties for the system designer and which may frustrate achievement of the solution. Sometimes they may be overcome by making a complementary change in the environmental condition (for example, by moving to a new location); they may require the application of more rigorous standards of control or testing to ensure that the planned system will perform according to its specification. The minimum implication for the system designer, as with the previous consideration of acceptability, is that the possibility of these elements absorbing planning resources and affecting outcome does need to be recognised at an early stage in defining the planning tasks.

Planning Effective Systems

To consider, relate and reconcile design factors in all their aspects requires a combination of factual evaluation, estimation and assumption, with a degree of extrapolation from experience. Little in system planning can be based on certainty because a project refers to future matters. It is begging the question to see a precise framework of constraints in the Terms of Reference (the guidance on objectives, scope, resources, constraints etc. given to the system planner at the start of a stage of analysis or design activity) for a system change as making it easier to carry through the development process, because that can only be so where the objective is clear and the path towards it certain. The reality of business information systems and, in particular, of those which require significant human activity and wide-ranging input and output functions, is that they will involve a considerable degree of design latitude and choice. There may be a number of major courses of action open and much more choice of minor variation in system detail; there may be also imponderables which have to be given substance as system development progresses. Typical business information systems are subject to shifting objectives and requirements because the environment in which they operate is always changing; therefore, the design factors will themselves change in nature and significance as planning progresses, and then throughout the life of the system, once in operation.

Any judgement about the effectiveness of a system must be in relation to the objectives of that system in the first instance, which gives emphasis to the importance of a clear definition and understanding of those objectives. It follows that the objectives must be specific and measurable, but this is not to say that measurement can always be a straighforward matter; where objectives are stated in terms of financial benefit such measurement is, more often than not, extremely difficult and this is one reason why evaluation of a system after implementation must be given due importance in any system planning schedules.

A second essential prerequisite for success is that the system be developed through a properly controlled and documented plan, with system design carried out to approved standards. Formalisation, and even elaboration of planning procedures, is often the only way to ensure proper control so that potential delays, additional costs, or risks of failure to achieve objectives can be identified in time to take corrective action.

One of the most important elements that should be included in a formally staged development plan (because it is the last line of defence against failure) is the acceptance trial, where the system is tested for the user before it is committed to production. This final test of the system before it is accepted by the user normally simulates live operation under conditions specified by the user.

A third category relates to the quality of judgement in decisions affecting system definition and specification. This is necessarily dependent on the experience of planners and on the interpretation of relevant facts. The most common errors of judgement found in system development are inaccurate estimation of system capacity and expected life, incomplete system design and over-optimism about achievement of planning targets and system benefits.

Capacity provision, as indicated earlier, must always be a 'trade-off' against cost or time, but any capacity assumption which risks a system life less than that required to produce a satisfactory return is obviously taking a risk with financial viability. Some systems are bound to have very short lives; in seasonal and fashion trades, for example, production and supporting systems need to change at very frequent intervals. The economics and other aspects of system design life must take these matters into account.

Inability to deal with valid exceptions or with unavoidable errors can lead to total or partial system breakdown. A system may not be designed to deal precisely with every variation from normal data patterns but it must be tolerant of them. At the very least, the system must recognise all the conditions it is likely to face and a vital element of protection must be that the full range of variations from normal data and procedures is taken into account in acceptance testing.

There is often a tendency towards optimism in estimating the time needed to complete the planning tasks and for savings to be achieved after the introduction of a new system. This has been particularly noticeable in the development of computer-based systems which carry the inevitable risks of exploiting new techniques and technology.

Three planning provisions are necessary to minimise risks from over-optimism

- Scheduling of planning activities with detailed time-scales for each stage
- Itemisation of costs and savings estimates in project appraisals, with planned review and evaluation after implementation
- Inclusion of substantial provision for unfavourable imponderables.

Business Efficiency

Improvement in business efficiency may be achieved by a lesser, or more effective use of resources, by more convenient methods of handling information, or by better control of information quality. It may be achieved indirectly as a result of improvement in other systems or by discarding superfluous or outdated activities. In any kind of business it should be possible to list a wide variety of benefits which might be derived from system change. There could be some savings in cost of working capital from reducing unnecessarily high stocks or accelerating debt collection; there could be cash savings from reducing bad debts or losses from pilferage or damage; there could be improvements in sales income from faster delivery or in profits from better ratios of revenue to expenditure; there could be all-round improvement as a result of better anticipation of unfavourable or favourable environmental factors. In other words, one can look for improvement under any design factor heading.

Consider a notional manufacturing business having various systems for handling Sales, Accounting, Production, Distribution and their supporting services. In selling, performance may be unsatisfactory because the sales force has inadequate information about products; marketing and sales promotion activities may be misdirected or otherwise incompatible; the process from order to delivery may be too long or too unreliable. In the processing of order documents, administration may be expensive or cumbersome because of the nature and method of handling transactions. Errors may arise because data has to be transferred to different media, or is misdirected. Delays may occur in authorising acceptance of orders or in establishing that they can be fulfilled. In the production process there may be delays because of differing capacities in various parts of machine systems; matching production with sales may be unsatisfactory because sales forecasts are inaccurate. Production delays may occur because of shortage of critical materials. Costs may be high because large amounts of capital are tied up in work-in-progress or in finished stocks awaiting despatch. Any one of these problems may be eased by finding a better way by introducing a more effective information system, by achieving more effective use of 'labour'.

Effective Use of Labour

It is generally true that the immense benefits in prosperity which have been achieved in advanced countries, and which are still accumulating, have been the result, in the main, of finding ways to make better use of the primary economic resource — labour. In the terms of the classical economists, this is ascribed mainly to better organisation and greater use of capital; today, we would be more likely to introduce concepts of technology and information. It may also be argued that so much of economic activity has been mechanised that continued improvement now comes more from replacing one machine by another — the mechanical by the electronic. Nonetheless, the objective underlying improvement in business systems is still to make more effective use of labour and, in reality, there are still very many business systems which have labour as a principal ingredient.

Experience

There are two ways in which labour can be used more effectively: through the improvement of human skills and through labour savings. Experience is one of the most notable human contributions to improvement of system efficiency (and often the least rewarded, such is the ineffectiveness of economic systems in handling remuneration). The capacity for remembering and repeating operations and for acquiring greater skills through such repetition, avoiding errors and refining techniques, can be carried to extremely high levels. If someone demonstrates a skill which is clearly superior to that of others, there can usually be found behind it a great fund of experience — practice, training and dedication; the virtuoso musician is likely to have a very much higher proportion of experience than of natural genius.

In the management and operation of business, experience is an equally vital ingredient. Influence of experience depends on the nature of the occupation and there is, for all occupations, a 'learning curve' of varying length and steepness which will bring most trainees to acceptable standards of perform-ance within a finite time (Figure 24). Experience goes beyond this, and is accumulative. It is said that human intellectual capacity is at its peak at the end of adolescence and thereafter a slow decline in mental powers ensues. It is experience which provides the compensation so that the intellectual capacity of the 18-year-old is not also associated with intellectual superiority over society in general. One way in which experience can show itself in very clear fashion is with tasks involving manual dexterity, where there can be demonstrated an enormous difference in competence between the unskilled and skilled. Keyboard operation as a professional task with business machines provides an example of these skills; when the punched card was the input medium for computers, trained operators could sustain typical speeds of 12 000 to 15 000 key depressions an hour with a very high standard of accuracy. Among the craft skills can be found equally impressive examples of quality (as opposed to quantity) which shows itself in the ability to produce an acceptable result at all, as opposed to producing a greater quantity.

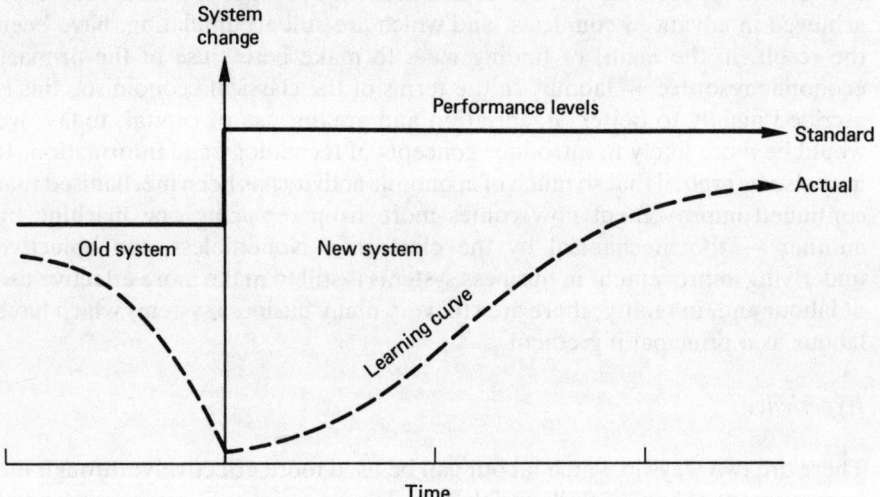

Figure 24   Learning curves

Experience is not the only ingredient in these aspects of human skills. Human beings have differing natural capacities reflecting different physical characteristics; inherited or environmental factors may also extend or limit the degree of skill to be acquired through experience. In business one would attempt to make use of all abilities brought to a task and, in many situations which involve the application of skill, aptitude and attitude may offer greater potential than experience.

When one talks of experience and dexterity, of course, it is rarely of people undertaking tasks without any kind of support for their physical effort; on the subject of excellence in the application of inherited and acquired skills unaided by artificial support of any kind, one really has to extend greater admiration to the animal world than to that of man. This suggests that the really distinctive skills of the human being at work have been in the creative and managerial fields — in the ability to plan, innovate, control and understand so as to be able to make better use of available resources and thus overcome physical limitations of unaided human endeavour.

Ability to Make Decisions

The ability to make decisions is one of the most valuable contributions to the exercise of human skill. Whereas dexterity may be demonstrated in a repetitive operation which has been learned thoroughly, the ability to make decisions is more remarkable when abnormal factors or unexpected events arise, offering choice and requiring judgement to select the best course of action. As with manual dexterity, these reflect a combination of natural and acquired skills but the significance of quality is greater in decision-making. One can improve the quality of decisions as the result of training and experience; management training in general is directed towards this end. The qualities of leadership — willingness to accept responsibility, firmness of purpose, authority and integrity — are a more subtle blend of human characteristics than experience or dexterity, which can make possible the development of high levels of skills but only within a narrowly defined area. That extra ability to face a new situation and produce a correct solution has been recognised as a special human attribute and is one on which, to a considerable extent, the successful operation of business undertakings has so far depended.

Adaptability

Unlike (most) machines, a human being is not designed for one specific purpose, and training in particular skills does not mean an irreversible commitment to tasks which use those skills. People may be retrained to undertake new tasks and can become skilled in a different field much more readily than most tools and machines can be adapted to other employment. There is not an absolute 'design limit' to human ability because it is, in principle, always possible to learn something new. For economic and physical reasons however, there are bound to be limits to the benefits obtainable from additional training and experience; age, physical characteristics, and educational background impose constraints on some individuals in comparison with others, and limit flexibility and potential achievement in any field of activity.

Labour Saving

The application of skill as a result of training and experience combined with natural aptitude can be described as a path towards labour saving. The person with skills is able to work at a faster rate, and to a higher standard but, in making better use of labour, it matters also how these special skills are applied. One obvious approach to labour saving is by making more effective use of the acquired human skills through specialisation, a concept at the heart of classical economic theory and of the 18th and 19th Century Industrial Revolution.

Specialisation, by reducing the range of skills that have to be learned and increasing the experience of the individual, leads to higher standards of performance, with one qualification: that specialisation is possible only under organised conditions where there is effective direction and control over resources. In the context of economic society and of business organisation, specialisation does mean organised specialisation — the factory, the office, or the organised production unit in which specialists are working to clear directions as part of a rational plan.

Labour saving can be achieved as a result of training: the deliberate input of special experience to accelerate the process of climbing to an optimal level of personal performance. The virtuoso not only practises but also has received training from someone who already has the skills. A necessary ingredient in the development of better systems is provision of training so that objectives and techniques can be understood more rapidly.

Another approach to labour saving is through 'motivation': the personal incentive to increase skill or to work harder. Whether the effect is to persuade some to achieve results beyond normal physical limits or simply to 'do an honest day's work', exploitation of individual objectives such as profit, competitive success or personal satisfaction has always had a place in improving productivity. Motivation is also a concept that reflects the subtleties of human behaviour since it may reflect any of the human characteristics such as greed, pride, or more attractive traits such as a desire to please. The ability to recognise what provides an incentive and provokes a favourable response is another of the special human skills which is so desirable for effective management.

Work Simplification

Specialisation, training and motivation, all building on existing human characteristics, can result in labour saving throughout the whole range of work activity; they are most significant in those occupations which demand individual skills — in the crafts and professions and, in particular, those which have a high intellectual content. In the broad mass of human occupations (the 'action' element of business activity) there are other means of labour saving which have proved more important. One of these is 'work simplification' which has become identified as a particular branch of business systems study. Organisation of production facilities, sequence of processes and work content in each job so as to eliminate unnecessary activities or to avoid waste of manual resources caused by extravagance or delay should be at the heart of any approach to change of systems involving use of labour. Human skills have to be channelled into the right direction by fitting them into an effective system environment.

It is one of the ironies of human behaviour that the benefits of dexterity and experience can be self-defeating in that they may allow people to become proficient in the use of an inefficient method. People will not always find the easiest way to complete a task; a better approach may not become apparent even when experience has been gained. To achieve work simplification itself requires special skill, the kind of objective analytical approach to a work situation which is not always the natural response of those engaged in the task themselves. Whether the inspiration for improvement comes from the application of work study techniques or directly from the working environment, work simplification should properly be regarded as the most valuable source of improvement in labour utilisation because it neither makes additional demands on human intellectual or physical abilities nor requires use of other resources. It is concerned with producing the same result with less labour because the new method is better. One of the criteria for effective business information systems already identified is 'simplicity', and it is a good principle to look for situations in which one step would serve as well as two, and where something could be discarded without any disadvantage whatsoever.

Mechanisation

However, it is difficult to dispute that, overall, the most powerful influence on labour saving has been the introduction of 'capital' or 'technology' — of tools to reinforce manual effort and of machine processes in substitution for labour. The achievement to date in the use of tools and machines to save human labour has been to carry substitution almost to the highest level of action and decision, and right through the input, processing, storage and output elements of many business systems. From the bare hand to the hand tool, to the machine tool, to the automatic machine process, to the totally integrated system, the functions of industry have had progressively smaller proportions of labour and greater proportions of machines and technology.

As everyone is aware, substitution of machines for manual operations is not always greeted with enthusiasm either by producer or consumer. It is often the variation or inconsistency which gives the end-product its special appeal, as with foodstuffs and works of art but, save for the question of scarcity value, economic arguments have usually pressed towards mechanisation sooner or later and, in the process, human skills are often discarded. In the earlier days of business machines it would have been said that the low skill, repetitive, monotonous jobs were those ripe for mechanisation. Now the upward movement of labour costs and the advance of technology have brought many more skilled tasks within the scope of machines; notably in the field of information systems and this is the prime topic in the next chapter.

Attitudes to Change

Reluctance to accept change is a normal human reaction. Although the human being is capable of adapting to new conditions, most people feel more comfortable in a familiar, stable environment than in strange, changing surroundings. Two reactions to change are notable: resistance to proposed or impending change and, once unavoidable change has been experienced, an aim to create new protective boundaries and landmarks. Resistance to change will be shown most strongly when the proposed new system contains many unknown elements, and will be allied to a desire to clarify the boundaries of the new system and to turn it into a routine once it has been implemented.

In the first part of this chapter the question of system change was considered as a possible constraint on system design; in this wider context, it needs to be counted as an influence on progress of the design phase and on implementation. Thus a conservative and hesitant approach expressed in the attitudes of managers and prospective users of a system may be further demonstrated in conscious or unconscious resistance to change itself. Such resistance probably reflects feelings of insecurity as well as personal resentment of people who feel threatened by impending destruction of an environment which they themselves may have been responsible for creating. More influential than this, however, is the implication for personal efficiency and the fears that it breeds. In the operation of any business system, familiarity with routines and procedures often improves individual performance to the extent that people with relatively limited ability and adaptability can maintain high levels of apparent personal competence. Because they operate within a system which they understand and which may have been moulded to fit the abilities they have, people of moderate competence may work with self-confidence, secure in the approval of their superiors: in principle, a very desirable optimisation of labour skills. To transfer such people to a new system environment, requiring them to learn afresh and to develop new skills may well affect not only their attitudes but also their actual ability to perform successfully. In a sense, people become victims of the measures that have been taken to make the best use of them in the past and it is a reminder that few people are likely to reach their full potential without a substantial investment in training and experience. Whatever the objectives and requirements for a new system, it must always be worth the effort and cost of turning theoretical acceptability into practice and of matching existing abilities to new needs so that former levels of personal skill can be restored in a new environment.

Loss of personal skill is not confined to people of limited ability; anyone will experience a fall in efficiency as an immediate consequence of any system change. Whatever the quality of people, and whatever confidence there is in the ultimate success of the new system, and however much care is devoted to ensuring co-operation and proper training to achieve that objective, the immediate effect when people are put into a new, unfamiliar situation is bound to be a lowering of personal performance. This will reduce benefits and increase costs of the new system until the people concerned have learned to adapt themselves to the new environment and acquired fresh skills and sufficient experience to restore their personal efficiency. This learning process starts when the new system is defined and extends through the period of system preparation and job training and then, from the time the new system is launched into operation, the process continues through the 'learning curve' of practical experience until a 'normal' level of efficiency is reached.

One of the contradictions encountered by designers of business systems is that those who have expressed doubts about changing systems will expect, once the proposal has been finally accepted, that change will follow promptly without fuss. The increased work load and transitional loss of efficiency associated with system change will all be regarded as unwarranted burdens. Any exceptional expenditure may attract resentment. The new system almost invariably will be criticised, using performance criteria which could only justly be applied to fully developed operations. Yet the full cost of the design process, including that of effecting the changes and creating the new system environment, must be taken into account in the overall system evaluation. If the new system represents a substantial change from the old, and the process of learning is elaborate and lengthy, then this cost may be the biggest single element in the total cost of development. The system development plan must provide for creating the right conditions and attitudes for successful implementation, for training and monitoring the system as it goes into service, and for the temporarily inefficient use of resources. To budget for full achievement of system benefits from the date of implementation without any cost of change is likely to be a most misleading and unrealistic assumption for any major business information system.

Consequences of System Change

The desired consequences of a change in system are identified as system objectives and expressed as a direct benefit such as reduction of cost or a potential benefit such as the achievement of a desired improvement in quality of information. The ultimate point in the chain linking the information system to the business purpose is the contribution to overall business objectives. Within the system area affected, the allocation and use of resources and the techniques employed will change according to plan as will interfacing systems, usually to lesser extents. There may be consequential changes in organisation, location of activities or even of products and business purposes themselves.

However, the business, through its management and those concerned with design and implementation of system changes, will find and therefore should anticipate the possibility that the system change itself may generate secondary consequences which may not be predictable in any degree. There may be unexpected benefits or costs to qualify the ultimate result; these are bound to occur to some extent however efficiently the system development has been carried through. There may be some 'organic' changes in the business organisation itself or in its environment. Organisational change may be necessary to accommodate the new systems (as with the creation of a data processing department to manage a computer installation). The optimum size of functions or business units may alter; greater economies of scale may increase the average size of business, causing some concerns to flourish and others to fail. Social habits may change; improvement in employee conditions in one area causes pressure for improvement in others and, ultimately, a change in the product and services available.

With any innovation of machine or method it is usually easier to find someone who is ready to reject it than one who can foresee its consequences; most technical advances start with a red flag in front. It is much easier to look back and see the consequences of earlier changes than to look forward and make a proper assessment of all possible secondary effects of change; for the individual organisation, true foresight would not necessarily affect the immediate decision. However, if one is to put the development of business information systems in perspective, it is essential to be aware of the chain reaction that any system change is likely to bring and which, with the growth of information technology, becomes more important with each successive advance. For the most part, and particularly with machines, there is no going back from any system change. The end result is not the implementation of the new system; it is merely part of a cyclical process of development, production and further development through successive system lives. In the contemporary situation of still accelerating technological development, the process of change itself becomes almost continuous.

Check List 7

An efficient system must balance a number of complementary or competing factors — time, cost, accuracy, capacity, acceptability, compatability. It must also be robust, easy to operate, and suited to its purpose.

The main reasons for changing systems are to improve efficiency or to adapt to changes in the operating environment. Improvement in efficiency may be achieved by a lesser, or more effective use of resources, by more convenient methods of handling information, or by better control of information quality. It may also be improved by discarding superfluous or outdated activities.

The desirability of modification and improvement in business systems may be qualified by the cost of effecting such change, which can be often the principal obstacle to increases in system efficiency.

Design Factors
   Cost of system change, running, relative cost.
   Time to develop systems, to complete processing cycles, to produce output.
   Capacity, to handle transaction volumes, for files, peak loads.
   Accuracy of data, system reliability.
   Acceptability at management and operating level.
   Compatibility with systems environment.

Human Skills
  Experience.
  Dexterity.
  Ability to make decisions.
  Flexibility.

Labour Saving
  Specialisation.
  Training.
  Motivation.
  Work simplification.
  Mechanisation.
  Substitution.

Further Reading

Drucker, P., *The Practice of Management*, Heinemann, 1955.
Radford, J. D. and Richardson, D. B., *Management of Manufacturing Systems*, Macmillan, 1977.

8 Information Machines

The Information Industry

The successive waves of development of technology over the last two centuries — in mechanical and electrical engineering, automotive systems and, currently, electronics — have brought huge changes in economic society which can be shown clearly by patterns of consumption and methods of production. Very little of what is consumed in industrialised societies today was available even a generation ago; typical patterns of current expenditure will show that most of the products and services consumed today then either did not exist or were confined to the very few because of the high cost. The labour content of production activity relative to output in all the prime industries of the 19th and early 20th Centuries — mining, transport, power, engineering, manufacture and (most notable of all) agriculture — has fallen steadily as technology and techniques have advanced. Some of the surplus resources of labour have gone into new kinds of production but most of the expansion of employment has been in what may be described as the information industry (figure 25).

Every organisation has its information elements — planning, recording, controlling, communication and general office systems — which constitute a substantial part of the typical organisation structure and activities, whatever the purpose, product or service. However, there is a very large group of organisations which can be considered as being in the business of providing information; their purpose is to supply the organisations concerned with

```
Advertising
Banking and Financial Services
Business Machines
Commodity Markets
Education
Entertainment
Insurance
Postal Services
Printing and Publishing
Professional Services
Public Administration
Telecommunications
```

Figure 25   The information industry

'production'. In this group are all the communication services (notably telecommunication and postal services which include some of the largest business undertakings), most of the professions such as accountants, lawyers, consultancies and all kinds of educational services, banking, insurance and other financial services, and a very large proportion of Government. There is also the substantial group of suppliers of general information comprising the news and entertainment media, the advertising industry and publishers. From a tiny fraction of the employed numbers a century ago, these industries and occupations now employ more than half the working population in advanced industrial countries. Some of the occupations are a consequence of greater prosperity, and some are a contributory cause of it. Prosperity has meant devoting a higher proportion of resources to the social well-being of the community; it has also needed the development of information services to support higher levels of productive activity.

Use of Machines for Information Systems

The relative transfer of labour from manufacturing and the other primary 'production' industries has been partly a matter of the relative growth in these activities, but is is also partly an indication that substitution of machines for manual operations has been slower in these new kinds of business activity than it has been in the 'production' areas. The information industry is not only a large employer of labour but it can be seen as 'labour intensive' in many ways, although the application of machine techniques has been very considerable. Until very recent times, it has been a fair generalisation that substitution of machines for labour has always tended to progress faster with predominantly 'manual' categories of work than with 'clerical' or 'office' work and employment involving direct contact between people. Machines for 'manual' work have tended to be introduced as fast as technology and social constraints permit and the typical manual worker has, for a long time, had a much greater value of capital equipment at his command than has had the office worker or the manager. Although business machines have been available for a wide range of purposes for many years, there has been (at least until recent times) an apparent reluctance to use them, despite the fact that clerical (and managerial) labour was often more expensive *per capita* than manual labour. Business information systems, being largely related to written and verbal communication of information were, for a long time, regarded as 'brain work' and therefore in some way less appropriate to the use of tools and machines than were manual activities. Three reasons may perhaps be advanced for this

- Large historical content
- Complex data and processes
- Conservative attitudes to capital expenditure.

'Paperwork' systems and management information generally involve a high proportion of historical content; in many organisations this has included personal knowledge of individuals operating in traditional systems in which their skills become a vital but intangible element.

Information systems are frequently complex, containing a large variety of data and of processes. These systems are often very difficult to change conveniently and it is usually true that mechanisation of a manual process involves a relatively greater change in the information systems which support it.

Attitudes to capital expenditure always have been much more rigorous in relation to proposals for business machines than for capital equipment in production or distribution environments. In this attitude the United Kingdom has been more conservative than many other industrialised countries, and has paid for it in lower productivity. In the delegation of responsibility for decisions on employment of labour and on capital expenditure, it is extraordinary to consider that the capital decision has usually been placed at a very much higher managerial level than that for the equivalent employment of labour, carrying with it the implication that capital expenditure is, in principle, undesirable. Yet if one calculates the annual cost of employing one person, with all the overhead costs involved, it will be found to represent the equivalent in capital spending power of a very considerable sum indeed. Moreover, the cost now of dismissing an employee is such that labour costs can no longer be considered as simple revenue expenses. Despite this, many businesses still refer to the highest level of management capital decisions equivalent to only a few days' wages. Where these attitudes persist the scope for improving business information systems is retarded, and there are powerful arguments for believing that it is only the impact of very considerable reductions in relative costs of information machines against labour that has produced a perceptible shift of attitudes in the last few years.

Information Technology

The main concern of this book is with computers because it is the introduction of the computer, and its association with other kinds of business machine, that has brought the current condition of accelerating application of technology to information systems. The computer has long been described as a 'data processing' or 'information' machine, which it is; the term 'information technology' is relatively new but has become generally accepted as a useful label for the association of communications and computers in a new range of machine approaches to information systems. All professions and disciplines like to create new languages and jargon and the computer industry has produced its own large, exotic and constantly changing vocabulary. No doubt 'information technology' will be superseded in due course but, for the time being, it is a useful description because it recognises that the computer is only one element in a number of associated technologies brought together in business information systems (figure 26). Business information functions have

```
Microelectronics
Computer Architecture and Design
Software Languages and Engineering
Telecommunications and Signal Processing
Television
Optical Data Systems
Printing
Copying and Reproduction
Data Encryption
Voice Processing
```

Figure 26 Information technologies

been described in earlier chapters as being concerned with recording and storing data, with editing, calculating, collating, printing and other forms of output and distribution of information. To link the processes within the information systems and the systems themselves to other decisions and actions, communication facilities are needed; to make sure that systems meet requirements there must be also a control element. Business machines may assist any of these functions.

Machines such as the typewriter, cash register, office copier, time recorder and calculator have been in common use for many years, as have the telephone, and the mechanical and electrical machine systems for accounting and other data processing. Many of these types of machine are still recognisable today although they have mostly changed from the metal, mechanical or electro-mechanical machines to the light-weight, largely electronically operated devices now to be found. The exploitation of electronics and the associated communications technology has dealt a severe blow to the light mechanical engineering industry but it has also brought into being many new kinds of business machine facility. Nowadays the typical business environment still has need of personal support or single process machines such as calculators and typewriters, but uses much more of the kind of machine facility that brings a number of elements together. The common feature of all these integrated machine systems is the microprocessor, which is found in its familiar role as the essential element of the electronic computer, comprising as it does the facilities for carrying out the programmed instructions, and also has wide application as the electronic control element of many other business machines, both familiar and novel. The telephone exchange is turning into a computer for handling all kinds of communication: digital connections for computer data and written communication as well as for visual communication and the original function of speech transmission. Television has moved from entertainment to business use for visual communication and surveillance, and as a device for general computer system input and output.

The designer and user of business information systems has become accustomed to such concepts as data networks, satellite telecommunications, computer workstations and terminals. Individual industrial and office machines are offered with ever greater ranges of facilities such that it becomes progressively more difficult to classify them in any meaningful way. The electronic calculator, in its basic form, may offer no more simple arithmetic than did its mechanical predecessor but, in other versions, it can be a clock, a monitoring and control device, a communications terminal and a portable computer. (In all these versions it may not appear to be very different, because all are primarily constructed of variations of basic computer circuitry with appropriately programmed, or programmable elements.) Similarly, the office word-processor can be a typewriter, a computer, a document store and a communications terminal. The label 'computer or communications terminal' can also now be applied to the cash register, factory time recorder and to the telephone itself. Between the familiar functions of the office typist, telephone and computer operator there is less and less superficial difference because they all may be found operating similar kinds of machine in a similar way. This universal video terminal, essentially comprising a key-board and monitor screen which can be linked to communication and computer facilities to provide terminal access for input and output, can also be found as much outside the office systems area as in it — the controller of a factory process, of a warehouse or a transport system has also become a computer terminal operator.

The microprocessor, with the associated integrated circuit technology, is used as the most dramatic illustration of the rapid advance in the application of technology to business machines over the last 30 years. It is rightly considered as a development of the utmost importance to business because this advance of technology has rapidly reduced the number of elements of information systems which cannot be transferred effectively to machines. It is now possible to conceive machine-based systems for supporting industrial office and managerial activities on the widest scale without necessarily demanding unacceptable simplification of systems. Techniques available for business information systems have now extended to the more specialised areas of management decision-making and it is probable that the only major constraints on development of more effective business information systems today are questions of attitude.

Information Techniques and Services

Machine-based facilities for business information systems may be grouped conveniently under four main headings

- Data processing
- Data management
- Data communications
- Input/output.

These correspond with the principal theoretical system elements of processing, storage, movement, and input and output. Data processing has been associated primarily with administrative systems — the processing of routine repetitive transactions such as sales and purchases and stock movements. Certainly, the early uses of business computers and their predecessors (the punched card systems — usually designed to hold 80 alphanumeric characters using single and double hole codes in 80 columns) were for activities which could be mechanised in 'factory' systems. In those days business use of computers was usually referred to under the headings of 'electronic data processing' or 'automatic data processing' and computer facilities were provided by central data processing departments. To a substantial extent this is still true because large data processing systems are the principal users of many business computer installations. However, data processing in a wider sense can concern all kinds of business information system, including those which handle data related to purely technical matters and systems for scientific, social, or professional purposes.

Data management is necessarily linked with data processing in any kind of business system; to process and store data in an information system makes it necessary to define, control and manipulate that data, applying appropriate techniques for creating file structures and procedures for access to these files. Data management has assumed a very considerable importance following recognition of the value of business information and the availability of techniques for convenient creation and integration of business files as 'databases'. When business data becomes easily accessible and increasingly valuable in supporting business decisons, then questions of security, quality and manipulation — of data management — also become important. Like the subject of data processing, data management is primarily associated with computers because it is computers that have given the capacity to manage data effectively.

Data communications is a necessary adjunct to processing and management of data but there is also a considerable part of economic activity which comprises information systems created simply to transfer data from one place to another. The area of special interest in this subject of business information must be telecommunications, which is both absorbing and superseding other methods of communication as well as opening up a wide range of new facilities. A few years ago the business of telecommunications shed its somewhat stodgy and bureaucratic image of a long-established speech and telegraph service which seemed to provide its services somewhat grudgingly, to be transformed into the major growth industry. It started to provide many additional types of data service, overlaying and extending basic telephone and telegraph networks. Many types of public and private telecommunication facility are now available (figure 27). There are various facilities for transmission of messages such as the 'electronic mail' Teletex services (in effect the Telex principle applied to higher-speed telephone network facilities, and operating through local office computer systems rather than from 'stand alone' key-board terminals), and 'Packet Switching' (a form of high-speed transmission of 'postal' packets of digital data — the user, in contrast to other systems, having

```
Public Switched Network
Leased Telephone Circuits
Datel (Data Transmission)
 X Stream (High Speed Digital)
PSS (Packet Switch Stream)
Teletex
Telecom Gold (Electronic Mail)
Radiophone
Telex
Facsimile
```

Figure 27   British Telecom services

to establish a connection only with the 'pillar box'). Videotex (Viewdata) services make use of computers, telecommunications and television to provide alternative public and private facilities for information retrieval. Telecommunications networks have expanded in capacity and speed of transmission to meet growing volumes of traffic and increasing use of computer-based system links which can benefit from higher transmission speeds. They also provide for transmission of graphical information with greater ease, overcoming the constraints which had held back the long-established facsimile services for transferring pre-printed messages or graphical data from one place to another across the telecommunications speech network. Telemetry, for remote monitoring and control of other machine systems, makes use of telecommunication circuits in much the same way as do data networks for all general business computer applications.

All these variations of public and private telecommunication service facilities are of current interest to business, and new facilities are becoming available as technology and economics offer opportunities for further advance. A different dimension which may have especial significance for business organisation and systems is the value-added network. This relates to the use of public telecommunication facilities by suppliers of business information for the sale of their (value added) services to telecommunication customers; it is not strictly a consequence of advances in technology but rather of the relaxation of public telecommunication monopolies. As this implies, Information Technology is not only a matter of exploiting the results of technical research and innovation; it is as much a question of taking advantage of improved economics to extend application of existing techniques and to bring different strands of development together to provide new kinds of facility.

Input and Output

Publication in information technology is principally printing and visual presentation through screen displays such as television and the visual display terminals used with computer systems. Both are, of course, long-established primary channels for information system output but the influence of computer systems and advances in technology have greatly extended the scope and form of printing and display techniques.

Broadcast television services have extended to cable and satelite links, giving increased numbers of channels, and to computer information services such as the Ceefax and Oracle services carried on television entertainment channels. The laser (using amplified light beam technology) and the fibre-optics cable (glass-fibre cable for transmission of data by means of light signals) have brought opportunities for substantial change in printing techniques (as well as in telecommunication and computer system input) with consequences for speed and mode of presentation which are opening many new information systems applications.

Specialised machines for provision of terminal access and system output (such as the bank cashpoint) change economics and social habits and also lead to new kinds of information service and facility. Where such machines can be used to interface two separate automatic systems the integration of those systems, changing the balance and characteristics of both, can be considered and this is probably one of the most significant aspects of development of information technology. The concepts of computer integrated manufacture involving co-ordinated machine control of associated systems in a large productive unit are in the process of rapid extension to manufacturing and processing plants of all kinds and could, in principle, be applied to much of office information systems and to publishing and printing themselves.

The Man–Machine Interface

The application of information technology to business systems and the resulting integration of manual and machine elements has brought special attention to the question of the 'man–machine interface' in the design of such systems. The buffers between separate processes or procedures which exist in purely manual systems or in machine systems made up of discrete elements (as in manual typing or in lathe operation), and in those computer systems which operate in 'batch' mode, are being removed as the systems are superseded by 'interactive' and automatic systems in which processing elements are linked together. With such systems, the only manual element may be at the points of system control and at the input/output interfaces with other systems.

As indicated earlier, a rapidly increasing proportion of business tasks involve operation of key-board/video units or other information-handling devices linked to computers and communication systems, and the sales clerk, typist, book-keeper, factory worker or laboratory technician will now more and more often be seen working at a computer terminal or workstation. However much the design of computer-based systems may involve technical questions, these 'man–machine interfaces' obviously concern the behaviour of people also. Interface design, marrying machine and human requirements, can be of fundamental importance to the acceptability of a system and to its economics. Acceptability must imply that operation at the interface can meet appropriate standards of convenience, physical ability, and the more abstract criteria of cost, time and accuracy. Since the cost of people who are performing input/ output operations may make up the greater part of the total in these days of relatively cheap electronic machines, miscalculation in this part of the system could have a decisive effect on overall economics. It is not surprising that the man–machine interface has become a major area of research in information technology as ever easier means of communication between people and computers are sought. This is consistent, of course, with the general business objective of making more effective use of labour.

Another of the major information technology research areas — that of 'artificial intelligence' and 'knowledge-based systems' — is also concerned with the relationship between people and information systems because it is aimed at extending the ability of computer-based systems to handle decision-making activities which were previously in the human sphere. Before these concepts assumed their present identity, the development of business information systems had been steadily encroaching on lower areas of decision and, as more sophisticated machines and techniques become available, so the extent to which man can be replaced by machine in decision areas has widened. It can allow machine–machine interfaces in place of man–machine, and man–machine in place of man–man in many areas of normal business communication and in the integration of systems to provide co-ordinated control over associated work activities.

Check List 8

The use of the term Information Technology has grown in recent years to cover the whole range of techniques and machine systems associated with use of computers for information. It reflects the expansion of industries exploiting micro-electronic technology — in contrast to the decline of the primary and mechanical engineering industries.

Information technology brings together micro-electronics, telecommunications, television, printing, recording and other technologies with computers.

Business Machine Functions
    Communicating.
    Recording and storing.
    Editing.
    Calculating and collating.
    Controlling.

Information Techniques and Services
    Data processing.
    Data management and databases.

Telecommunications:
  Electronic mail.
  Teletex, Packet Switching and Videotex.
  Facsimile.
  Telemetry.
  Value-added services.
  Lasers.
  Fibre-optics.

Man–Machine Interface

Further Reading

Awad, E., *Introduction to Computers*, Prentice-Hall, 1983.
Silver, G. and Silver, J., *Data Processing for Business*, Harcourt Brace, 1981.
Spencer, D., *An Introduction to Computers*, Merrill, 1983.
Zorkoczy, P., *Information Technology — An Introduction*, Pitman, 1983.

9 Evolution of Information Technology

Origin of Computers

An historical perspective

If a student is invited by a teacher to write an essay on the history of computers, the probability is that it will begin with a collection of potted biographies from the pantheon of computing: Blaise Pascal, Leibnitz, Babbage and his remarkable associate Ada, Lady Lovelace, not forgetting Turing and Von Neumann whose names have become part of the fundamentals of computer science. We can and should regard their intellect and achievements with the greatest respect, and find the accounts of their work interesting and absorbing, but if one asks how much this aspect of computer history will contribute to a practical understanding of computers and their uses at the present day, the answer is — very little.

For research scientists and technicians seeking to explore new forms of computer architecture or develop new approaches to software design, the theoretical base of the subject is a necessary field of study. For the business managers and system designers it is still true, as it was in the beginning of computers, that it is much more important to understand how a computer may be used, and why, than to know what is inside the box.

Nevertheless, an objective view of the history of computers is relevant (as is history in general) to a proper understanding of the present day. Today, a business manager who knows no better may think a computer is a cheap portable magic box of tricks obtainable from any good stationer; the school child may see the same computer as an exciting toy. In consequence, the one soon becomes disappointed and the other bored, and the machine facilities both have so eagerly acquired cease to be used. An historical perspective alone is not likely to ensure sound business decisions about computers and certainly will not help to prolong the lives of such ephemera as electronic toys, but a knowledge of economic history and of the effect of technological and economic change on the means of development and practical usage of computer systems can help a great deal.

There is a natural tendency (particularly when we are young) to believe that the past represents folly, ignorance and stagnation, in contrast to the new ideas from new intellects which demonstrate the sudden discovery of wisdom. In the world of business machine systems, the new challenges the old in much the same way. The seller of the new compact personal microcomputer invites us to look with contempt at yesterday's manufacturer of the 'mainframe' who could conceive nothing better than that slow, lumbering and expensive antiquity. The systems analyst, anxious to produce the best-ever new system, is often tempted to treat the old system as unworthy of any regard whatever. Yet the truth is that, at the time, the intellectual skills and judgements applied to design problems may well have been as good as, or better than those of the present day. Moreover, the apparent advantage of present knowledge and skill may not be as great as it seems. There is still not a personal microcomputer which can handle as much work as the first business machine installed by J. Lyons & Company and, of Systems Analysis, it has often been said that the principal element is the science of 'antithetics' — where old systems are reborn in another re-invention of the wheel.

The specific advantages of the present are hindsight and a starting point of greater knowledge. As often as not, these advantages may be thrown away through refusal to truly learn from the past. No doubt individuals can have some significant impact on historical events but it would be quite another matter to argue that the state of the art in computers would have been grossly different if such people as Babbage, Von Neumann, or Thomas J. Watson had not lived. A consideration more important than the actions and achievements of individuals is the general flow of events in economic history and the relationships between economics, technology and, to a lesser extent, politics.

The Punched Card

The most useful starting point for an examination of the history of computers in business is the end of the Second World War, when the punched card was reaching the zenith of its development as the prime machine system for business use. The successors to Hollerith and Powers, the American originators — International Business Machines and Remington Rand and their imitators, representing the 'square' and 'round' hole punched card concepts — developed their ranges of machines during this immediate post-war period to a peak of achievement in electro-mechanical and mechanical engineering techniques respectively.

These were not the only business machines available at that time but, for the most part, these other machines were in what would now be the category described as 'personal support tools', allowing an individual operator to work more efficiently. In contrast, punched card systems were designed to handle large volumes of repetitive transactions in a machine installation. Wherever accounting transactions had to be processed, or quantities of data analysed, punched card machine systems showed themselves capable of handling large numbers of similar transactions rapidly and economically, and thus could offer significant cost and time advantages to the business user.

These systems operated essentially as 'process' systems because of the nature of the predominantly mechanical devices used. Each of these machines was designed to produce the optimum result for the process: the key punch to make most effective use of the skills of an individual operator; and other machines, freed from the limitations of human capacity, to sort or print at the maximum rate obtainable from mechanical card feeds and electro-mechanical processing facilities.

The basic elements of a business system — input, processing and output — could easily be demonstrated in the individual machine processes of punching, sorting and tabulating, with the storage element represented by the punched card (figure 28). Some installations would comprise perhaps no more than a sorter and a tabulator and a few punches, other installations could be huge. (The UK Government installation which processed social security records boasted at one time 112 punched card tabulators.) Any business having a large number of transactions to process would use punched cards and, through ingenuity and sophistication in the design of systems and use of machine facilities, punched card installations were able to deal effectively with a wide range of data processing needs.

A punched card installation usually operated as a 'factory', providing a data processing service to other departments. It would be organised as a specialised

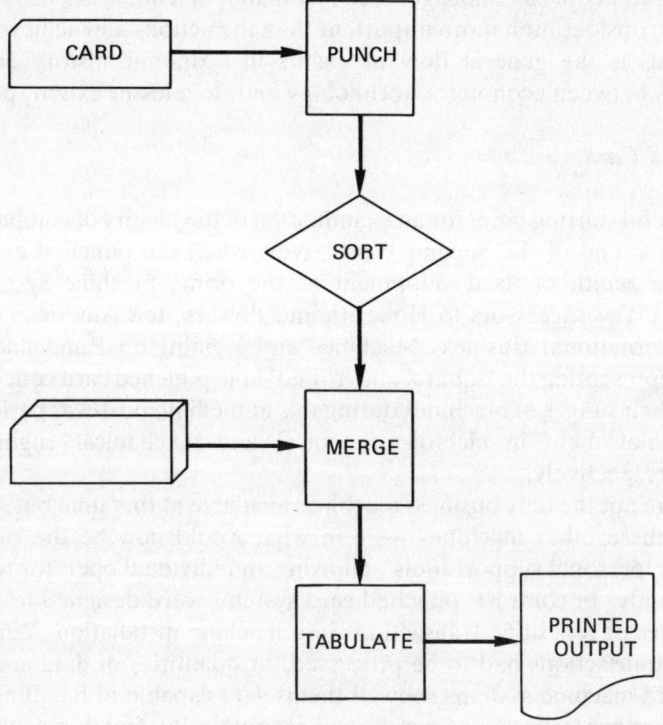

Figure 28   Punched card system

machine section of the business, receiving data from originating departments and distributing complete information in the form of tabulations or other printed documents to user departments or external destinations. Such a central service offered the same advantages as any factory over a 'cottage' industry unit: economies of scale through exploiting capacity of machines, and the benefits of discipline and control in pushing up labour productivity and permitting effective planning.

The punched card installation had a major impact on the efficiency of business administration and on the theoretical concepts of business information systems. Although business systems were moving firmly away from the earlier view of office work as 'individual' and not subject to performance criteria, the punched card was not a universal solution to business information problems, even for accounting. The key-board accounting machine which allowed book-keeping to run in much the same way as manual ledger systems, with immediate access to 'up-to-date' records, might have the disadvantage of being limited in speed to that of the single key-board operator, but gained in that records could be held and be accessible at the point of origin of the transaction data. Since this was often the point of use also, the key-board machine could fit conveniently into other parts of the business systems. In contrast, to send original documents some distance to a data processing installation might be very inconvenient. Such a central installation could only operate effectively on a 'batch' basis of accumulating data over a period and producing results at fixed intervals; this could cause delay and difficulty in dealing with queries because there might be significant periods when access to individual records would be difficult or impossible.

Even where access to records between output 'runs' was not required, punched card processes were too cumbersome and expensive for many processing jobs where the data volumes were small. There was certainly nothing to be gained from using punched card techniques for correspondence, filing, communications or copying. The punched card was primarily a medium for mechanised accounting and, even there, it had very limited ability to edit, calculate or deal with exceptions to normal routines.

The First Computers

Serious attempts were made to overcome some of these limitations and to extend the economic range of punched card systems. In the early 1950s the business machine industry, although reaching the limits of mechanical engineering, was still moving forward steadily with the introduction of more and more sophisticated calculators. Using simple electronics, these calculators could hold stored constants and short program sequences, apply calculations (such as $a \times b + c - d = e$) to data input on cards and produce results on those cards ready for the next process. This was a step towards the business computer and, for the punched card suppliers, towards their transformation into computer manufacturers.

The impetus behind the development of computers did not come only from the business machine industry. The electrical industry was making increasing use of electronics, and in academic and applied research laboratories in universities and industry, both before and during the Second World War, much was being done to harness new electronic techniques to problems of calculation. The result was a number of machine systems designed, for scientific purposes, to be able to undertake complex and lengthy calculations. These computers, although not intended to be used in large-scale business data processing, attracted immediate attention from the business world because of their calculating power and programming flexibility. The two machines which are, probably rightly, regarded as the most important pioneering ventures in business computers were the Univac I in the United States and the Leo I in the United Kingdom. The Univac was marketed by Remington Rand, the 'round-hole' punched card company in the USA, and the Leo by J. Lyons & Co, the food suppliers, who installed the first for their own use in their bakery division; both machines were based on experimental work in academic research centres in the respective countries. IBM followed quickly with their own first computer systems, also derived mainly from academic research.

The electrical industry moved to exploit the commercial potential of the business computer; throughout the industrial world major electrical manufacturers started to launch their own computer systems and, for a short period, led the innovation and marketing of computers for business. They were also instrumental in the rapid development of computers for scientific purposes from the original areas of research. Ferranti, the UK electronics company, which is still a major supplier of computer systems, developed the Ferranti Mark I with Manchester University for the scientific market before the Univac and Leo. Although there is a tendency to think that these first computers were quaint and amateurish, the architecture of computers has not yet changed radically from the early concepts. Programs were prepared externally by specialists, using the set of machine instructions able to be organised in any desired sequence and pattern. These programs were then held in a computer internal storage location from which they could be withdrawn for automatic processing of transaction data fed into the computers. Internal storage was of two kinds: main (immediate access) storage for data and programs in current use, and backing storage for file data and programs not immediately required. The central processing unit in which the program instructions were carried out was linked to these storage areas and to the input and output devices so that they could all operate under the control of the program. Admittedly, much of the technology was different from that of the present day, and machines were very large and costly. One could walk inside the Univac I or Leo I, a necessary arrangement for engineer access and heat dispersion from the thermionic valves used as circuit switches.

The size of machines and the cost of special accommodation obviously would have precluded use for many of today's computer applications but, for scientific calculation, or for business data processing at that time, size was not a significant disadvantage. Cost was a consideration, since computers were relatively expensive; at a time when the average industrial wage in the United Kingdom was less than £500 a year, the Leo I marketed commercially by Lyons was priced at over £100 000 compared with £5000–10 000 for the typical punched card installation. The work undertaken to justify such expenditure had to be substantial, and computer systems and programs needed to be designed carefully to produce the maximum benefit. In the United States, computers were accepted more readily than in the United Kingdom and elsewhere, not because the inhabitants of that country were necessarily more enlightened or more efficient in their methods but because US labour costs were higher and a computer could be justified at a lower level of savings. Use of punched cards was also more extensive in the United States for the same reason, and the introduction of computers for business was justified often because they cost less than the punched card installations that they displaced.

The business applications using punched card systems offered a ready market for the new computers and much of the punched card equipment was soon displaced, although the punched card itself remained as the prime source of input to computer sytems for a long time.

In comparison with the present day, when we have become accustomed to virtually complete reliability of 'hardware', there was a significant need for preventive maintenance and repair, but the many successful computer systems fully matched in reliability the electrical and mechanical devices they had superseded and such loss of usable time as there was could usually be accepted. One can think of many computer tasks today which would not be attempted in a situation where there was a risk of interruption through failure at any time but if one considers the kind of batch processing operations typical of early computer installations, uninterrupted performance was not essential. This is still true for routine batch data processing; provided that there is sufficient time between receipt of the last batch of data and the time for the first output to accommodate both the machine processes and any reasonable loss of time through failure, the overall system can work successfully.

The Computer becomes a Business Machine

The first types of machine did not last long. Experience of production and usage quickly brought improvements, starting the business computer on the continuous and rapid development which still goes on. Valves and 'delay lines' were replaced by new switching and storage devices, bringing improvement in computer performance with every measure — cost, capacity, speed, reliability and size. The business computer, having absorbed much of the old punched card business, started to expand beyond it. It was found possible to break away from earlier constraints as it became feasible to bring together business functions which had been previously performed as separate machine or manual processes.

Competition between suppliers contributed to the rate of advance but also brought immediate pressure on the weaker manufacturers. Even at that early stage, the importance of 'economies of scale' were apparent not only in their effect on direct costs of manufacture but also on the ability to spread overhead cost of the essential large investment in continuous research and development. One by one, the electrical manufacturers dropped out of the market or reverted to a role as supplier of components. Within a decade of the first commercial computer systems, most of the business of supplying computers was in the hands of the old business machine companies, dominated, as before, by the United States: by IBM and Univac, the punched card companies, and by Burroughs and NCR, the suppliers of keyboard accounting machines. The only UK supplier of any significance was International Computers and Tabulators (now ICL), formed by amalgamation of the two British punched card companies — Powers–Samas and British Tabulating (Hollerith) — together with computer off-shoots of various electrical companies which had entered the computer market.

The machine companies knew, and customers soon learned, that dependence on the supplier did not end with installation of the equipment; the customer would need maintenance support, technical advice, extra machine capacity and, eventually, a suitable replacement. A vital consideration was confidence in the supplier — in technical knowledge and experience, in financial stability, in belief that the supplier would be able to offer a solution to a problem whenever it was needed. IBM understood this; they did not 'sell' to installation managers but to managing directors and financial directors: that is, to those who made the investment decisions. This combination of its understanding of customer motivation, supported by its vast customer 'base' from the punched card era, its enormous experience and its effective marketing organisation ensured IBM's continued dominance in the business machine market. It was larger than all its competitors together, and still is so.

The importance of IBM in the historical context and in any understanding of computers and information systems is not as a story of business success but in the pervasive influence their dominance of the computer industry has had on the nature of computers, their software languages and techniques, the use of computers and the attitudes towards them, even on the actual vocabulary of computer jargon itself.

Computers were used for any business data processing application which was appropriate in size and nature to justify the investment. Typically, these were applications with a large number of repetitive transactions leading to periodic output of lists, summaries, or otherwise edited information involving processing sequences which could be identified precisely as a series of algorithms and, consequently, be programmed. Payroll was the first choice for many installations because it had these ingredients, and a special element of urgency which would place great demands on a clerical organisation over a short period. To such organisations as the National Coal Board, which had at one time some sixty elements in calculation of employee gross pay, the computer was a very welcome invention indeed and, for a brief period, the NCB was renowned among the computer pioneers.

The processing of sales transactions — order processing, invoicing, sales accounting and sales analysis — were extremely important computer applications too. Airlines used computers to analyse revenue from millions of passenger journeys, public utilities for billing their huge numbers of customers, and local authorities for preparing rate demands.

The computer demonstrated its advantages over previously used methods where data was required for more than one purpose; for example, pay information for cost analysis as well as for payroll, and order information for billing and for sales analysis. The computer provided an easy means of analysing data for management information because of the very small additional costs of sorting and assembling information in different ways. Sales could be analysed by area, by representative, and by product: comparative figures and projections could be presented combining the functions of routine recording for accounting and control purposes, and generation of management information for decision making.

By the mid 1960s, scarcely ten years after the first business computers went into operation, the computer industry was firmly established. Use of computers in business was widespread and the technology had made substantial advances. Many of the constraints of cost, speed, capacity and reliability which had restricted markets for the first computers were gone or much reduced.

Landmarks of Computer Technology

The first decade of business computing should in no sense be regarded as a purely experimental period with tentative steps in limited areas. Development of technology and extension of applications was a continuous process spreading as rapidly as experience, techniques and economic argument permitted. Computers had their limitations, but they offered many advantages over previous means of solving business problems and these new opportunities were grasped with tolerable promptitude by many business undertakings. On the whole, too, they exploited opportunities of devising better systems with efficiency and success despite the novelty of the technology and of the techniques for designing and operating computer systems. Even so, this achievement was minute compared with what was to come; over the next two decades the pace of development continued to accelerate with ever-widening scope for computer application as limits were quickly extended or removed.

It is normal practice to describe the advance of computer technology in terms of 'generations' of hardware and software. Technological advance does not work in quite such an ordered way and it is really more appropriate to see the development of information technology in terms of landmarks. In the mid 1960s, following the emergence of business machine companies as the major force in the computer industry, there were two such notable series of events: the introduction of modular ranges of standard computer products by the business machine suppliers and the installation of the first major communication-based systems.

Modular Computer Systems

In 1964, IBM introduced its new '360' series of computers, and ICL its 1900 series; existing computer products were superseded by these ranges of advanced modular systems which offered users the opportunity of 'growing' with the same supplier. The modular concept of computer families was a series of compatible central processors of differing power, associated with a range of storage and peripheral input/output units which could be grouped in differing configurations (figure 29). It became possible to cater for many differing customer requirements through one family of computers, and suppliers could obtain and offer to customers the benefits of significant economies of scale in production and marketing. Modular systems had the added attraction that computer investment decisions could now be taken with much greater confidence. It was not necessary to ensure that the capacity of equipment installed at the outset would be sufficient for the life of the business system; one

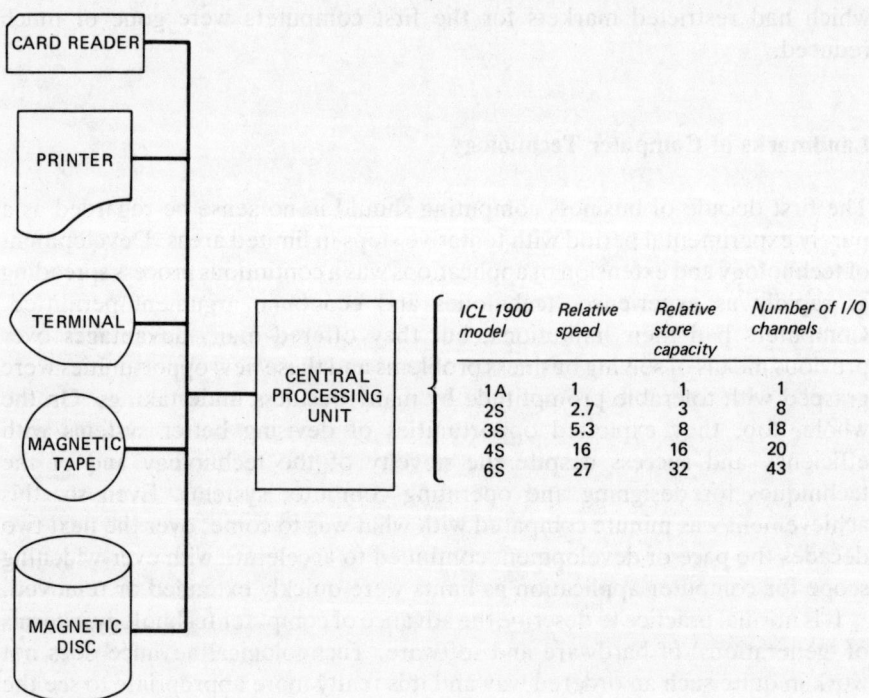

ICL 1900 model	Relative speed	Relative store capacity	Number of I/O channels
1A	1	1	1
2S	2.7	3	8
3S	5.3	8	18
4S	16	16	20
6S	27	32	43

Figure 29   Modular computer system

could now plan to add elements of storage, input or output as required, and then advance to a larger computer model with greater basic power without having to replace system or programs. This 'upward compatibility' was not as great as it might have seemed from manufacturers' selling arguments, but it was nonetheless real and important.

The modular concept was a response to three important lessons which had been learned in the preceding years

- All computer applications tend to grow
- If a computer is available it will be used for new tasks
- The real investment is the system and its software, not the equipment.

Once a business acquires a computer, however satisfactory or disappointing the early experience, the computer is usually 'there to stay'. It becomes an essential part of the business organisation and its use grows and extends; in consequence, demands on computer capacity grow also. Experience points to new applications and gives confidence in tackling them, adding further to the demands on capacity. Eventually the time arrives for the original equipment to be replaced. This brings a realisation that the important investment is not in equipment but in the business system itself, represented by programs and procedures. New machinery may be substituted with comparatively little physical strain but if this new equipment cannot handle the old programs, files and other system 'interfaces' without difficulty, or without unacceptable interruption of operation during the changeover, then the business is faced with a very considerable re-investment in new system design. This might be unavoidable if the original system concepts and programs are no longer appropriate to existing requirements and are incapable of modification but, in general, it is clearly advantageous to be able to look forward to easier growth paths: to avoid the trauma and expense of changes in systems which affect most aspects of a business administration and around which much of the organisation may have been reconstructed.

These are problems to be faced by computer users at any time; perhaps they were particularly important in the 1960s because so many users were then planning to replace computer systems for the first time, and faced the realisation that, even if the original supplier had not gone out of business, a compatible replacement was not readily available.

Manufacturers had their own view of this dilemma; to take advantage of technological developments and to be competitive, it was prudent to produce systems which were the best for future needs. But these, almost inevitably, were incompatible technically with their predecessors. A first principle of marketing in the business machine industry has always been to protect the existing 'customer base'; computer suppliers attempt to retain their customers despite changes in computer architecture, by providing software or hardware 'bridges' to allow new systems to emulate or simulate old systems until these can be reprogrammed at leisure.

Important though existing users were in the 1960s, the potential market was more important; the combined effect of modular systems, lowering the entry level and offering easy growth paths attracted many users and applications and set data processing on a period of firm and rapid expansion.

Telecommunication Systems

The second landmark is most memorably related to the introduction of large 'real-time' systems for airlines. The use of computers for airline seat reservation is still the most quoted 'classic' example of the application of 'real-time' systems. Studies leading to the introduction of these systems started in the early 1950s — very soon, indeed, after the first commercial computers were available. That they took some years in development reflects the complexity of system problems: even to define the nature of these problems required considerable application of scientific method. It also indicated the limitations of available solutions to several important technical problems.

One problem was to obtain a high standard of performance, so that a computer could be relied upon to function continuously as an integral part of the whole information system. The term 'real time' was coined to express some important differences from the normal (batch) computer systems used for general data processing: that the computer was actually operated directly at the time a transaction arose, that its file records would be updated immediately, and that a response on which further action depended would be received within a very short time. If, for any reason the computer failed, then the whole system would fail. (For the batch system, in contrast, input data and the action resulting from output of information are separated from computer processing and, provided there are adequate time buffers between processes, a computer failure need not be noticed by users.)

Another problem was that transactions would arise at any time and would require action without delay. It would not be known when a customer might call for a reservation, or which destination would be sought, or whether the call was simply an enquiry or was to make a booking or cancellation. For this the system would have to be designed so that programs and data files were available constantly and immediately accessible. This random nature of input data was one of the reasons for the use of operational research techniques to establish what the input data patterns and their demands on the system might be. (In the event, the first large real-time airline seat reservation system collapsed in production after a few hours because these data problems had been incorrectly appreciated.)

The problems of developing appropriate software, of constructing reliable storage devices with adequate capacity and access speed, and of providing input/output facilities capable of handling large varying numbers of transactions from many directly connected points undoubtedly did extend the limits of computer technology at that time. But, in retrospect, it was this direct linking of computer facilities to remote points that was the real landmark — the introduction of telecommunications. In technical terms perhaps this did not involve any really notable innovation; the seat reservations systems used public telecommunication facilities (as systems still do) with appropriate adaptation for digital information which was generated at terminals for transmission accurately, at the required speed, to and from the centre of computer operation (figure 30).

These first successful uses of telecommunications were quickly followed by others, soon establishing telecommunications as essential for any computer installation. 'Teleprocessing' — using a computer for production jobs or system development with terminals linked on-line to the central computer facility — overcame the handicap of distance. Where benefits of computer speed might have been lost in transporting transaction data from a remote point by post or courier to a data processing centre, the installation of direct communication links could allow the needs of geographically spread organisations to be met almost as easily as those of centralised organisations. It also made it possible to use a computer for systems requiring operation to time standards more exacting than those possible with any 'batch' approach. This applied not only to commercial systems such as airline seat reservations where action is generated by customer contact but also to 'technical' systems for monitoring and control, where input might be a reading from a meter or gauge and output the operation of a switch.

Computer Terminals

Much of the growth of telecommunications for computer systems was related to the 'on-line' concept; that is, having a physical communications link between an input/output terminal point and the computer processing and storage centre. Such a link is essential for real-time working but the two terms are not synonomous. Direct input links can be used simply as a means of 'capturing' transaction data quickly and storing for processing at a later time, without the immediate file updating and response of the real-time operation. Used as an on-line input device, the Visual Display Unit (VDU) Terminal competed with punched cards and paper tape and soon replaced them for general business data (figure 31). These two media had been the principal means of converting original data to computer machineable form, and the nature of this data preparation process was such that it paid to organise it on a 'factory' basis, using a large group of (female) punch operators working in a disciplined environment and capable of producing very high standards of speed and accuracy.

At first sight the VDU as a means of data input does not appear to offer any advantage over the key punch. Certainly there was no gain in rate of keying but it could offer two important economies: less data need be entered and verification was easier. With any computer operation some verification of input data is essential to minimise the risk that inaccurate information enters the system. Verification of key punching was achieved by repeating the task — duplicating the punching operation to overlap the errors; when a VDU was

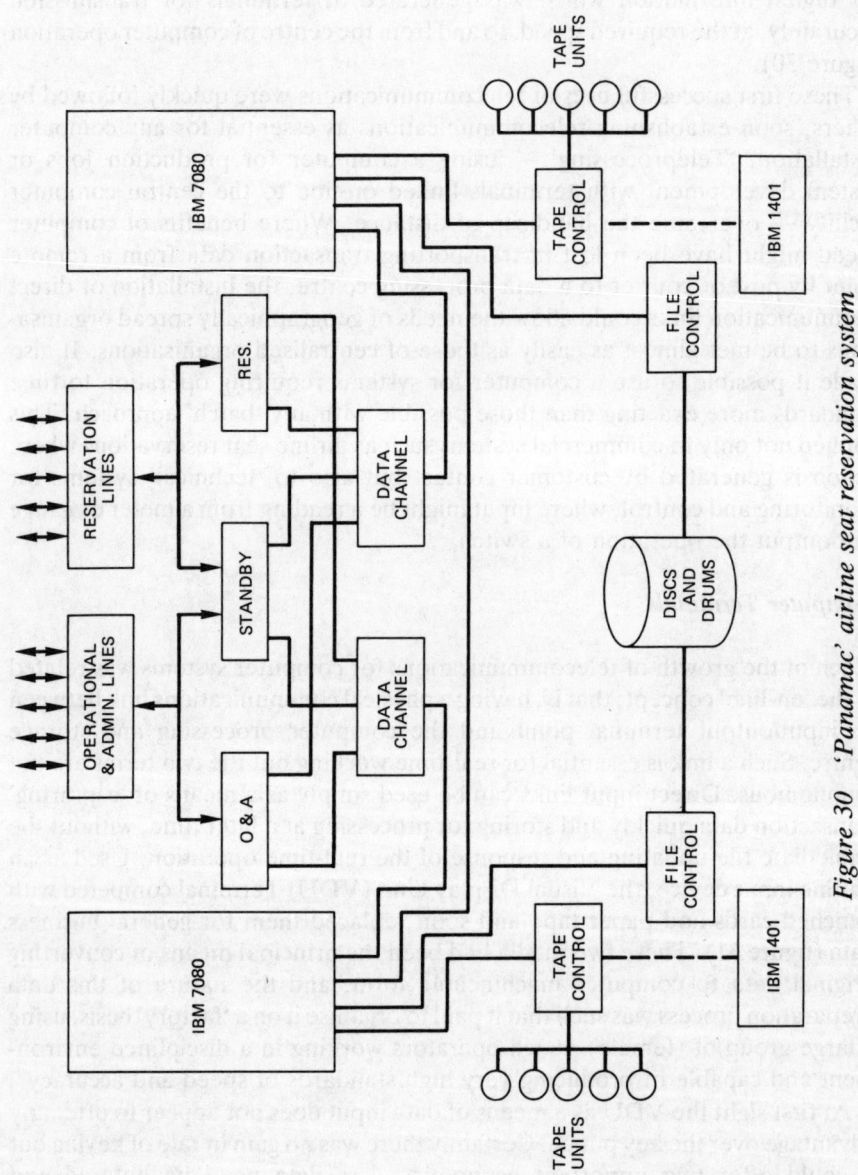

Figure 30 'Panamac' airline seat reservation system

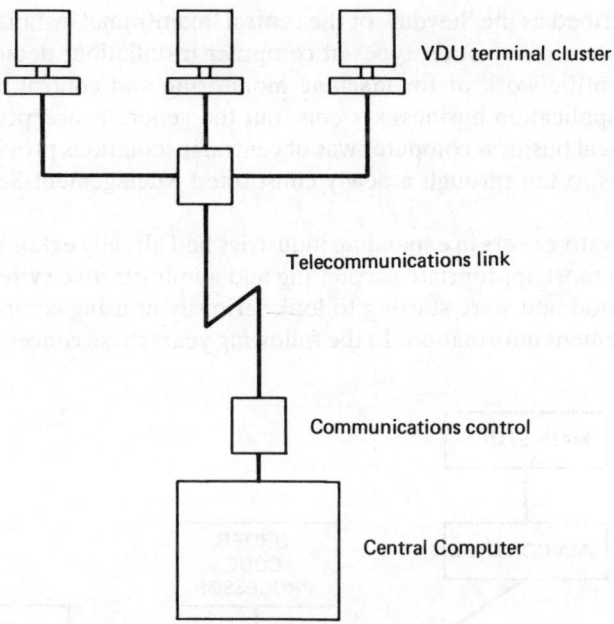

Figure 31   Visual display unit terminals

used, 'sight verification' — comparing data displayed on the screen with the original — made a second operation unnecessary. The verification process could be helped further by the use of programmed routines to identify data errors, and the slower keying rate of the VDU could be offset by taking advantage of information already in the computer system to allow input data to be abbreviated. This facility for 'interactive' working could be used also to eliminate earlier stages of data preparation. Key punch operators always worked from transaction documents; to obtain the best performance it was often necessary to transcribe data from original documents, which were difficult to read, to forms from which punch operators could work swiftly and accurately. The real-time seat reservations system had shown how it was possible to take the transaction data entry back to the point of origin, perhaps eliminating the need for any kind of written document. To bring the point of computer system input/output close to the 'interface' with other systems is still an important principle in the design of computer systems: the closer to the origin and destination, the more effective the system is likely to be.

The Computer Centre

The period following the introduction of modular ranges of business computers and the joining together of computer and communications technology was one of rapid development in every aspect of business computing. It might perhaps be described as the 'heyday' of the central 'mainframe' installation (figure 32). There were many other types of computer installation: dedicated computers for scientific work or for machine monitoring and control and many small, single application business systems, but the generally accepted conception of the typical business computer was of central installations providing a service to all users, often through a newly constituted Management Services organisation.

Innovative users in expanding industries had already extended their applications to most appropriate accounting and administrative systems very early in this period and were starting to look seriously at using computer systems for management information. In the following years these concepts spread rapidly

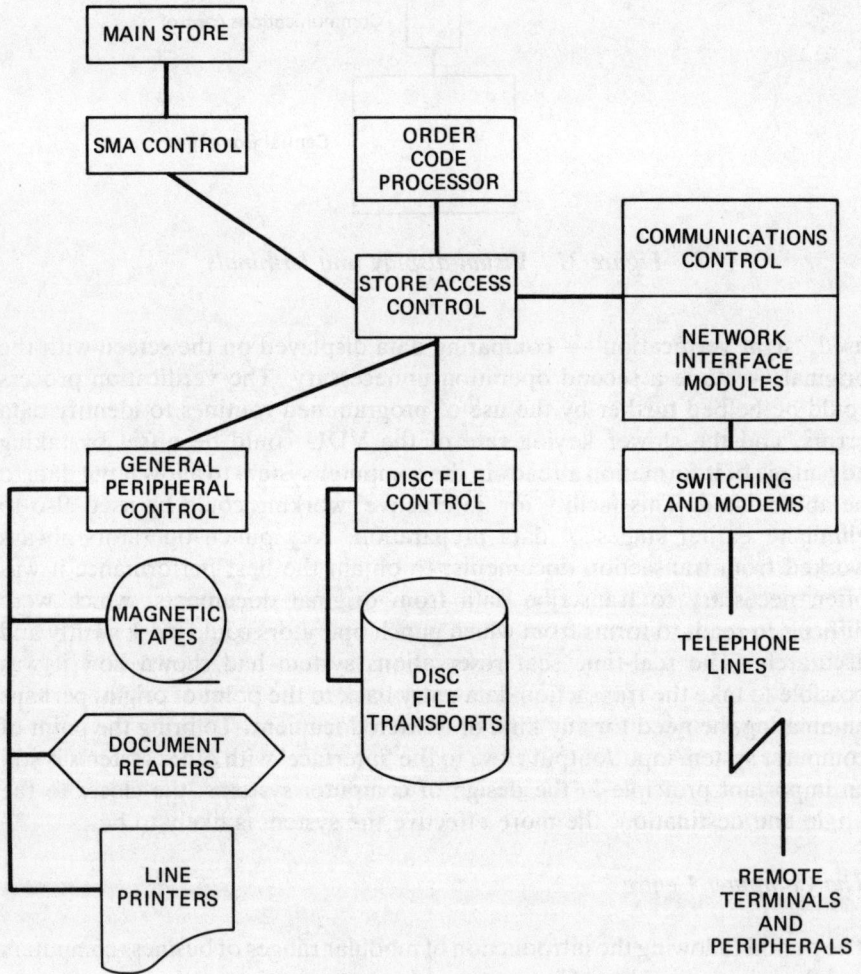

Figure 32   Mainframe

to most of the medium and larger business organisations — manufacturers, retailers, public utilities and local government authorities. The economic arguments against computer use for minor transactions and for alphabetic information were reducing steadily, leading to the integration of all types of data and process within computer operations, and to the introduction of systems specifically designed for 'information retrieval': that is, the computer as a library rather than as a data processing factory. Most business systems now contain both 'data processing' and 'information retrieval' elements.

Packaged Software

Reduction in cost of computer capacity, while making the economics of computers generally more favourable, also brought a change in the balance of costs of developing and running computer systems. As equipment reduced in price, the cost of employing people was rising which meant that designing systems, writing programs, entering data and operating computers became relatively more expensive. Moreover, the extended range and scope of computer systems brought about by the cheaper, better hardware meant more complex, and therefore still more expensive, software. These extra costs clearly did not cancel out the gains in hardware costs; they did cause greater and greater attention to be directed to ways of reducing labour costs. Much of the progress in this direction was through the software itself.

Where previously the 'Operating System' (the programmed facilities provided with the computer) had been intended primarily as an aid to more effective use of equipment (as with 'multi-programming') the changing balance of cost brought moves to reduce the need for operators; ultimately to make it possible for computer users to manage without specialist operators at all. This 'system software' which provided these operating facilities also began to be used to reduce the work of the programmers; more and more pre-programmed facilities were made available so that, in this field also, the user eventually found himself able to dispense with the services of the specialist.

To identify all the aspects and variations of Operating Systems and other system software concepts which developed in rapid succession is a major subject in its own right. It is sufficient at this stage to point out that Operating Systems quickly became an essential part of computer facilities. When we look at a modern general-purpose business computer and note that it has several million characters of mainstore (or 'immediate access' storage — containing data and program elements in current use) available to it compared with the several thousand of its early predecessors, we must remember also that a very large part of this huge storage facility may be essential to accommodate the Operating System which makes it possible to use the computer for a wide range of purposes with minimum effort and skill.

Exploration of software techniques also extended to the computer languages themselves. New program coding and compilation techniques (the 'higher level' languages), aimed at reducing needs for technical skill in programming and saving time for writing and testing programs, superseded the 'machine code' (repertoire of instructions which can be performed by the computer processing unit and which are executed through the program sequence) and 'assembler' (which convert the low level assembly language to machine code) techniques in most general commercial applications practice. Common needs in applications programming were met by the introduction of 'utilities' (computer programs provided, often as part of Operating Systems, for *ad hoc* use or incorporation into application software), for such repetitive activities as sorting and control of printing output. Packaged application modules for the most popular applications — payroll, sales accounting, stock control etc. — became available, offering substantial savings in cost and development time over programs written specifically for individual use.

Higher level languages and their successors, and all the application packages, are less efficient in their use of machine capacity than the precise and detailed machine code languages and the 'tailored' application programs, but that does not matter if the end result is cheaper, more quickly produced and close enough to user needs to offer an acceptable system solution.

Increasing use of packaged software led to the growth of a new type of organisation in the computer industry — the 'software house'. There had always been consultants able to supply expert assistance in developing and programming systems but the production of packaged software became as much part of computer supply as the hardware itself; in fact, much of this software eventually became indistinguishable from the hardware because it was supplied already 'wired in'. At the lower end of the market the argument for choosing cheap packaged software eventually became unassailable when it was apparent that the employment of one programmer would cost as much as the acquisition of a computer system of very considerable power.

Database Management

Of all the ready-made software facilities which have been changing people's conception of computers and the way systems should be constructed, none has become more familiar than the Database Management System. The idea of a 'database' arose out of the linking of computer and communication technology in the late 1960s and the concept of a truly integrated business system: a 'total' system in which the computer would be used to hold a central file of all data needed for running the business. This file would be updated, as changes arose, from the point of origin, and would provide information to users, when required, at the point of action or decision.

Some businesses have achieved this goal, including some that have reconstructed their organisations around a central database, but there are not many truly integrated data management systems; most business organisational structures of any size have so far proved to be too complicated. Nevertheless, Database Management software, as a necessary addition to the basic operating system facilities, has become an essential feature of business computers.

Separation of 'management' of business data from use of that data, which is a central feature of database concepts, offers considerable advantages. It means that one can buy, much more cheaply than the one could design, flexible software facilities that are able to provide the file-handling element for any computer application, so avoiding the need to write special routines for each new application. There is the ability to alter existing applications, and to add new ones, without having to change file organisation or risk corrupt data affecting other applications.

From its origins as a means of creating large file structures for the management of integrated computer systems, database management has become a necessary part of computer software facilities, indispensible for even the smallest system. As much as any other aspect of computer hardware and software, it has evolved from something that has a very considerable influence on the way systems are designed and run. The realisation that 'data', as a valuable resource, must be managed and protected is largely the result of the development of computer database management systems (as is the paradoxical concern for 'Data Protection' — if we need legislative control to protect 'sensitive' records from corruption and misuse, then we must have needed it rather more when such records were kept on manual, insecure and error-prone systems).

What then does a Database Management System do? It provides, in the form of a ready-made computer software package, a means of storing file data so that it can be located and retrieved rapidly from any 'key' that is presented. There is no concern about location or sequence of data in the store; all the programmer or operator need do is present the new item of data or the interrogation request in the right way, and the data management system will do the rest. The system may also offer protective facilities: to prevent unauthorised access, to prevent corruption of data through error, and to restore file data damaged because of a computer failure. It may include facilities to edit file data and to prepare report formats, data extracts and summaries; in short, to provide all software needed to develop and run complete basic business systems.

It scarcely needs to be said that, behind such a powerful and sophisticated set of software tools, there will be a great deal of research and development. It is an important area of computer expertise in its own right and the first database system certainly deserves to be identified as a major landmark in the history of computers.

Micro-electronics

The emergence of software as the dominant and decisive element in the choice of computer facilities was also closely associated with the introduction of the personal microcomputer. The 'microchip' which encapsulates the essential computer processing and storage elements was not a dramatic discovery nor the personal microcomputer a revolution in itself. Historians may look back after the first 100 years of business computers and describe the changes that have taken place over that period as a revolution, but the personal microcomputer itself should be seen as no more than an important stage in a rapid and continuous process of computer technology development. The huge success of the personal microcomputer pioneers (Commodore, Apple, Tandy and Sinclair) should not be noted only because they introduced personal computers to the public at large. Although the personal microcomputer created (at last) universal interest in the computer, it probably caused as much misconception as it did true enlightenment. Of the huge numbers of personal microcomputers which were sold initially, the great majority were diversions or ornaments; they were useful if they led to acquisition of skill and understanding which could be put subsequently to practical use, but aimless when used for puerile games.

What was significant about this mass distribution of personal microcomputers was that it was a practical demonstration of the mastery that had been achieved in the design and manufacture of integrated circuits: principally the techniques of applying layered circuits to semiconductor wafers for the production of integrated circuit 'chips' containing all essential elements of a computer in a unit of minute size and at negligible cost. This technology is not applied only to the personal microcomputer, of course. Any new computer, of any size, will be designed to take maximum advantage of the latest technology. Improvements in cost, size and speed have been obtainable by all computer users and for any size or type of application. As a broad generalisation, it might be said that the arrival of the microcomputer has meant that cost and technical considerations have ceased to restrict the application of computers for any business purpose. From mechanised accounting to general data processing, monitoring and control, and information retrieval systems to word processing and personal support, it is becoming difficult to visualise any work situation which could not benefit from the use of a computer in some way or other.

Micro-electronic technology did not find its only expression in computer information systems. Large-scale integrated circuit techniques which were applied to all kinds of business computer were also extremely valuable for many kinds of industrial machine, process and product. The miniaturisation of circuits, combined with the ability to manufacture microprocessors as sealed units containing built-in programs, greatly expanded the application of micro-electronic technology to industrial machines — to replace electro-mechanical systems, to provide new facilities, and to create new products. There is no more telling illustration than the manufacture of watches; an industry which had reached the ultimate refinement of mechanical skills was destroyed, and replaced by a new industry using the electronic skills and technology of computers. The watch industry was a relatively easy victim of simple micro-electronic technology; for 'watch' one might read almost any kind of meter, switch, register, measuring, recording or control mechanism. Externally it may still look the same but inside it is driven by a microcomputer containing a sealed program.

If one were to identify a landmark related specifically to the personal microcomputer (as opposed to the micro-electronic technology) it should be the entry of IBM into the personal computer market which, because of IBM's immense reputation and influence , quickly brought the standard for microcomputer software to be based on IBM's own equipment. As mentioned in the earlier context of large systems, once a business user found that dependence upon a computer system became established so quickly, the main fear for the future would be that support from the supplier would no longer be available, or that it would be impossible or very costly to replace the computer equipment when necessary. These things can be expressed in terms of confidence in the supplier and a feeling of security about the future; whatever else might be said of IBM, one could always be sure that it would still be there and that it would offer new products to meet the future need of users. Thus, when IBM launched its personal computer in a sector of the market previously supplied by many small companies, the reaction was the same as in higher levels of the computer industry; other suppliers of equipment and software quickly adapted themselves to IBM dominance and, with some notable exceptions, 'IBM compatibility' was upmost in everyone's mind.

Workstations

The IBM personal computer was extremely influential in rationalising the lower end of the industry and in persuading managers that the microcomputer could be brought into business use with confidence. This establishment of a firm market for 'personal support' machines led to a further rapid expansion of the range of uses for microsystems; such 'add-on' facilities as graphics, audio response (converting human speech and other sounds to recognisable digital information for processing within a computer and generating synthetic speech or other sounds as output) and machine tool control brought down the cost threshold for new kinds of computer application. It also led to what may be seen as another major landmark in the development of computer usage: the conversion of the personal microcomputer to the 'workstation'. The personal microcomputer was not itself very important economically; a million microcomputers would still represent only a small percentage of the total computer market, and the impact on business efficiency of these machines, although not insignificant (and certainly spectacular in particular cases), still represents a relatively modest influence on business information systems as a whole.

The microcomputer really became very much more important when it started to affect the major areas of employment, and this is the great significance of the workstation. The implication of the term is that the personal microcomputer becomes a terminal, still capable of use as an autonomous unit but also able to be connected through communication networks to other terminals and computers. Through a workstation one might have access to a central computer where major applications are processed or a large database is held, to computer systems in other organisations for transfer or retrieval of data, through public telecommunication services for despatch and receipt of messages, or to a network of integrated computer systems controlling an entire industrial operation.

'Convergence' of Information Technologies

Micro-electronics has brought together computers and all kinds of other machines in industrial and commercial applications covering the whole range of business activity. The business computer is now familiarly associated with many other types of industrial and business machine. All the information machine facilities which existed separately when computers were first introduced have now come together — copiers, typewriters, printing machines, calculators, telecommunication services, audio and video communication devices; a 'convergence' of separate streams into the new concept of 'Information Technology'. These reflect the extension of the range of information systems into the integration of communications, the linking of business information systems on a 'total' system basis, and the expansion of technology into the area of complex business decisions.

The concept of the computer itself is no longer meaningful; one cannot talk appropriately of a 'computer' when even a personal microcomputer may contain several computer units and new architecture concepts for larger systems link many processors in multiple arrays.

It also has become inappropriate to see the computer as a machine which will only provide a useful service when someone has designed and constructed a program and fed it into the computer store. Business computers still have this facility and many business systems must be tailored with the precision that only sophisticated language facilities can offer but there are now many other kinds of software product, giving a choice of means of constructing information systems. Hardware and software, and information systems, all mean something very different from that with which business computers began. New machine facilities and techniques offer opportunities of improving systems in general and of resolving specific system problems in particular. In examining aspects of business information systems, it has been affirmed at a number of points in this book that the significance for the business manager is not the improvement or the solution, nor the means by which they are achieved, but the consequences of those changes. Whatever the extent of application of technology to business systems this remains true, although there is no doubt that it becomes increasingly difficult to look at the consequence rather than the machine. Thus we argue that the important matters for consideration are the effects on use and allocation of resources on other systems, on organisations, decisions and objectives. However, we cannot ignore the technology and see no difference between the introduction of the hand tool and of the automated office or factory.

The special significance of the convergence of information technology is in the extent of this potential impact on all aspects of the business undertaking. The bringing together of different kinds of machine can be matched by the bringing together of systems and organisational functions, of separate businesses, and even of industries. The technology not only permits change on a widening scale, it also causes change. One may resist all temptation to engage in fanciful speculation and even see an early end to the present phase of technological advance but still be able to visualise the probability of radical change in the nature of business activity, merely by drawing conclusions from contemporary events and a relatively superficial examination of the feasibility of further change in the immediate future. The IT revolution is not the technology but the changes it will bring.

This has to be seen in two ways, still no different in principle from the beginnings of business machines but greater in impact. The first is the results which have been planned, or taken into account in the development of plans for the new system; the second is the further consequences which the system changes set in train. Organisation is one illustration. The early, large, central computers produced various benefits resulting from improvements in cost, speed and quality of data processing operations; they also led to organisational change, creating the need for new central data processing departments. The arrival of low-cost computing, capable of being managed by the user, offered the opportunity to decentralise system operation and to revert to the kind of organisation which existed with manual systems. The joining of communications and computers offered a further opportunity for change through the ability to develop integrated organisation structures, so that no valid assumptions about organisational hierarchies, departmental boundaries or allocation of management responsibility can now be assumed.

The convergence of technology also has much greater implications for the nature of business itself. Technological advance always leads to change in products and services — disappearance of those which cannot benefit from the new technology and introduction of new products and services which become economically or physically feasible. Information technology continues this progress in all kinds of goods and services, with some special importance for information itself. Reference has been made elsewhere to the dramatic consequences for the engineering industries of the supersession of mechanical and electrical techniques by electronics. Equally dramatic examples can be found in information industries such as banking and other financial services where information technology is forcing change in the industries and all their constituent business undertakings. These questions are taken up further in the examination of system development in chapter 14 because the most important consequence of this 'convergence' is that one can no longer make secure decisions about system change unless they fit within an overall strategy. With such possibility for change, it becomes impossible to look at any department, function, system or business problem in isolation.

Since the introduction of business computers, much of the advance in technology and economic feasibility has shown accelerating pace of change: in computer processing and data transmission speeds, in the size of integrated circuits and of data-storage devices, and in the ratio of cost to speed, capacity and power of computers and communication systems generally. Historical parallels provide the assurance that these rates of change do not go on for ever, and there are already indications that the rate of acceleration is slowing down. That is a long way from saying that any technological plateau is in sight because the momentum of current change and the fruits of current research may be expected to further transform the economics of information technology within a very short time. Furthermore, the potential of technology has so far outstripped the application that the potential for changes in systems and in the whole structure of business economics has no foreseeable limit.

Check List 9

The nature and uses of computer-based machine systems may be traced to origins in three distinct areas of activity:

- Data Processing
- Scientific and Technical Calculation
- Communications.

The development of information technology has brought these three areas together and has led to the extension of computer applications into every aspect of business activity.

Origin of Computers
  Punched cards.
  Electronic calculating machines.
  Batch data processing for accounting.
  International Business Machines.

Landmarks of Computer Technology
  Modular computer systems.
  Teleprocessing.
  Mainframes.
  Operating Systems.
  High level languages.
  Databases.
  Packaged software.
  Microcomputers.

Convergence of Information Technology

Further Reading

Awad, E., *Introduction to Computers*, Prentice-Hall, 1983.
Foy, N., *The IBM World*, Eyre Methuen, 1974.
Silver. G. and Silver, J.,*Data Processing for Business*, Harcourt Brace, 1981.
Spencer, D., *An Introduction to Computers*, Merrill, 1983.

10 Computer System Concepts

Language of Computing

To understand the place of computers in business one needs to see their development in proper perspective, and have some grasp of the theoretical concepts applicable to computers and other information machines. It is desirable to appreciate the differences between the kinds of computer system available and the ways in which they are used.

There is some danger in making specific comments about the contemporary situation because it changes so quickly, not least in the labels attached to machines and modes of use. Any new industry, profession or field of study brings with it an irresistible temptation to create new words and expressions to describe concepts, activities and objects for which existing language is considered inadequate. As in other special fields, the use of jargon is found advantageous by computer industry theoreticians, technicians and marketing experts to create a scientific aura and to distance themselves from the 'lay' public. Computing may have dubious claims to be classified as a science when one studies its theoretical base but the huge library of proposition and record it has accumulated in a few years can match any science in its incomprehensibility to the majority. Sales presentation of computers follows conventional marketing wisdom that there is advantage to be gained by labelling or branding to create a unique identity which can then be invested with superiority.

The business manager should not need to enter fully into this world of computer designers and academicians. It is essential for the manager to be able to communicate with these technical and sales experts so as to understand the specifications and proposals upon which computer system decisions will be based and, to this extent, he must have some familiarity with the jargon of computing, recognising meanings and implications of words and expressions which are currently popular as well as noting when they change.

Of the words and expressions created by the computer industry to fulfil a need at a particular time, some become established in the language, some last a short time and then become outdated, while others remain but change their meaning. For the most part, they originate in the United States and thus are readily absorbed into the English language, although sometimes with not quite the same flavour as in the country of origin.

We have adopted 'hardware', the American term for ironmongery, as a general heading for computer equipment of various kinds, and 'software' as a satisfactory label for all the complementary elements of computer programming facilities on which the computer depends to perform its functions. Where the software is embedded in the hardware and indistinguishable from it, we have been offered, somewhat less convincingly, the intermediate description 'firmware'. The word 'program', using the American spelling, means a computer program in contrast to other kinds of 'programme' in the conventional English spelling; an easy and elegant means of distinction.

Much of the new language comes, as one would expect, from IBM. Among the IBM words, one of the most enduring is 'byte', coined to give special indentity and implied superiority for the 8-bit stored data unit in a new range of computers, in contrast to other existing machines which employed techniques based on 'words' of varying bit size. Since then 'byte' has also become synonomous with 'character'. In the microcomputer world the terms '8-bit machine' and '16-bit machine', relating to the comparable area of unit data storage and transfer, have become generic descriptions and we now discuss these terms with familiarity, agreeing that the 16-bit 128K byte machine is better than the 8-bit 64K machine, without necessarily understanding why.

We encounter terms and abbreviations like 'picosecond', 'K', 'M', 'MIPS' which indicate aspects of speed or capacity, and 'upwardly compatible' or 'CAFS' and 'VM' which designate some special characteristic of a machine system that may be considered important to the user. All these do have some significance and need to be decoded, but none is meaningful unless in proper context.

Any attempt at an explanation of the vocabulary of computing is beyond the scope of this book. This aspect should be pursued through appropriate reading, and more particularly by linking their meanings with their use in practice, but it is desirable to draw attention to some of the more common terms which describe the principal categories of computer and modes of use.

'Mainframes', 'Minis' and 'Micros'

For some time business computers have been labelled under three broad categories: 'mainframe', 'mini' and 'micro', representing successive marketing waves of new products which exploited changes in technical feasibility and manufacturing costs. The types of general business computer sold in modular product ranges at some point attracted the label 'mainframe', to distinguish them from computers designed for technical applications by the Digital Equipment Company and others. These machines were called 'mini' computers because of their notable compactness and cheapness. The cheap personal computers founded on the micro-electronic technology became the 'micros', for similar reasons of cheapness and size.

From the first introduction of each new computer range or type it starts to 'grow', with successive products in the series offering greater capacity and better value. As design and manufacturing techniques advance, today's 'mini' becomes more powerful than yesterday's 'mainframe'. The mini becomes the 'super-mini' and the micro the 'super-micro', and the mainframe becomes larger and more powerful than before. The small and medium sized general-purpose computer attracts different labels in different environments.

It is now probably unwise to treat any of these descriptions at face value, or even attempt to fit types of computer neatly within formal classifications. There is still as wide a gap as ever between the smallest and the largest computer in power and cost, and there are still the ranges of general machine systems: 'families' of machines from individual manufacturers which offer a growth path through a series of compatible models from the relatively small to the extremely large. There are also various types of 'descendant' of the original minis which are aimed at more specialised markets — machines adapted particularly to real-time monitoring and control systems and to scientific applications.

The business microcomputer, epitomised by the IBM personal computer, was (briefly) a clearly identifiable category, but its evolution into the 'intelligent workstation' which can be linked to any other computer through a communication network means that it now may be associated with any technical specification and information use. The continuing advance of technology is removing size and cost category distinctions, offering as much power as may be needed to the workstation, whether in the form of a local facility (the '32 bit' micro) or through communication systems which place the capacity of the largest 'mainframe' at the disposal of the local terminal.

If and when the development of business computers reaches a condition of reasonable stability, it may be possible to see the only distinct types of computer outside the general range of modular facilities to be those applied to separate, specialised purposes. In the meantime, the prudent course is to take less account of the label than of the use to which the computer is put.

System objectives and requirements identified at the investigation stage of a computer project lead to decisions about the mode of use; this then leads to an evaluation of software requirements and of computer characteristics, and then to the actual choice of equipment. For example, before reaching the stage of deciding to use a machine labelled as a 'personal computer' one needs to consider first whether a computer with those characteristics is appropriate at all, and then what kind of personal computer it is. If the proposed system relates to the work of one person and, effectively, all transaction data and information output could be handled through a single terminal point, then an autonomous, personal microcomputer might provide the physical means of running the system. But even at the 'micro' level there is a very substantial difference between demands on storage, processing speed and software of, say, 'computer-aided design', with its needs for superior processing power and complex software facilities for graphics and calculation, and the much simpler needs of a very small, personal book-keeping record system. It should be remembered that, whatever has happened to the cost and power of computers over the years, there is yet a difference of more than 1000:1 between the largest and smallest computer system in cost, speed and capacity, and this no more than reflects the wide differences in size and scope of computer application.

Modes of Use of Computers

Just as one cannot generalise safely about types of computer, so with modes of use; but there are current terms used to describe particular concepts, appropriate to certain kinds of application, which have a bearing on the nature of equipment and software facilities to be used. These are described under the following system headings

- Data processing
- Information retrieval
- Batch, interactive, on-line and real-time
- Integrated
- Dedicated
- Telemetry, monitoring and control
- Communication networks
- Distributed
- Office systems
- Decision support
- Microsystems/end-user computing
- Point-of-sale
- Expert Systems
- Embedded.

Data Processing

The topic of Data Processing is referred to frequently throughout this book. It started as the most important use of business computers, picking up from other machine systems, and has continued to be the principal use for business computer capacity. Methods change with technology and economics but the basic applications do not disappear. Much of business activity in any kind of organisation does consist of processing data for records and reports as part of routine administration, as output to other systems and as information for management planning and control decisions.

The term 'data processing' is often applied generally to the use of computers for business purposes; computer service facilities have most commonly been organised in data processing departments. Recently, with the increasing popularity of the newer concept of 'Information Technology', associated with the rapidly growing importance of communications, the general label has tended to disappear and 'data processing' has been used more narrowly to describe those kinds of application which involve repetitive processing of substantial numbers of transactions. (figure 33). However, since such applications are to be found in every business situation and are always likely to represent a very large proportion of the use of computers, data processing or an equivalent description of this primary area of computer application is here to stay.

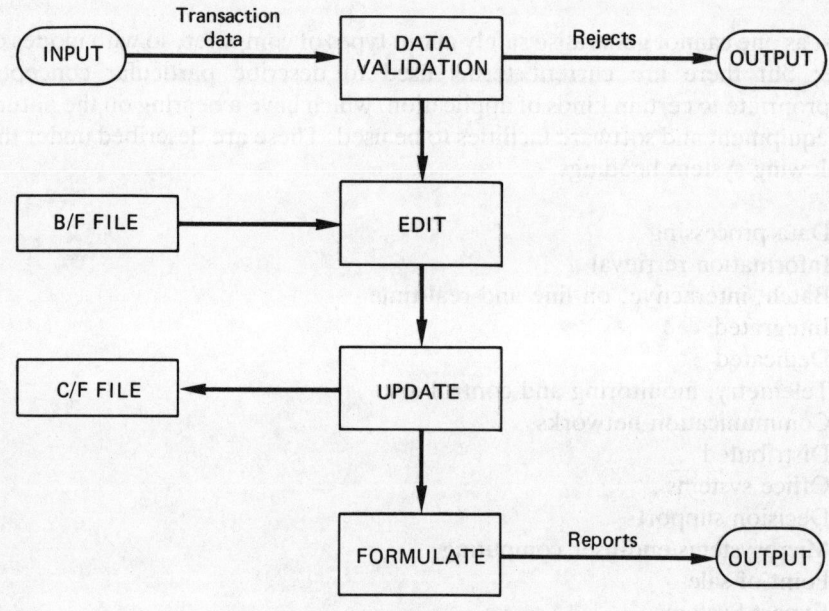

Figure 33   Data processing

Information Retrieval

'Information retrieval' was coined to describe a new aspect of computer applications which developed as a result of the fall in unit cost of storage and the introduction of reliable means of accessing data directly from input/output points. The information retrieval concept is essentially one of answering enquiries — setting up a file of information which will be available and accessible when needed. It might be superimposed on routine data-processing operations to provide access to accumulated records for status enquiries and extraction of information for decision and action, or might be complete in itself where a business objective can be achieved simply by having some data available in the right place at the right time. Business operations are surrounded by records created to meet information needs which, although known to arise, may occur randomly and demand rapid response; diaries, timetables, price lists, dictionaries, technical specifications, stock balances, are all of this kind.

Batch, Interactive, On-line and Real-time

These terms describe broadly some of the ways in which information is handled in computer systems and indicate particular system requirements and needs for hardware and software facilities.

The first use of computers for business applications was on a 'batch' basis. Each stage of the job would be separate (not greatly different in principle from the earlier punched card systems) and the computer operator would set up programs, feed punched cards into card readers, load magnetic tapes to tape units and paper to printers, and 'run' each stage in sequence. Subsequently, much of this operational work has come under the automatic control of Operating Systems but the batch approach still involves separating jobs into 'buffered' stages and the whole operation is essentially sequential. Batch systems are still commonplace and very large users of computer capacity, not, as in early days, because of limited technical options but because this approach is most appropriate to many data processing needs.

The typical characteristics of batch systems are the accumulation of input transactions in batches, and the processing of these batches together, matching transactions in sequence against master files of brought forward data. Processing takes place between the input of the last data item of the batch and the output of the finished results. (For example, data about sales accumulated by a retail store might be entered into the computer in daily batches, stored on temporary files and, at the end of the week, sorted and analysed to update customer account and stock records. This data might then be edited and summarised to produce weekly sales reports and monthly customer statements.) Except in terms of overall time constraints, therefore, input transactions for computer operations in batch mode are not tied directly to output. A computer file only has to be up-to-date when information is extracted from it, which will be at pre-determined times. Any failure in the system will be of importance only if it uses up all spare time between processes and causes delay in output (for example, if an analysis of last week's sales is not on the manager's desk on Monday morning as required by the system.)

In contrast, the 'real-time' approach involves processing each transaction as soon as it occurs; input data is added to the file record immediately and any response required to the input is produced within a very short space of time (figure 34). Thus the whole process from input to output is effectively continuous. The computer centre must provide a facility which will be available whenever a transaction occurs, be able to accept and process any of these transactions (of whatever kind) and produce results within a set standard time. For example, a typical real-time system dealing with external customer enquiries or order transactions might need to be accessible throughout normal business hours. With enquiries coming in by telephone, the maximum tolerable delay between input and output will be a matter of a few seconds. Thus, accurate up-to-date files have to be available awaiting these enquiries; when they arise, the programs and the physical data communication facilities to

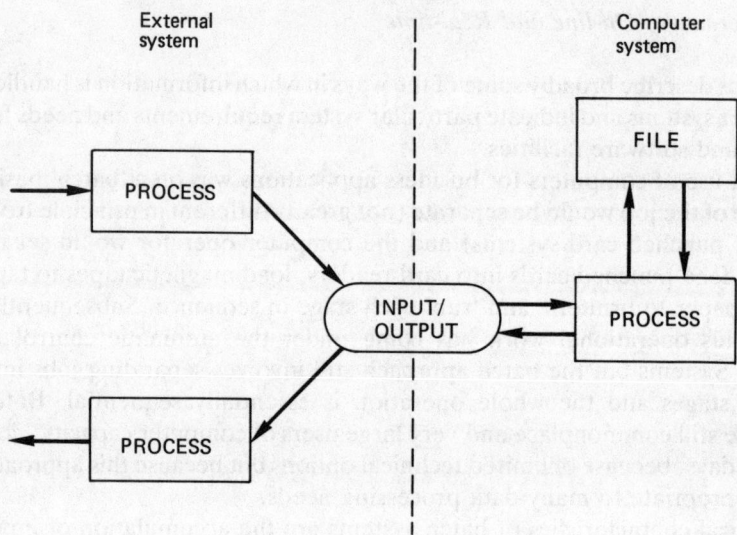

Figure 34   Real-time system

handle them must be ready and must be capable of completing the transaction within the standard time allowed, regardless of how many transactions occur during a given period. Furthermore, the nature of real-time systems is such that, if these requirements are not met, then the external aspect of the system cannot function; the customer's enquiry or order cannot be processed. The whole system depends entirely on proper functioning of the computer operations.

A real-time system must have an on-line facility with an input terminal connected to the computer so that, as soon as a transaction arises, data can be fed in and processed without any delay. 'On-line', therefore, means that when it is desired to enter any data to a computer system, the computer is switched on, and the necessary software is available and can be activated by action from the terminal point. One could still use such a facility in connection with a batch system; for example, in situations where a VDU terminal system has superseded a punched card or key-to-tape off-line system for data input, the input process may involve feeding data directly from terminals to a temporary file which may then be used to update the main file at a later time. Real-time systems impose heavy demands on computer facilities, much greater for an equivalent volume of data than the relatively simple batch system concepts. In the earlier days of computer systems there was a heavy cost penalty which would not be easy to justify; now the economic picture has changed, and equipment designed for real-time working and ready-made software often make the cost differential (in situations where either a batch or a real-time approach might be feasible) a marginal consideration.

Real-time mode, however, is rarely essential. Its use is more often a matter of convenience; other things being equal, for any 'transaction-based' operation it is likely to be more convenient to have it dealt with immediately. This applies particularly with personal computers where typical uses for information retrieval, planning and design work, and office activities do require rapid response, not because a delay would be catastrophic but because it would waste the time of the operator, which constitutes the main system cost.

The development of operating software which provided computer operators with versatile 'command' facilities for data and file manipulation (and the widespread use of the personal microcomputer for which these kinds of facilities are essential), led to the popularisation of the term 'interactive' to describe the method of handling these facilities. An appropriate description of interactive working is where much of the input and output consists of a dialogue between operator and machine system, with question and answer, instruction and response. Interactive working is equally applicable to large and small systems and, in real-time mode, a system must be working interactively. It is becoming the norm that business computer systems contain a large element of on-line, user operation and that system building (putting together software facilities to construct the systems) is an 'interactive' computer operation. Much of business system development has become a matter of using software tools for preparing screen layouts, input/output messages, file and record para-meters and report formats — interactive system design for interactive systems.

Integrated Systems

For the mass of business information systems under the general headings of Data Processing and Information Retrieval (run in batch or interactive mode), data files are of central importance. The 'database' has become a firmly established feature of business computing and 'data managment' an essential function of any computer installation. Once there were no longer reasons of cost or technical difficulty for limiting the size or use of computer files, the database concept began to evolve. With this concept, the practical possibility arose of achieving theoretical goals which had been in the minds of computer specialists from the outset — the 'total' system integrating all elements of business information handling. In essence, the idea of an integrated system would be one where all data relevant to the business was collected at its point of origin, stored as a central library of information, and made available to any user when required. This was the 'true' database concept, sweeping away all the ramifications of separate departmental systems, duplication of files, and multiple copies of transaction documents, with their inherent costs, delays and errors. Much more than applications based on former manual system bound-aries, the integrated system concept takes the information element away from the action and decision elements of a business, Instead, it envisages providing information as a general service, comparable with basic business services such as heating, lighting and telephones, available to hand when needed. Telecom-munication facilities, of course, are being merged with computers and the idea of Information Technology implies an extension beyond the integrated 'systems' concept to one of integrated 'services', where both information output derived from a common business system and physical facilities for data transmission processing and storage are also integrated. A telecommunications channel, for example, can provide integrated facilities as a common carrier for all the information signals — computer data, speech, Teletex, Videotex (see the section on Communications Networks later in this chapter).

An interpretation of 'integrated' systems which differs from the idea of a central database serving a communication network is the integration of separate systems through machine/machine interfaces so that the systems can operate automatically under co-ordinated control. Such an approach might be made to the control of the operations of a production plant or other large complex business environment. Thus, an integrated manufacturing system might link computer aided design, production control, materials management, plant scheduling, automated machine and process control, materials handling, quality monitoring and environmental control so as to achieve high performance standards within each system and for the plant as a whole with minimum labour cost. Such an operation is most likely to be undertaken when a new production unit is set up, because that would make it much easier to harmonise all the physical elements and incorporate appropriate computer and communication facilities in the right way, but it is by no means a matter only for new plants or new industries, nor is it applicable only to manufacturing environments. The section on Telemetry, Monitoring and Control later in the chapter indicates some of the areas to which integrated system concepts can also be extended.

Neither the 'logical' integration of business systems nor the 'physical' integration of information-handling facilities is as simple as it sounds. Physical integration involves technical protocols and software structures capable of linking dissimilar devices and carrying different types of data, but perhaps the more difficult in the long run is the business system aspect with all its implications for reorganisation of information flows, operating procedures, and attitudes and responsibilities of people in organisations.

Dedicated Systems

The idea of a 'dedicated system' is the use of a computer installation for one purpose only. (It is an example of the semantic confusion which surrounds computer jargon that the word 'system' in this context refers to the machinery — one business system on one machine system.) A general-purpose business computer might be used exclusively for one application but dedicated systems are most often associated with special equipment for special applications. A virtue of the dedicated approach is that a system can be designed for optimum efficiency and yet require less complex software and hardware facilities because it is freed from the complications of sharing users and applications. Dedication also makes it easier to achieve guaranteed levels of reliability because greater simplicity reduces the number of sources of potential failure.

Dedicated systems are likely to be the appropriate answer for industrial applications of computers, many of which involve continuous operation over long periods in real-time mode.

Telemetry, Monitoring and Control

Under this heading one may find systems which might as easily be labelled 'dedicated' or 'expert', and which involve also aspects of data processing and information retrieval. Although there is overlap between these headings, it is still useful to identify this group separately because it has been an important market for suppliers of real-time minicomputers. A common characteristic of these systems is that input and output are often part of machine processes, with manual system interfaces only for action outside the routine operation of the system. Thus, computer-controlled conveyors and machine tools found in flow and assembly line manufacturing receive much of their input from monitoring movement, temperature, pressure or other physical conditions, and produce output to control other machine operations.

This is an area of application in which the computer makes it possible to take previously separate monitoring and control activities, link them together and eliminate the need for human intervention (with its consequent costs and delay). A sensing device might be linked to a telecommunications line which can transmit readings as computer input from which an output signal can be used to operate a switch. This is a concept which could be applied to a single machine or industrial location, or could be extended, for example, to control a highly complex distribution network (figure 35). Telemetry demonstrates one of the benefits of bringing together communications and computers so as to make possible a complete information picture of all associated elements of a business system spread over a wide area. This implies that distance is the key factor, but one can find very suitable applications for the techniques in relatively confined areas where advantage can be gained from a more rapid and more reliable response than is possible from a human operator. In military aircraft, which employ computers in dedicated real-time mode for operational systems such as navigation, communication, weapon systems and flying control, the purpose is to enable a pilot to control a complex machine in a way that would not be achievable at all by purely manual means. (This is also an extreme example of the dependence of a real-time system on machine reliability; in such a system, failure would cause the aircraft to crash.)

Monitoring and control systems are not to be considered only as automatic, machine-to-machine systems. There may be display outputs to allow manual intervention, and there may be manual inputs both for original data and to over-ride automatic outputs. Many examples can be found, particularly outside the area of purely industrial applications, where emphasis is more on communication than control and the output interface is with manual, not machine, action. Industrial machine and process control systems usually have visual outputs for manual supervision and intervention and often printed

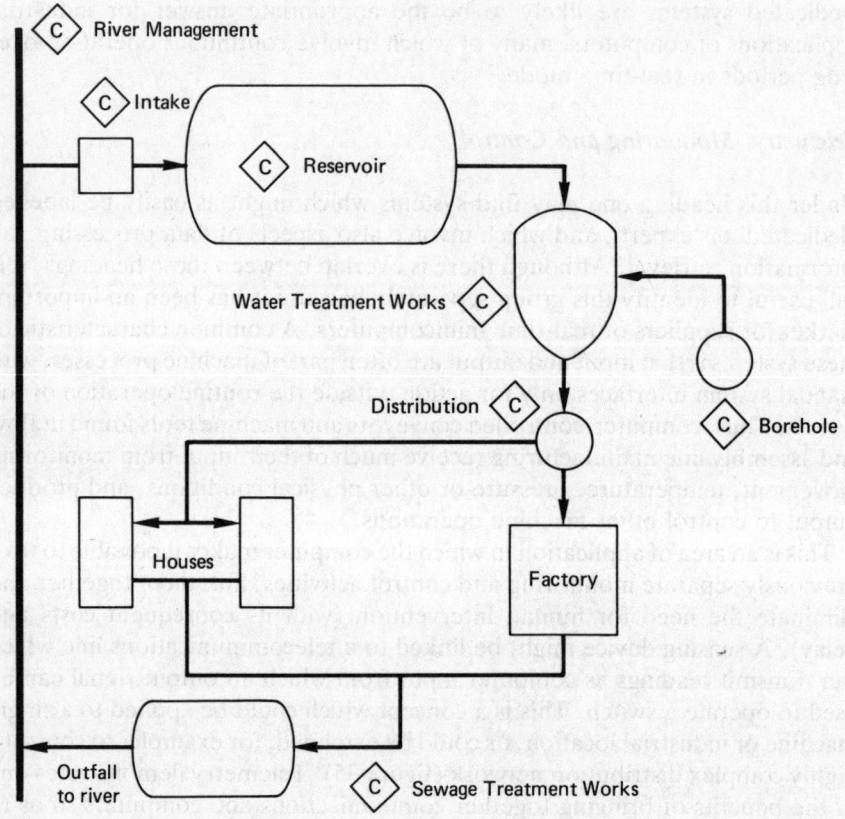

Figure 35   Water cycle control

output information for performance analysis. Examples from other areas, such as environmental control for modern office blocks, automatic warehouses, and the many signalling and control applications found in transport and energy industries, have similar features. There are also systems such as the 'command and control' applications for fire and ambulance services, where automatic output may be little more than the ringing of alarm bells, but which provide vital information to operators (about location of resources etc.) so that prompt decisions can be taken.

Many of these applications may be described simply as 'knowing what is going on' — providing information in the right place at the right time — but their importance to the computer industry and to business generally cannot be overstressed. Whether or not they contribute to the more effective use of material, machine or human resources, their benefits are often much more tangible and substantial than those from administrative systems, and the average size of investment is usually greater than for the average general business computer installation.

Communication Networks

The focus of interest in computer equipment has shifted twice in its history: from the central processing unit to the data management system and then to the communication network. The effect of this second shift has been that the computer has ceased to be seen always as the centre of the business information system but has rather become a 'node' in an information network, functioning as a processing or data storage unit, as a switching centre or as a terminal workstation. Network concepts, which are still evolving, combine telecommunication facilities with software routines and protocols to permit transaction data, messages, files or programs to be transferred from one computer node to another or to be accessible from any point.

The idea of a communications network is familiar enough; public networks for speech and telegraph communication existed long before computers. Computers started to acquire their own forms of network when remote input and output devices were connected with central computers, using public service telecommunication facilities (sometimes called 'star' networks). Communications networks have now become one of the most important issues in Information Technology (figure 36). Private and public service networks are expanding rapidly, providing new services and evolving towards an ultimate goal of a common facility for all kinds of telecommunication — the integrated services (digital) network.

The 'star' network is still the most common form of computer communication link within an organisation, but is being supplemented by new kinds of network which have been given the label 'Local Area Network' (LAN). Using different techniques and protocols, these LANs might take the form of a 'ring' or a 'bus' (communication highway) to which terminals, file stores, printers and all kinds of computer processing units might be connected, providing communication links for transfer of programs, files and messages to form a co-ordinated facility for information handling (figure 37). The introduction of complex information structures such as integrated, monitoring or distributed systems implies joining computer facilities through some form of local area network. For separate identification, external private and public service networks are often described as 'Wide Area Networks' (WAN), linked with LANs through telecommunication exchanges or other 'gateway' connections.

Business organisations are able to link their data communication and processing facilities through these wide area networks to other organisations — terminal to terminal, terminal to computer, computer to computer. The attractions for computer-based business information systems are the opportunities for systems integration and the freedom from constraints of distance and technical compatibility. For example, in addition to the remote terminal as a computer facility for data transmission available from the 'star' network, an organisation might use its computer and communication facilities for any of these functions

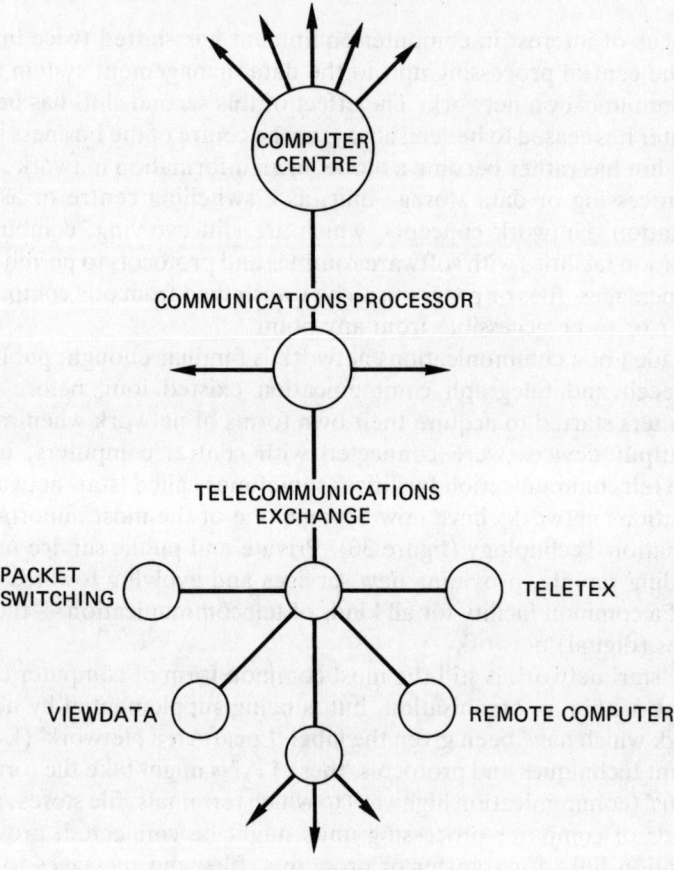

Figure 36   Communications

- To interrogate a file held on another computer
- To transfer data from one computer file to another
- To generate a message from a computer to Telex or other public message switching system
- To allow two or more computers to work as one system.

Computer and communication facilities within an organisation can be linked together also by private local area networks, offering facilities for internal resource sharing and data transmission, including such uses as

- Sharing storage units, printers and other 'peripherals' between a number of computers
- Interdepartmental message systems (electronic mail)
- Distributed processing (see next section).

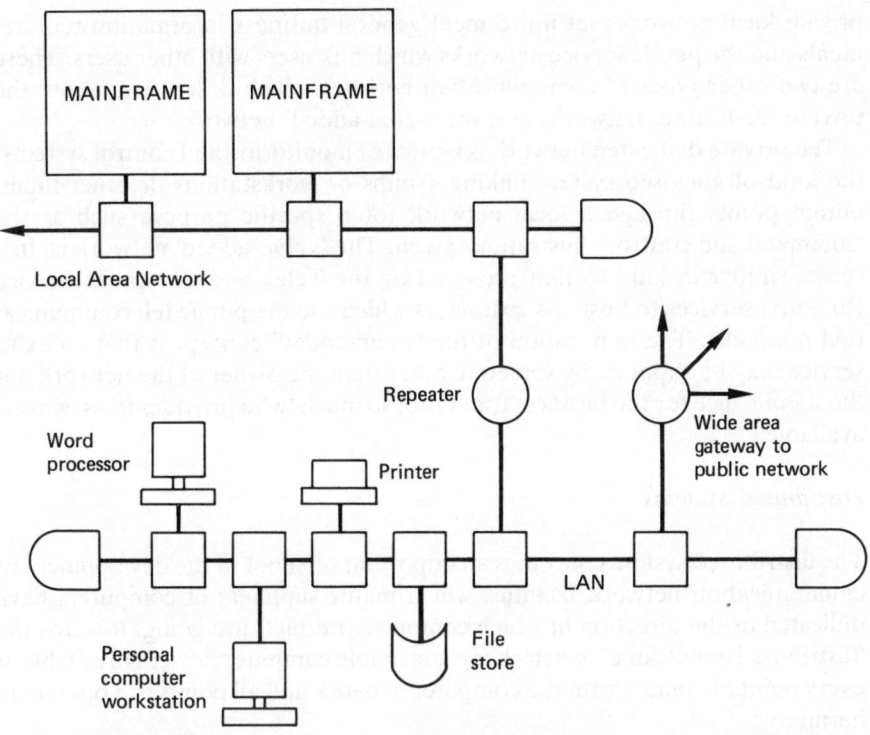

Figure 37   Local area networks

Networks impose complex design and construction problems. There must be physical compatibility between all equipment used in the network and the rules for identification and control of all data along network paths must be no less rigorous than those within the computer itself. With public telecommunication services where the supplier sets the rules and ensures compatibility, and with the user-controlled private 'star' network, technical problems are contained without difficulty. With local and wide area networks which involve bridging gaps between incompatible machine architectures and system software, there is a need for special rules to create standards and appropriate software to allow different facilities to communicate with each other.

The ultimate solution to problems of incompatibility for wide area networks is an extension of the principle of international standards which apply to existing public service communications, and this is being followed through the International Standards Organization. Adoption of a set of rules for this 'Open System Interconnection' and implementation by all suppliers in their software will make the user's choice of solution easier, and confidence in building information systems with integrated communications networks will be greatly strengthened.

Most of what has been said so far about communication networks relates to

private local networks set up to meet general business information requirements and the public service networks which link users with other users. There
are two other types of communication network which deserve mention: the
private 'dedicated' network, and the 'value-added' network.

The private dedicated network is typical of monitoring and control systems:
the kind of enclosed system linking groups of workstations or other input/
output points through a local network for a specific purpose such as the
'command and control' illustrations given. The 'value-added' network is, in a
sense, similar in kind to that provided by the Telex and Computer Service
Bureaux: services to business customers which use the public telecommunication networks. The implication of the 'value-added' concept is that an extra
service may be supplied by someone other than the owner of the network but
the significance for the business user is not so much 'who provides it' as 'what is
available'.

Distributed Systems

The distributed system concept is an important offshoot of the development of
communication network facilities which major suppliers of computers have
indicated as the direction in which computer products are going: towards the
'distributed mainframe', when cheap and ample computer power is available at
every point of contact with the computer network and all points can operate in
harmony.

Whether a computer installation input and output facilities are clustered
around it or are at remote points and linked by telecommunication systems, the
concept of having one computer controlling a group of satellite devices is
reasonably simple, both technically and operationally, even though that
centralised system may be used for many different applications and receive
data from a very large number of terminals. The linking of two or more
compatible computers to work effectively as one has for a long time been a
valuable way of increasing power and improving peformance, and also poses
no great problems for system designers and users (nor does the software
subdivision of one computer to work effectively as two or more).

In contrast, to link two separate computer systems so that they can both work
autonomously or transfer data between themselves under automatic control,
or for one or other system to act as the controlling point as desired, brings
considerations of equipment compatibility, of Operating Systems and of other
system software as well as more detailed questions of format, organisation and
control of data transferred between machine facilities. As with the other
sophistications of computer software, the practical solution for most users of
distributed systems has been to make use of packaged facilities supplied by
manufacturers. Within the boundaries of one organisation such packaged
facilities may be sufficient, without any dependence on the creation of
international networking standards, for a move away from centralised or
totally separated installations to the kind of internal network which allows a
choice between a localised, centralised and distributed approach.

The term 'distributed system' implies that, in place of a centralised system which handles all data processing, computer power is distributed to the user locations (figure 38). The (smaller) processing facilities at user locations are linked to each other to provide general computer facilites (for example, by ten small linked computers each with ten terminals, instead of one large central computer with 100 terminals). The progressive development of distributed system concepts has come about partly because the communication and software facilities became available, and partly because changing costs of hardware have meant that the economies of scale in computer size are not quite so marked as they were. There is now often a genuine economic choice between centralised and distributed approaches, independently of other considerations.

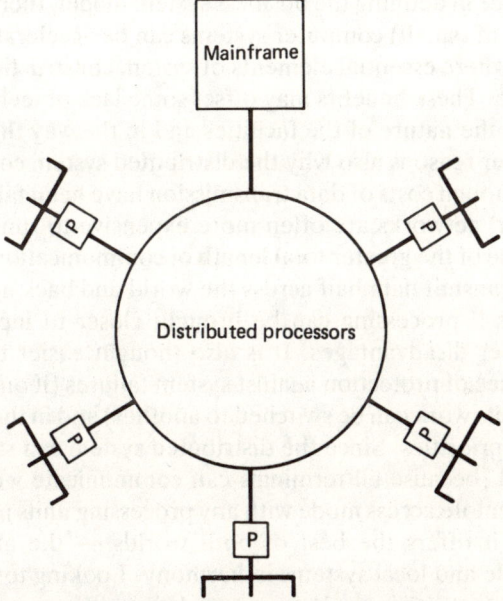

Figure 38   Distributed systems

Some of these other considerations are matters of attitude and some are more tangible. Attitudes have always played an important part in the development of computer systems. The importance of organisational boundaries goes beyond any demonstrable systems convenience; boundaries are also matters of personal status, influence and allegiance. Thus, we are always prepared to tolerate our own mistakes more readily than those of others, we assume that we can handle problems more efficiently and that our judgements are sounder. The classic conflict between centralisation and decentralisation is fundamental to business organisation and has shown itself as strongly with computers as with any other aspect of business activity. There always has been some criticism levelled at central computer services about difficulties of communication between user and technical specialist, long waiting time for attention to user needs and lack of concern for user priorities, and it is not difficult to find examples of these kinds of problem. It never has been an inevitable consequence of centralised data processing that there should be an unsatisfactory standard of service to users; where there is a deficiency it usually can be traced to other organisational or managerial shortcomings. However, there is no doubt that the coming of packaged software to ease the task of developing business computer systems has reduced the dependence of users on technical specialists and this, with the shift in 'size' economics, undoubtedly has given users encouragement to bid for control over their own computer resources. An added argument is that software has moved a stage nearer complete user control through the extension of packaged software to facilities for system building by unskilled users. Provided that there has been proper technical guidance in defining the business system model, there is no doubt that implementation of (small) computer systems can be accelerated (and satisfaction increased) where essential elements of system construction and operation are in user hands. These benefits may offset some lack of technical refinement and economy in the nature of the facilities and in the way that they are used.

There are other reasons also why the distributed system concept has gained acceptance. Although costs of data transmission have been falling steadily, it is argued that 'star' networks are often more expensive to run than distributed networks because of the greater total length of communication lines. There are systems which transmit data half across the world and back again, but there is no virtue in this if processing can be brought closer to input/output points without any other disadvantages. It is also thought easier to ensure a good standard of service of protection against system failures (if one processing unit is out of service, its work can be switched to another) and in the management of communication priorities. Since the distributed system can still behave as if it were centralised (because all terminals can communicate with common files and operate in remote access mode with any processing units in the network), it is claimed that it offers the best of both worlds — the ability to operate organisation-wide and local systems in harmony. Looking towards a situation when computer 'power' is no longer a question of cost so that substantial computer capacity can be located at every terminal workstation, one can understand the argument that the concept of a computer 'installation' could be discarded completely.

Office Systems

'Office system' is a label which has been attached to 'packaged' machine configurations which are offered for use in offices although, in application, it can also refer to software applied to general-purpose business computers and to major integrated office services. It is worthy of separate mention because the business office has been one area of rapid exploitation of computer techniques in recent years.

Although it is perfectly true that much of the use of computers in business information systems to date has been in the administrative area, most of the work handled in business offices is very varied in nature and pattern and is organised in relatively small units. It is also particularly concerned with communication and it is only since the linking of computers with telecommunications, the fall in computer costs and the introduction of cheap packaged software facilities specifically for office work that the extension of information technology into this area has gained momentum.

The most widely adopted type of office computer equipment has been the 'word processor', which has evolved from the original (IBM) magnetic store automatic typewriters to specialised office machines for a range of typing activities, as well as to packaged software facilities attached to ordinary computers. The current concept of word processing is a combination of facilities. One aspect relates to improving the effectiveness of typing operations: easier correction, avoiding unnecessary keying and speeding up effective output by use of stored data and program facilities for repetitive typing. Another is the provision of aids for the preparation of reports and formal document layouts for direct duplication or as 'masters' for printing. The word processor is potentially much more versatile than the specialised typing machine. It does not always compete as successfully against the typewriter as is sometimes supposed in those tasks for which the typewriter was really designed but it assumes much greater significance as part of wider office systems, and as a special-purpose workstation linked to other computer facilities.

A word processor might fit into a local office computer network as a means of eliminating the need for handwritten drafts or audio tapes for typing work. This can have the effect of replacing professionals with part-time amateur typists, because the convenience and the elimination of intermediate data-preparation stages are worth more than the skill of the professional operator.

Communication is a primary office function, and another opportunity for change opened up by the 'office system' concerns the transfer of messages. In large business undertakings one may expect to find that most 'paperwork' is for communication within the organisation — inter-office memoranda, works orders, stock requisitions, and other action documents. Except in occupations where it is the prime instrument of communication, the telephone is often an unreliable means of transmitting information to other people, let alone of ensuring that they take the requisite action.

The memorandum, as a means of passing instructions, convening meetings or reporting events has so far survived all the developments of office technology despite the high cost of typing and of the (internal or external) postal method of passing information from one person to another. Even long-established telecommunication services offering 'hard copy' such as Telex and facsimile have been largely confined to specialised areas. Computer office systems offer a new channel, based on two necessary propositions: that each potential recipient of a memorandum has his own workstation and that it is adopted as the normal method of receiving and transmitting such information.

This is electronic mail. By providing an external link from the telecommunication system one can extend this to communications with other organisations. The same office system can also act as a terminal device to a computer. It can absorb the function of the Telex machine, removing the buffer between the creation of the original message and the keying of the teleprinter message.

With filing and duplicating facilities attached to the office system, one can glimpse a view of the 'paperless society' as the proportion of incoming, outgoing and internal messages handled through the integrated services network increases. One cautionary note deserves repetition: unlike many other modes of use of computers, the office system does demand substantial change in organisation and allocation of responsibility in fragmented areas. These areas are also very much concerned with human 'interfaces' to other systems which cannot be easily modified to be compatible. This applies particularly to offices dealing with customers or members of the public, and to managers whose prime responsibilities involve personal communications with other people.

The ultimate prospect seen for office systems is 'office automation': the introduction of integrated machine systems for the business organisation as a whole. As indicated earlier, the first phases of computer application excluded much of office administration because this tended to be fragmented and specialised. Much of the recent application of technology in such fields as word processing has been to support, with moderate changes, these specialised areas with increasing reference to the decision functions of managers and skilled specialists. For these applications the use of information technology is seen from the point of the individual function; office automation views all these functions as part of a communication network.

The communication network, of course, existed before office automation in the form of telephones and other conventional communication links. Office automation systems absorb these functions and see each office, manager and specialist as part of this network and provide facilities for communication between them with local workstations for decision and processing support.

Office automation is expensive and difficult to implement successfully. While this might not be an apt comment in an environment where office automation was firmly established, in areas where new applications of technology are being considered the problems of change which affect organisational structures, allocation of responsibilities and performance of individual tasks are likely to be substantial. In the office environment they are greater because every part of the business is affected at points which are themselves often difficult to control. (The most intractable problem likely to face the advocate of system change is to alter the habits of a managing director.)

Decision Support

Since the primary function of business information systems is to assist decision-making, it follows that the application of technology to decision support must be designed to supply relevant historical and current information from within the organisation and from its environment to the decision points. In some senses, therefore, all computer-based systems are for decision support and a system with this label clearly must contain these elements.

However, in the more precise application to management activities, decision support systems are seen as including facilities to discern trends and examine the implications of information, as well as means of examining alternative courses of action and evaluating potential consequences. Decision support also carries the implication that there will be a convenient way of distributing the instructions which result from the decision, providing information to support and explain those instructions, and also providing feedback to the decision point of information about the consequences of the instructions which have been carried out. In other words it implies a view of the complete information cycle for each separate decision area, with the necessary links to general information systems and the addition of personal support facilities to the manager. In practice, this last is the key point: the provision of a workstation having appropriate software facilities (such as the 'spread-sheet') and communication links to other decision and action points, and to databases which carry the full range of information from which decision material is distilled.

Microsystems/End-user Computing

Although it has been argued that the manufacturing and marketing separation of microcomputers from larger systems was a transient phase which is coming to an end, the separate identification of microsystems probably will be important for some time to come because these cheap systems do represent a huge number of sales, mostly involving simple applications, small investments and a wide range of choice. As a result the microcomputer has almost become an industry of its own, with specialised manufacturing and distributing outlets and a complementary software industry to supply suitable user products. The element which holds this part of the industry together is the price range. However, as soon as the user requirement goes beyond the personal 'tool' level which can be satisfied by a stand-alone microsystem, the rest of the computer industry comes into the picture. It is notable that once the major business machine manufacturers extended their ranges to include microcomputers, larger computer users started to dominate the customer end of the market as well.

Microsystems, by definition, are applications with small data volumes, concerned either with very minor processing applications or with personal support to an individual task involving calculation, information retrieval or data organisation and communication. Typical examples are book-keeping, financial planning, word processing, personal records and technical design. All these systems are likely to have in common that they are designed and implemented largely by the end user, with cheap packaged software.

The absorption of the personal microcomputer into computer networks as the workstation, to which attention was drawn in an earlier section, has brought a combination of the 'end-user' computing and the professionally planned and managed major systems. Where the workstation is used as an autonomous system, running applications tailored specifically for the individual end user, it is appropriate that that user accept full responsibility for management of the facility. When in the 'terminal' or 'communications' modes, the user is bound to operate under control of the network and any 'host' computer facility.

A typical business application will be company-wide systems (either centralised or distributed) which handle the major data processing and management information systems from which end users at workstations can extract, edit and manipulate information for their own purposes. Only when attempting to input data and alter central files will it become necessary for control to be relinquished to the central facility. In this specially defined sense of end-user computing, it seems likely that the kind of software and approach to system development which has been applied to the independent personal microcomputer systems is likely to be retained and expanded, although within policy and general control frameworks of the wider computer network.

Point-of-Sale

The term 'point-of-sale system' is most properly applied to computer terminals which combine the functions of cash register and sales data computer input device at the point of sale in a shop. They are likely to be found in large turnover wholesale and retail establishments such as cash-and-carry stores, supermarkets, and department stores. They operate as satellites of a local computer in a 'star' network for updating stock and sales records, or as part of local area networks linking order, stock and despatch points where these are separated. The special features of such systems are the point-of-sale unit and the technical and ergonomic problems associated with it. As a generalisation, the effectiveness of point-of-sale systems depends on the extent to which the equipment and its handling have been tailored to the job, and to the operator (in contrast to the standard VDU which takes little account of either).

Other specialised input/output devices can be grouped under this heading because the concept of a special terminal integrating computer input with other functions, or producing computer input as a byproduct, is not confined to shops or to selling. Factory data collection systems for job costing and labour time 'clocking', bank cash dispensers, ticketing machines, security systems and library systems are all typical examples of application of 'point-of-sale' techniques.

The essential purposes of specialised input/output machine systems are to improve the efficiency of operation at the man/machine interface, usually by linking actions with computer input functions which were previously separated. In practice their significance may be much greater because they may produce other gains from integration of system elements as well as producing beneficial changes in the environment. For example, the point-of-sale system in a shop may be seen as the means of improving revenue through added customer convenience or more radical changes in selling techniques. The bank cash point, which offered a means of providing customer service outside the (inconvenient) banking hours shows signs of becoming the normal method of dealing with routine banking transactions such as cash withdrawal and account enquiries, with significant implications for the general provision of customer services by the banking industry.

Expert Systems

Three popular phrases — 'Knowledge Engineering', 'Artificial Intelligence' and 'Expert Systems' — all circle around the same area of meaning, concepts which are moving software towards the ultimate achievement of the selection and decision capability of the human brain. No doubt more new terms will be coined as the techniques and software products extend their range. In chapter 3 it was noted that all human activity can be seen in terms of decisions, even at the very simplest level of activity, but that there is a vast difference in quality and complexity between those at the lowest level and those which demand experience, skill and judgement, as in the highest levels of management decision and in the complex technical areas of business activity. The computer has extended to most of the data processing activities necessary to provide information for business decision-making, and also absorbed many low-level decision elements in commercial and industrial applications. More sophisticated applications involving selection and decision have been developed with considerable success. For some years it has been possible for a computer to fly an aeroplane from take-off to landing, and to play a very competent game of chess. A patient can also obtain a better (although somewhat impersonal) diagnosis from a computer than from the average general practitioner. Such systems were devised before the term 'Expert Systems' had been coined.

However, it would be quite misleading to suggest that the only new element is some jargon and fresh outbursts of computer science research and literature. To approach the subject of 'Artificial Intelligence' seriously implies having the ability to meet the very large demands on software and data storage that this subject will make. The significant advances and the justification for giving this topic a separate identity are the progressive introduction of more complex software tools, associated with removal of storage and capacity limitations and the linking of automatic input/output devices which are not operated externally. With conventional key-board/screen entry, a machine system can be expert only if somebody decides to put into it all the information it needs to make the decision — such a substantial task that the range of decision inevitably will be circumscribed and the economic justification only realised if repetitive use can be made of the facilities. If a machine could be provided with sensory facilities to see, hear and feel as events occurred, the problem would then change to one of deciding, not what information to put in but, of the information received, what is useful and what is not. There are also the considerations of modifying decisions by learning, reaching conclusions based on partial information and inference, and the subjective elements in decision-making. All these imply much wider dimensions of data storage, analysis and selection, greater sophistication as well as size of software elements, and moving away from the sequential processing which has been a fundamental part of computer techniques so far.

As one looks more closely at the subject of Expert Systems there are interesting questions to consider about the implications of removing external constraints from computer input, processes and output and economic and ethical speculations about why one would wish to go beyond making human beings more effective, to design a more expensive alternative to that superb and elegant mechanism which comprises the human brain. On the other hand, one may also wonder who would wish to take from a machine its characteristics of tireless and dependable response to human instructions, and corrupt its precision with the quixotic, emotional, biased and incompetent behaviour which also is a part of truly human decisions.

Much of the development of Artificial Intelligence is still at the academic research stage with the study of sophisticated language facilities, computer architecture and interface areas of image and voice processing. There is clearly a long way to go and we may not wish to go all the way, but in the 'lower level' field of Expert Systems there is no doubt that more than enough potential value to business operations can be found.

For the business manager, the practical interest in Expert Systems lies in their application to business problems. Much of the very considerable current research and development leading to the practical application of Expert System techniques has been given the label 'Intelligent Knowledge-Based Systems' (IKBS). Such systems have three principal elements: the 'knowledge base' containing the information acquired from human experts, the 'inference engine' which provides the machine ability to derive appropriate answers to questions put to the Expert System, and the 'natural language interface' which provides a link with the system user (figure 39). The systems offer a direct contrast to the large-scale communication systems being applied to computer integrated manufacture and office automation in that the knowledge-based systems may be related to a very small area — which is now often the function of one human 'expert', so that the machine element may be quite small. Nevertheless, as indicated earlier, it draws on the achieved advances in information technology of cost, capacity etc. and also on the current areas of new development of advanced software languages, very large-scale integration of circuits, parallel processing and speech and image recognition. It also does not have to be an isolated application. Much of the potential development of integrated systems and of robotics will depend on the ability to introduce IKBS elements to remove the need for human interfaces and allow machine-controlled operation over wider areas of associated systems.

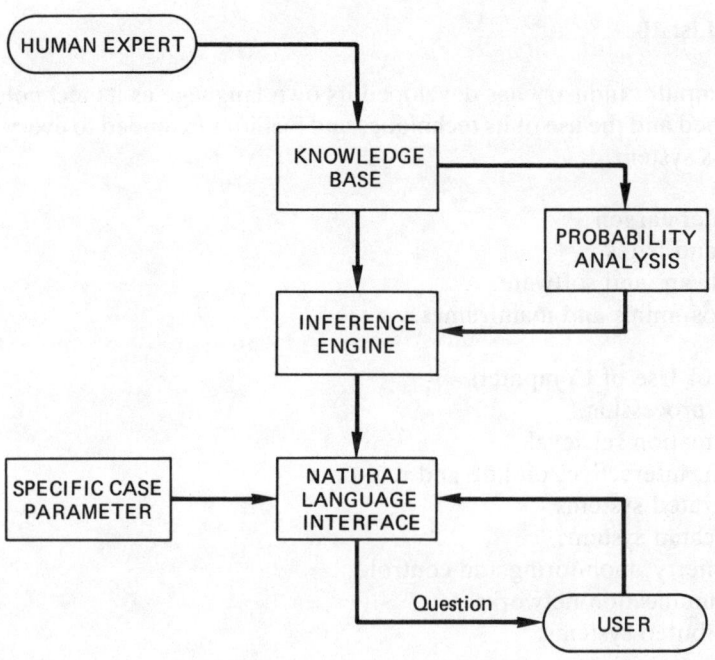

Figure 39   Expert System

Embedded Systems

As a postcript, there is one category of computer application which may well
exceed all the others put together in terms of the number of computer devices
— the systems 'embedded' in other products. They contain all the elements of a
computer together with the software designed to carry out their purpose — the
ultimate extension of minaturisation and packaging: automatic systems fitted
to other machines or physical systems to provide control and data-handling
facilities. They are usually designed to be cheap, reliable and inviolable, and
are to be found in all kinds of tools, industrial and domestic equipment,
vehicles and consumer products. They often provide subsidiary functions in
larger computer-based systems; computers themselves contain embedded
systems. Sometimes they replace electrical or mechanical components or
linkages to improve reliability or operating convenience; sometimes they may
be installed to improve performance, as in systems to improve fuel economy.
We may know that they are there (as when the output is a synthetic voice);
more often we do not.

Check List 10

The computer industry has developed its own language as its technology has developed and the use of its techniques and facilities extended to every kind of business system.

Computer Jargon
  Bits and bytes.
  Hardware and software.
  Micros, minis and mainframes.

Modes of Use of Computers
  Data processing.
  Information retrieval.
  Batch, interactive, on-line and real-time.
  Integrated systems.
  Dedicated systems.
  Telemetry, monitoring and control.
  Communication networks.
  Distributed systems.
  Office systems.
  Decision support.
  Micro systems/end-user computing.
  Point-of-sale.
  Expert systems.
  Embedded systems.

Further Reading

ICL, *Basic Concepts in Data Communications*, Heinemann, 1983.

Kroeber, D. and Watson, H., *Computer-Based Information Systems*, Collier Macmillan, 2nd edn, 1986.

O'Leary, T. and Williams, B., *Business Data Processing*, Addison-Wesley, 1985

Lee, B., *Data Processing Methods*, Hutchinson, 1984.

11 Computers in Business

In this chapter some applications of computers to information systems are described, illustrating types and modes of use of computers in different business organisations

- Industrial: cement manufacturing and engineering
- Wholesale distribution: builders merchanting
- Retailing distribution: departmental stores and supermarkets
- Transport: airline
- Public utilities: electricity distribution
- Professional services: engineering design
- Business services: advertising and insurance.

Distributed Data Processing (Case A — Cement manufacture)

Case A is a large cement manufacturer, typical of the industry. It has central sales and administration and a number of production units located at or close to the sources of supply of raw materials. Like many other businesses in extractive industries, its activities do not consist solely of moving material in its original state to the market; the company produces a range of cement, decorating and other products for the building industry. Cement itself is produced in different forms (for example, rapid hardening, sulphate resisting, high alumina), changing chemical content and production processes to meet differing market needs.

It operates a general data processing service through a central computer installation which handles a number of major applications, including

- Order processing: receiving orders from customers, instructing delivery from depots and cement works and producing invoices
- Sales accounting: posting customer accounting records and administering collection of balances due
- Sales analysis: preparing analyses by product, area, etc.
- Purchases accounting for engineering supplies, vehicles, consumables and services for general company needs
- Payroll and employee records.

The company benefits from central computer systems for these applications because of the volume of transactions and the similarity of processes required throughout the production and distribution organisation. Firm control of financial resources is obtained through bringing together all information about debtors and creditors. Of great importance too is the ability given by a central database holding all essential transaction records to make information readily available for management.

The main economic factors which influence the company's success are

- Price: requiring the lowest cost production
- Product reputation: requiring dependable quality
- Product suitability: requiring optimum coverage of the range of market needs
- Cost of product storage: requiring close balance between sales and production to minimise the need for (protected) storage
- High investment in capital resources: requiring optimum use of production units.

All businesses can produce comparable lists of key areas of management information and decision which affect cash flow, working capital requirements, profit margins and, ultimately, achievement of overall objectives. Often the needs are conflicting, as between the last two items above, and in these situations the value of having prompt access to useful historical, comparative and projected information about sales and production costs and volumes is even greater. To meet these, the company uses its computer facilities also to produce from its basic records

- Analyses of direct, indirect and overhead production and sales costs
- Comparative analysis of sales trends
- Operating profits of production units
- Industry models and projections of total market demand patterns.

On-line data links to works, depots and sales offices away from the administrative centres have been created to minimise processing time and to provide feedback facilities to management at these operating centres for retrieval of up-to-date information from central files.

The cement industry is regarded as traditional and conservative because of its long establishment and substantial dependence on employee experience and skill. In consequence it could be expected to be relatively resistant to change, both in its own technology and in the application of computers. However, the company recognised the dangers of relying on tradition and experience and saw a need for more accurate and up-to-date information to control quality and produce reliable cost figures, and to identify means of improving plant productivity. To meet these additional needs the company introduced a number of local computer-based systems

- Stock records for control of locally held engineering and consumable stocks, using business minicomputers
- Laboratory and production control records and analysis, taking basic production data from manual records and automatic recording devices for processing through a multi-user microcomputer system to produce information for quality control and production statistics
- Production analysis: routine reports for management on output, performance and breakdowns
- Production costs: calculation and accumulation of standard and actual cost, and preparation of works cost ledgers from production figures, local expenditure and overheads
- Office communications: local area network workstation facilities (linked to the multi-user production system) to provide word processing, internal mail, Telex and 'gateways' (or network links) to the general stock records facility and to the central computer.

Thus computer facilities were developed in three tiers, linked through networks but each capable of working autonomously: microcomputer local area network and distributed business 'mini' systems at works level and, centrally, a large general-purpose 'mainframe' installation (figure 40). The

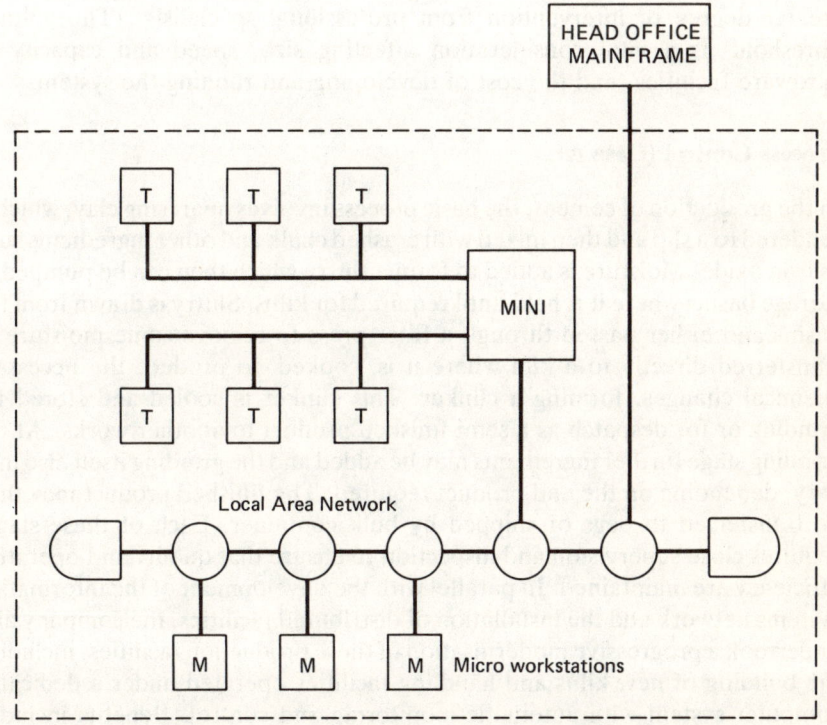

Figure 40   Distributed data processing

company could have considered replacing its central systems entirely by distributed facilities located at its main operational points, to accommodate both mainstream data processing operations and small local systems. It chose to add small systems at the periphery for new applications, avoiding any need to make costly changes in established centralised systems and overcoming two of the classical problems of communications in geographically spread organisations.

It gave local managers the ability to develop their own computer operations within the overall corporate framework and ensured that network links were such that, at any terminal, files were available easily and promptly wherever they were held. The use of microsystems for small volume applications was found attractive although, in principle, such applications could be handled perfectly well on larger systems. The decision was made to tailor these facilities to data volumes and individual needs rather than to adopt time-sharing policies at this level because the cost of software development was less and the systems were easier to bring into use. They were able to take advantage of available cheap, packaged, 'user friendly' (that is, specifically designed for the end user to handle without the need for specialist technical assistance) software tools from which systems tailored to local needs could be created by the users themselves. In contrast, equivalent facilities or tailored software on larger systems would have been substantially more expensive and require a much greater degree of intervention from professional specialists. (The volume 'threshold' is a vital consideration affecting size, speed and capacity of hardware facilities, and the cost of developing and running the system.)

Process Control (Case A)

In the production of cement, the basic process involves quarrying clay, which is rendered to a slip and then mixed with crushed chalk and other ingredients such as iron oxide. Moisture is added to form a slurry which then can be pumped to storage basins where it is held until required for kilns. Slurry is drawn from the basins and either passed through a filter press to remove some moisture or transferred directly to a kiln where it is 'cooked' to produce the necessary chemical changes, forming a clinker. This clinker is cooled and stored for grinding or for despatch as a semi-finished product to another works. At the grinding stage further ingredients may be added and the grinding itself also may vary, depending on the end product required. The finished product may then be transferred to bags or shipped by bulk container. Each of these stages requires close supervision and inspection to ensure that quality and operating efficiency are maintained. In parallel with the development of the information systems network and the installation of distributed facilities, the company also undertook a progressive modernisation of these production facilities, including the building of new kilns and handling facilities operated under a dedicated computer system with automatic monitoring and control. Benefits included closer and more accurate control of processes, using less labour as well as bringing improvement in the general operating efficiency through a greater degree of automation in the operation of the plant. The computer facility also provided an input of laboratory and production-control data to the local management information system, thus reducing the time-lag in analysis of production data and eliminating a further stage of manual operation.

On-line Data Processing (Case B — Manufacturer of electro-mechanical assemblies)

The company manufactures (for stock) a range of temperature and pressure recording devices for sale to other businesses, mainly for fitting into their own products or processes. The company has fewer than 100 employees and, because of its size and the nature of its business, is vulnerable both to competition and to general economic conditions which affect its customers. Such a business has a need to ensure optimum operating efficiency and to be versatile in sales and marketing. It could have made effective use of microsystems in a number of ways to produce marginal savings in labour costs and other benefits but it elected to concentrate its efforts initially in two main areas

- general-purpose on-line system for production management
- embedded systems for company products

Stock control, whether of raw materials, finished products or office stationery, is a necessary function for any business. Too much stock increases the cost of working capital, too little means waste of other resources and loss of income through inability to process or deliver. Production management is concerned with two key areas of stock control: raw materials and parts for manufacture, and finished products. Control of stocks is not simply a matter of having reliable information about what is available and what has been consumed; it also involves linking this with information about what will be required. Forecasts of sales determine the requirements for stocks of finished goods and for production of those goods in a given manufacturing period. This production 'plan' will then determine requirements for labour, assembly machine capacity, materials and parts, and other resources. The materials requirement plan will affect the need for part stocks and for purchase action.

The company acquired a small business computer with on-line terminal facilities for end-user operation in the Stores, Assembly and Office areas. Software was a packaged system providing the following modules

- Stock control
- Materials requirements planning
- Shop loading
- Work in progress
- Costing

Working from sales targets and forecasts, the production manager would use the software facilities to set up long-range plans from which purchase orders on suppliers, bills of materials, stock issues and job ticket issues for manufacturing assembly shop loading would be generated as required. Information to management about stocks, production and costs would be fed back for adjustment of planning and operating decisions. Advantages of such a computer system are the rapid evaluation of alternative courses and a reduced risk of error or delay because of lack of knowledge or time. Investment in stocks can be reduced because requirements are predicted with greater accuracy. With manual stock systems it is often found too costly to keep detailed records and undue reliance is placed on subjective assessments; if full records are maintained, the time lag between the transaction event and its recording is such that any information, however accessible, is likely to be out of date. When these problems are eliminated by using an on-line computer approach, detailed plans can be prepared and adjusted whenever necessary to provide reliable means of deciding on provision and allocation of resources. Case B is a situation where greater effective control over stock levels alone was sufficient to justify the entire investment in computer systems.

Another effect of reconstructing production management activities round a computer information system was to make possible a more optimistic view of other computer applications; the marginal cost of such additions to the installation work load was low, and computer links between production and other business systems offered added convenience in operation. Further applications implemented were

- Sales order processing and accounting
- Word processing systems for customer mailing and sales promotion
- General ledger accounting.

The company employed no specialist computer staff either for system development or for operation, the software being bought in packaged form and the operation being entirely under the control of the user. The successful introduction of systems covering all the main administrative functions created sufficient confidence for the company to start developing new applications, using software designed to allow building of computer routines by end users without programming skills. A long-range plan was also drawn up for replacement of the existing computer installation at the appropriate time by a networked facility, which would permit incorporation of additional work-stations for internal communication and independent use for specific decision support and other personal applications.

Embedded Systems (Case B)

The embedded systems project was entirely separate from the general computer systems. Introduction of embedded microcomputer systems to the products meant, in effect, a new range of products; not only were the composition of the products and the manufacturing processes changed in detail but also the application of the products could be extended. (They could, for example, now become computer input devices for telemetry systems.) Once the technical problems had been resolved, manufacturing processes proved to be simpler than before but the major benefit was to the company's competitive position. As well as opening new sales opportunities, the better presentation and added convenience given by the computer element made the products more acceptable and improved the company 'image'.

These different applications within one business illustrate sharp contrasts in approach. As a user of business computer information systems, company B had no need for its own technical expertise, relying on suppliers for hardware and software support and its own staff for operation of equipment. For the embedded systems, however, the research and development function of the company was fully concerned with systems design, technical specification and programming in a comparable way to that of any other technical specialist concerned with a computer project.

Real-time Data Processing (Case C — Builders merchant)

Case C concerns another large national business, serving the building industry and the public directly as wholesaler and retailer through an organisation of central warehouses and local branches. The company, which is an amalgamation of a number of separate firms, supplies all kinds of building materials and products including cement and sand, ironmongery, sanitary ware, electrical goods, plumbing, timber, decorating materials and tools. In the process of assimilating its constituent businesses it undertook a major review of organisation, systems and policies, taking advantage of its new size to develop a corporate image, rationalise product ranges, create brand identities and introduce bulk central buying.

To achieve some of the desired changes, the company embarked on the development of a number of basic computer systems. After first setting up batch accounting and administrative systems at a company computer centre, it then created a network of real-time and on-line systems linking 'main-stream' information flows through order processing, despatch, invoicing, stock control, sales and purchases. The principal applications were

- Customer order processing
- Branch stock replenishment
- Sales accounting and sales analysis
- Warehouse stock recording and replenishment.

Since the computer project was itself an element of the rationalisation, any costs and benefits relating to computer systems would be difficult to distinguish from other changes. However there were some areas of specific weakness in previous systems which computer systems were intended to overcome. The builders merchant carries out the classical wholesaling function of holding stocks whereby, on the one hand, the customer (in this instance, normally, the small builder) can deal with one supplier instead of many and can rely on that supplier to meet needs as they arise and, on the other hand, the manufacturer can distribute in larger volumes to fewer customers and avoid having to hold stocks to meet retail demands. In builders merchanting, the function goes beyond that found in most other industries: notably, many customers expect to have any requirement met on demand and, through favourable credit arrangements, to rely on the supplier for a substantial proportion of working capital needs.

Because of these customer attitudes (which are encouraged by competitive pressures), the builders merchants finds that two aspects of costs — working capital tied up in customer debts and in stocks of goods for sale — and two special influences on sales (apart from price) — stock availability and prompt delivery — are of exceptional importance. A primary objective of computer use was to assist with these problems.

Interactive VDU terminal facilities were set up in main sales offices to receive customer orders. These terminals were linked directly to regional databases containing up-to-date customer account records, stock balances and prices. On receipt of an order, the VDU operator would confirm customer identity and credit-worthiness, establish stock availability and price for the items ordered, and then transfer accepted orders to a suspense file, awaiting the next stages of warehouse 'picking' and despatch, and billing (figure 41). This basic system covered orders for direct delivery to customers, which orders might be received by post, telephone or Telex, from field sales representatives or from customers directly.

With the object of minimising the time-lag between placing the order and warehouse action, the original procedures (involving transcription of written and verbal orders received to 'key punching' documents) were superseded by interface procedures adapted to the order origins, making the fullest possible use of new technology

- Microfiche copies of computer-produced price lists for sales representatives and major customers to reduce need for preliminary screening of orders
- Direct telephone selling contact between order originator and input operator
- Direct input from Telex
- Audio response system for (controlled) direct speech input from sales representatives
- Direct terminal access for major customers
- 'Calling out' telephone sales techniques.

Use was made also of interactive facilities to give terminal operators access to information about special discounts and promotional offers, making it possible

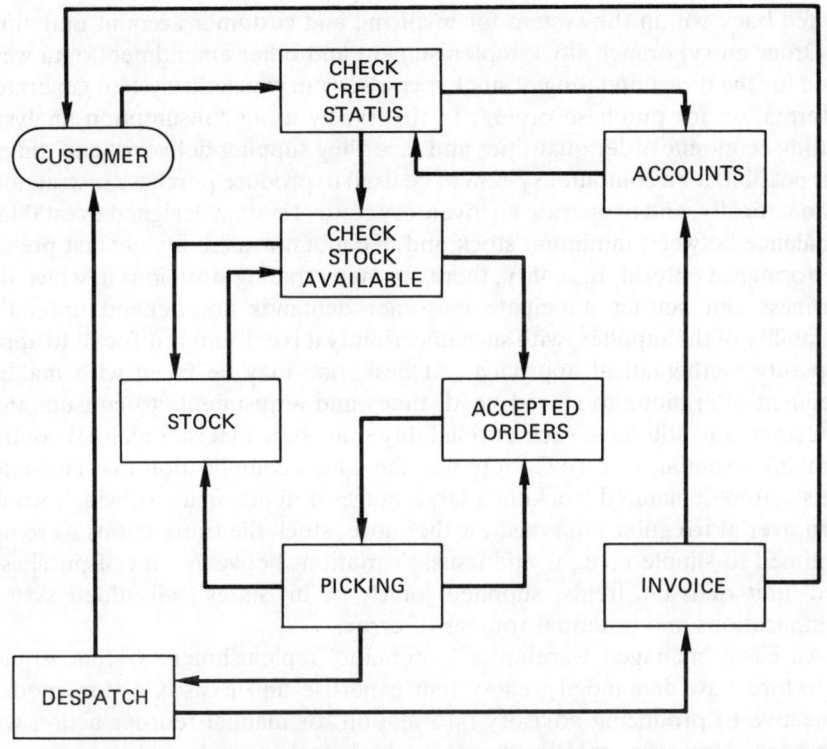

Figure 41   Order processing

for them to act in a direct selling capacity as well as to receive orders.

Branch stock replenishment (the transfer of sale items from central warehouses to branch stocks) and orders for the direct supply of materials from manufacturer to customer could be handled through the order entry system. For the 'light side' items (as opposed to 'heavy side' sand, cement, bricks, etc.) which could be stocked in 'supermarket' branch outlets, stock replenishment techniques appropriate to food retailers were used. These involved attaching computer-printed labels to shelves and gondolas showing stock codes, minimum stock and order quantities. At fixed intervals (usually weekly), branch staff would check physical stocks and record totals for each product item on a portable terminal. The terminal would then be attached to the branch order-entry terminal facility for transmission of stock data to the computer centre. From this information sales and replenishment quantities would be calculated, and warehouse instructions prepared for despatch of fresh stocks to the branch, to which revised shelf labels and sales summaries were sent directly. Warehouse picking and despatch operated as a real-time system linked to order entry. On demand, picking instructions would be prepared to meet vehicle loading deadlines, and delivery sheets produced to control vehicle loading and to provide information for customers. Despatch data would then be fed back within the system for invoicing and customer account updating.

Order entry, branch stock replenishment and other amendment data were used for the direct updating of stock records, from which the system generated information for purchase orders. In theory, by using consumption analysis, setting economic order quantities and recording supplier delivery 'lead' times, it is possible for a computer system to be used to produce purchase instructions automatically, and to operate an inventory control system designed to establish a balance between minimum stock and maximum availability against pre-set performance criteria. In reality, there are many trading situations in which the business can neither anticipate customer demands nor depend upon the reliability of the supplier; with such uncertainty it is extremely difficult to apply a purely mathematical approach. At best, one may be faced with making frequent alterations to stored 'lead' times and adjustments to consumption forecasts, and still have such unreliability that some external manual control remains essential. In case C there was the added complication that customer satisfaction demanded stocking a large range of items, many of which would turn over at irregular intervals. Furthermore, stock file transactions were not confined to simple receipts and issues; variations between 'unit of purchase' and 'unit of issue' items, supplied jointly or in 'suites', all added system complications and potential sources of error.

An easily managed warehouse 'automatic' replenishment system would, therefore, have demanded great system 'expertise' and in case C a more modest objective of producing advisory information for manual reorder action was accepted. However, creating 'machineable' stock records and linking stock control with the other machine systems do offer potentially substantial advantages over manual (or purely autonomous) stock-recording systems. In case C a number of clear benefits were derived

- More accurate records from rapid updating
- Automatic generation of information for purchasing management concerning out-of-stock items and abnormal demand patterns
- Cyclical and sample stocktaking to reduce year-end disruption and cost, and to identify physical stock discrepancies more promptly
- Value analysis allowing a policy of discrimination in replenishment of stockholdings to concentrate attention on items which were significant for availability and for inventory value.

The limitations of the computer-based inventory management system, the need for retaining a substantial clerical element and the partial success in improving control over stocks led to pressures for rationalisation of warehousing operations in a number of respects. These included a greater degree of product 'packaging' to eliminate differences between receipt and issue handling and the introduction of semi-automatic replenishment procedures for key items identified by value analysis. These special systems involve the establishment of direct data links with major suppliers and feedback of delivery information.

A large business of this kind could be expected to use information technology for many other administrative and management information functions, and among the case C computer applications were the preparation of corporate planning models, budgeting, vehicle maintenance and performance management, and control of electronic warehouse security surveillance systems. However, one of the best general arguments for computers in a substantial multi-location organisation is their ability to overcome problems of distance, thus reducing conflict between the centre and the periphery and eliminating communication failures and delays. There are added advantages where the geographical separation is also a separation of function: between selling branch, central warehouse and head office administrative and support functions. In case C, extension of on-line terminal facilities to all branch locations gave the same speed of processing and ease of access to information as is possible with a completely unified organisation in one place. Transactions could enter the computer system at the point of origin and output be received where it was required. Files could be updated without delay so that, when stock items were unavailable in one place, it could quickly be established that they were available elsewhere. The very substantial problems of bad debts and 'shrinkage', endemic in the building materials industry, could be managed much better because there was up-to-date information always available to control credit in time, or to identify causes of stock discrepancy. As a result the company was able to increase both its sales volume and profit margins.

Two disadvantages of the systems in operation were that communication costs were very high because open access was necessary from each terminal to the computer centre throughout every working day. Much of the transaction data required a response to the point of origin. Line costs could have been substantially lower if there had been processing facilities at warehouses and major selling branches. This system could also tolerate very little failure; interruption of operations lasting an hour at a critical time could be sufficient to disrupt the pattern of warehouse deliveries for up to a week, which was not acceptable to user departments. The risk of failure of hardware, software or communication links could arise at so many points in the network that a substantial investment in protective and fallback measures proved desirable. The concentration of computer facilities at a central point also held back the development of other applications and placed a heavy penalty on the 'batch' system, to the extent that routine payroll operations were found to be more effectively handled by a computer service bureau. The consequence of this experience led the company to decide, on a second phase of development, to add peripheral processing facilities at key points for local processing with reduced links to the computer centre.

Point-of-sale System (Case D — Supermarket)

Large grocery supermarket chains have many functions appropriate to computer-based systems. The case D example principally concerns point-of-sale systems and the interaction of the special terminal with the external customer and internal information flows, through branch computer centres for local processing, to warehouse centres and thence to administrative centres and external suppliers. The company's computer strategy had some similarities with that of case A where there was an evolution from central batch-based systems to a combination of central and distributed systems linked through networks covering all data communication channels. The point-of-sale system represented the ultimate extension of this communication chain to the limit of the selling system within the business. However, it was not simply a question of extending computer systems to the point of origin of sales transactions, in pursuit of optimum system principles: it was also seen as part of an aim to use computers to improve the general performance of a supermarket branch as a separate organisational unit. Main features of the system were

- Branch stock recording and replenishment
- Branch sales analysis
- Customer sales information
- Product shelf labelling
- Checkout cash audit.

The system involved replacing 'checkout' cash registers with computer terminals linked to a small business computer in the branch. This computer held a record of all stock items in the branch, with prices and descriptions. A price and description label was attached to the shelf where the product was displayed, but there was no longer a price label on the product itself. At the 'checkout', the terminal operator, instead of keying in a price from the grocery item label to produce a tally roll and cash total, would pass the item over a 'laser reader' built into the checkout which scanned a bar code on the product label (pre-printed by the supplier). The bar code identified each product precisely, producing input data to the computer which fed back a responding tally-roll print of price and description. The customer received an itemised list; the machine operator had a much simpler task (only keying input data for products which were not bar-coded), product labelling was saved and the branch had up-to-date information about stocks in hand without the need to check shelves and reserve stocks. With information about sales and stocks available for feedback to the warehouse computer system, automatic stock replenishment became possible, comparable to that described in case C. The computer facility also provided the opportunity for firm cash control by establishing computer totals at the time cash was removed from the till.

The benefits expected from the point-of-sale system included improvement in stock control, reduced costs of product price labels, greater efficiency at the 'checkout' points and indirect benefits from customer satisfaction. However, because of the difficulty of reaching valid theoretical conclusions, the novelty of the techniques and the importance of obtaining reliable information about customer attitudes, the company undertook prolonged trials with pilot systems in locations considered representative of the trading patterns. These trials led to technical modifications and to a significant reassessment of costs and benefits. It was found that the critical factor in handling customers was the packing of purchases into shopping bags and the only way that the full potential of the point-of-sale system could be achieved was by having a second person at the checkout point to assist the customer in packing. Benefits which proved to be more substantial than expected were the ability to introduce discriminatory pricing (for example, by offering quantity discounts which could be calculated through the computer systems) and in giving effective control over losses in profit margin from sale of 'time-expired' items.

Communication System (Case E — Department store)

Although in a number of ways departmental stores have moved closer to supermarkets in recent years, this illustration points some of the differences in system requirements between the two types of retail business which arise from the nature of their sales transactions. Instead of selling relatively few items in large numbers, the department store tends to sell in small quantities; stocks of many items are small (notably clothing and furniture). The number of items bought at a time by an individual customer is also much fewer than in a supermarket. A substantial proportion of sales is on credit, through the store's own credit system or through credit card companies. Restocking is not an automatic process, because of the greater influence of such factors as local market conditions, changes of seasonal fashion and sales promotion. In consequence there is less emphasis on rapid throughput and stock replenishment, and more on capturing accurate data for management information and for control of payment.

Case E relates to a multiple departmental store group which has a distributed processing network, with computer centres located in each store linked to point-of-sale and general-purpose terminals at main input/output points. In this illustration, two particular aspects of the credit sales accounting system are examined

- Electronic Funds Transfer (EFT/POS)
- Credit control.

The EFT concept as it is applied to a retail store involves, in effect, a banking transaction whereby the customer pays immediately through a current bank account. By means of a direct data link to the bank system, the amount of the debt is transferred from the customer's account to that of the department store. While the ultimate effect is the same as for payment by guaranteed cheque, there are the additional attractions of convenience and security, but this illustration should not be seen as an endorsement of EFT as a conventional means of payment since these kinds of application are necessarily developed with caution because they cross system boundaries. There is, for example, less tangible advantage to the customer than to the store since the customer is paying more promptly. There is also a significant cost of a communications link to the bank; the economic (as opposed to the technical or convenience) consideration is whether or not usage of the connection and the compensating savings will be such that a mutually acceptable arrangement between store and bank can be achieved.

In this application, the customer's bank card or store account card would be used to enter customer identity information at the point-of-sale terminal, while sales codes and value would be entered manually or from a machineable garment tag (this tag being detached and the data input through a special reading device). Sale data would be transferred to the store computer or, in some cases, to a data switching centre from which EFT information would be routed to the bank computer system and internal information to the appropriate store computer system. The system would respond to the terminal with an appropriate transaction acceptance signal allowing the terminal to release a customer receipt.

Store customer credit accounts were updated in real time so that credit limits automatically reflected the current situation. The benefit gained from controlling credit risk was regarded as more important than the improvement in cash flow and the better management information. Provision of any credit facility poses a dilemma for a departmental store: on the one hand it is clearly established that allowing credit does increase sales because many people are prepared to buy on credit where they would not pay cash (even when they have funds to do so), on the other, allowing credit without checking a customer's account position involves high risk of bad debts. This risk is greater with a multiple store because transactions arising in different locations must be collated, hence the attraction of a communications network with real-time updating of accounts.

This could, of course, be done with a centralised system. In case E, the preferred solution was to locate a distributed centre in each store, to hold the accounts of customers whose business was predominantly at that store with 'on-line' or 'dial-up' (that is, via the public telecommunications network) data links to other store centres for account enquiries when 'out of town' customers buy. This approach had the advantage of reducing the volume of data communications traffic and concentrating processing predominantly in the location where the transaction occurred.

Dedicated System (Case F — Airline)

Although airline seat reservations is probably the most well-publicised (and most extensive) application of computers in the civil aviation business, it was not the first application, nor was it the last. Airlines, because their business involves handling very large volumes of transactions in many administrative and control systems and because, for a vital period during the early development of business computers, they were expanding rapidly, both needed and could easily absorb new techniques. They have proably made as great a use of computers as any industry in the world since the very early days of computer systems. Passenger and cargo sales and revenue, inter-airline billing, payroll, general ledger, engineering maintenance, stores accounting, fleet planning, timetables, flight control and many other applications have been handled by computer for many years. Only one application has been chosen as an illustration under case F.

● Passenger 'check-in' load control.

A number of real-time systems for handling passenger traffic grew out of seat reservations; case F is one of these. It is a dedicated system using specialised equipment for handling the recording and information flow tasks arising from 'check-in' processes at airports. The computer system has its own network to terminals at the 'check-in' desks but it is also linked for transfer of data to Reservations, Flight Information and other computer facilities (figure 42). The starting point is the setting-up of flight and passenger booking information for each period coming under control, against which data may be entered through

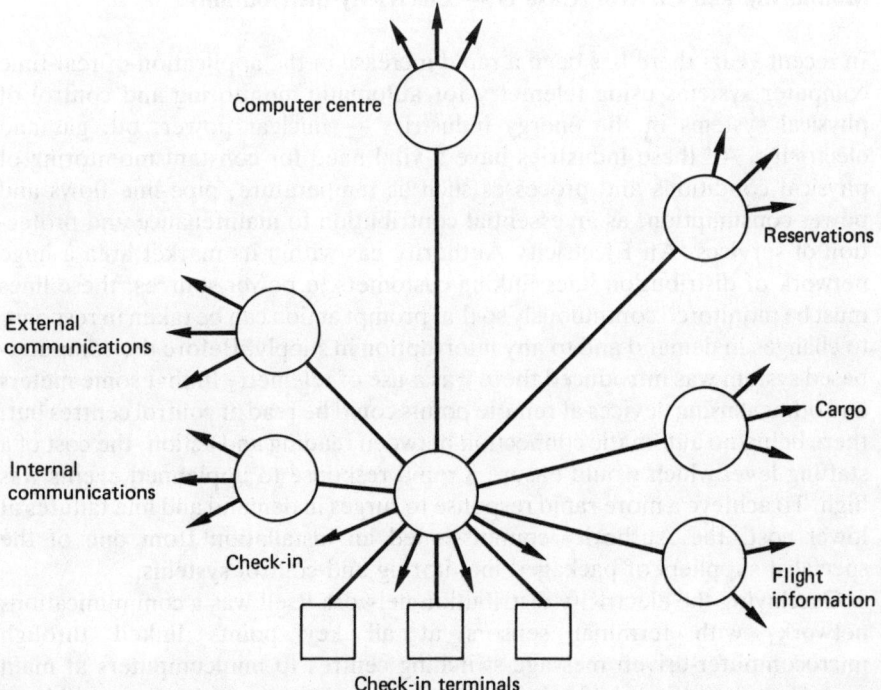

Figure 42   Passenger 'check-in'

special-purpose terminals at 'check-in' and ticket desks, to confirm the booking, prepare passenger lists and, where appropriate, notify baggage weight or count required for aircraft loading calculation.

The advantages of a dedicated system are that it is possible to tailor equipment precisely to the requirement, to simplify the software facilities (since there are no applications sharing time on the equipment) and to make it easier to meet the need for very rapid throughput at peak times. Although the theoretical cost savings are marginal (as in many physical control systems), the benefits from reducing delays, permitting later flight closure and having immediate transmission of important messages to different parts of the airport, build up to a very substantial improvement in operating efficiency.

Even the connection to airport departure display information generates benefits in speed and convenience because there are no incompatible interfaces between the systems concerned.

Apart from the general advantages of more effective passenger handling and accelerated communications, the particular benefits found in case F were increased traffic from business passengers without luggage (who could be offered delayed check-in at boarding exits) and 'stand-by' passengers without reservations (because of precise knowledge of seats available at critical times).

Monitoring and Control (Case G — Electricity distribution)

In recent years there has been a rapid increase in the application of real-time computer systems using telemetry for automatic monitoring and control of physical systems in the energy industries — nuclear power, oil, gas and electricity. All these industries have a vital need for constant monitoring of physical conditions and processes such as temperature, pipe-line flows and power consumption, as an essential contribution to maintenance and protection of services. An Electricity Authority has within its market area a huge network of distribution lines linking customers to power sources; these lines must be monitored continuously so that prompt action can be taken in response to changes in demand and to any interruption in supply. Before the computer-based system was introduced there was a use of telemetry in that some meters and other sensing devices at remote points could be read at control centres but, there being no automatic connection between reading and action, the cost of a staffing level which would ensure a rapid response to unplanned events was high. To achieve a more rapid response to surges in demand and line failures at lower cost, the Authority commissioned an installation from one of the specialist suppliers of packaged monitoring and control systems.

Overlaying the electricity distribution network itself was a communications network, with terminal sensors at all key points linked through microcomputer-driven message-switching centres to minicomputers at main control centres (figure 43). Information from the network was accessible to control staff through VDU terminals and mimic display diagrams, and there

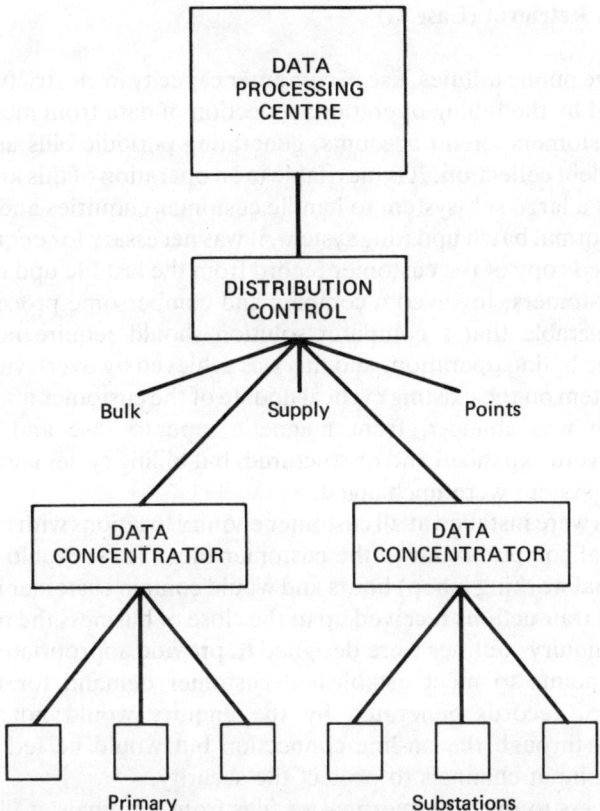

Figure 43 Electricity distribution control network

were output links to switches and other control points where automatic responses to input data were required. Supplies might be re-routed as an automatic reaction to a detected circuit break, or additional supplies automatically switched in as a response to a surge of power demand. Manual intervention was necessary only to over-ride automatic controls in exceptional situations or to arrange for the repair of a physical break which had been located precisely from computer information. (The system described would not be totally self-correcting, but one can find examples of comparable control systems having duplicated facilities which can be brought into use under computer control to ensure that there is never an interruption. Such systems may be found where failure is critical, as in aircraft control systems and in the design of microprocessor circuitry.)

It should be noted that this type of telemetry system, to be fully successful, must provide real-time facilities which can respond to automatic data input and must take system reliability virtually to the point of infinite time between breakdowns.

Information Retrieval (Case G)

As in all large public utilities, use of computer capacity in electricty distribution is dominated by the billing operation: collection of data from meter readings, updating customers' credit accounts, generating periodic bills and recording progress of debt collection. It is inevitable in an operation of this kind that there is a need for a large sub-system to handle customer enquiries and complaints. Under the normal batch updating system, it was necessary for enquiry clerks to have a printed copy of the customer record from the last file update which, for 1 500 000 customers, involved a complex and cumbersome procedure.

It was desirable that a computer solution should require no substantial change to the billing operation, and this was achieved by overlaying an on-line retrieval system on the existing cyclical update of the customer master file. The file medium was changed from magnetic tape to disc and the records themselves were expanded and restructured, but billing cycles and the external parts of the system were unchanged.

Terminals were installed at all customer enquiry locations with on-line access to the central computer and to the customer files. These would be available during normal working (shop) hours and would contain customer information, including all transactions received up to the close of business the previous day. Real-time enquiry routines were designed to provide appropriate file extracts at enquiry points to meet established customer demand for information. Alteration of records generated by the enquiry would not be effected immediately through the on-line connection but would be fed through the normal data input channels to protect file security.

Direct access to the customer master files from terminals at district offices made it possible to deal with personal telephone and letter enquiries related to any account. It was not necessary to introduce real-time updating because the great bulk of queries were generated by the issue of bills and, therefore, the record at the time of the enquiry was effectively up-to-date. Apart from reducing cost of handling queries, the system offered quicker rectification of errors and intangible benefits of greater customer satisfaction resulting from the prompt response to their enquiries.

Another information retrieval system illustrated by case G is the use of private Viewdata facilities in showrooms, linked to a database containing information about prices and descriptions of electrical appliances available for sale. The system is an autonomous customer service facility which is a typical application of Viewdata. It had the merit of being inexpensive with cheap terminals, no line cost (because it used the authority's existing private network) and no need for complex processing. All purposes of the system could be met by interrogation and display of a particular part of the central file. The benefits were to Sales as a convenient, inexpensive and rapid alternative to using combinations of printed price lists, descriptive literature and telephone enquiries to other parts of the organisation when information was not available in the show room.

Computer-aided Design — Personal Microsystem (Case H — Engineering designers)

The use of computers as personal support facilities for engineering designers, architects and other technical professions has become extremely important. Although described as a personal system having relatively limited input and output, the power and capacity of the microcomputer for computer-aided design (CAD) in engineering is likely to be considerable, and the use of graphics, particularly with three-dimensional displays and colour, and the need for complex calculation facilities (both of which would be provided by packaged CAD software) are substantially more sophisticated than the typical business microcomputer system. The benefits, however, are not dissimilar in principle.

The essence of a personal support system is that it allows the user to achieve a given result in a much shorter time, sometimes to the extent of bringing within the capacity of an individual tasks which previously would have demanded much wider and greater effort. It also extends intellectual scope by creating the ability to consider with ease the question "what if?" The designer and planner can consider alternatives, modifications and variations which previously would have been virtually as costly in time as the original concepts and which, without such an aid, might well not have been explored. The use of computer power to generate three-dimensional images and to examine and manipulate them also adds considerably to the power of the individual designer. A manual alternative might be to construct a physical model and test it, introducing a series of modifications as each aspect of performance was explored. Similarly, construction of a mathematical model which, in a computer design facility, could be examined effectively through an infinite series of iterations or variations would, in a manual system, soon exceed time, if not cost, limits. The whole area of sophisticated package design tools using computer facilities for calculation and presentation can show some dramatic impact on cost and range of application.

Case H, which is related to the design of electronic circuitry — effectively, the computer designing the computer — took the CAD process a stage further. The designer used a combination of visual displays and a 'drawing' pad, which could be manipulated by key-board entry of parameter changes, by touch-sensitive screen surfaces and by a 'mouse' (a hand-held cursor control device for manipulation of graphical information in particular) to construct, alter, and test circuitry to specific characteristics and output requirements. Having completed the design, it would be consolidated into a manufacturing specification which could then be transferred to a computer-controlled manufacturing unit.

In such an example, the 'business system' is relatively simple and the investment in the design facility not unduly costly (in comparison to that in the designer) but the technology behind the software and equipment is sophisticated, as is the overall conception of the integration of design and manufacturing processes. When one associates this approach to engineering design with automated production concepts and the introduction of microprocessors into products themselves, it can be seen that the impact of computers on the production field is certainly not to be considered any less significant than the impact on the administrative and general management fields.

IKBS — Personal Microsystem (Case I — Advertising)

Case I relates to a directory publisher whose revenue comes mainly from the sale of classified advertising. Much of the advertising space is sold by telephone; although not as effective in terms of the ratio of sales to sales 'contacts' as is direct selling by sales representatives, use of the telephone allows four times as many contacts per day. In consequence, telephone selling offers better value except in relation to the large customer. Telephone selling is a skilled business; to persuade someone to buy something that they did not think they wanted at the start of the telephone conversation demands a high degree of experience and skill in selling.

Personal computers have demonstrated their value in these kinds of selling situation as a means of providing the sales person with a source of rapid reference to information about the customer and about the 'product'.

The case I illustration goes beyond this to the fringes of Expert Systems. The system run by the 'telesales' representative during the selling contact provided direct support to the sales dialogue through a 'script' which offered alternative response to prospective customer queries and objections. The expertise built into the software was derived from analysis of past experience, and indicated to the telesales clerk the point beyond which it was not worth pursuing the matter. The benefit derived was greater sales productivity, not through an increase in the effectiveness of the sales message but through more effective use of time, thus permitting a greater number of sales contacts per day (with the success ratio maintained).

The successful application of personal computer support in an occupation which had been considered to depend on individual skill and experience can lead one to the conclusion that there are now relatively few occupations which could not benefit in some way from computer facilities.

Portable Microsystem (Case J — Insurance)

The insurance industry is a major user of computers; large central database systems holding customer policy and premium account records, with 'star' networks to terminals located in branch sales offices, are typical of insurance. Apart from the economies resulting from rapid access to records and from efficient handling of large numbers of transactions, computer systems also can assist selling activities through machine handling of customer correspondence and direct mail sales promotion, using the more professional and flexible presentation now possible since the introduction of economical colour graphics and laser printing. The insurance industry is also a potentially substantial user of knowledge-based systems.

The specific example taken from case J also relates to sales, and may be contrasted with the use of a microcomputer for personal support in the previous illustration. One of the most important methods of selling personal insurance is direct sales contact; the case J illustration is an adaption of a (very cheap) portable, personal computer designed for the hobby market to the selling of life assurance to prospective customers in their homes. The sales technique used by the company's representatives took advantage of the ability to use a domestic television set as the 'monitor' to which the portable computer is attached, and of the greater susceptibility of people to a message displayed on a TV screen than to other forms of persuasion. Instead of explaining potential benefits verbally, referring to printed leaflets and offering quickly prepared manual calculations on paper, the sales representative would be able to present examples and options rapidly and effectively with the support of professionally designed graphical displays on the television screen. The technique brought two tangible advantages: in a better success rate in selling policies, and in the increased number of sales contacts recommended by clients.

Influences on the Use of Computers

The illustrations given are not intended to give a comprehensive picture of the current uses of computers. No mention has been made of the extensive and varied applications in the Health and Medicine, the Education and the Leisure industries, and many others. Such are the opportunities offered by information technology that only a sample selection can be presented within a reasonable space. Moreover, since the momentum of change is not yet slackening, tomorrow's reader will soon find new applications.

As a conclusion to this survey, some additional comments are made on the future economic condition in which the computer will have a paramount influence over the shape and structure of business information systems and, through them, over much of economic and social life.

Momentum of Technology

It may be said that it was necessary to invent the computer; without it, many of today's business problems could not have been resolved. That is an easy speculation, but it is also possible to demonstrate the mirror image of that proposition: that the introduction of the computer has created situations in which it has become essential. Beyond that, it can also be said that use of computers feeds the development of computer technology and (at least as long as we are in an 'upward climb' in this electronic era) that there is a momentum which leads managers to accept and encourage development of progressively more sophisticated facilities and applications.

The basic theoretical proposition offered in the first chapter is relevant: that there is inherent in modern economic society a pressure for growth and change which impels developed economies and the organisations which they comprise to seek continued improvement. Thus, the computer is introduced because it offers improvement over the punched card system; before long there is a better computer solution and, when the time comes to look at system requirements again, the better solution will be adopted. It is inconceivable that a computer user will contemplate replacing obsolescent equipment by something identical; further, whatever is offered must be demonstrably superior if it is to be considered at all.

The process of advancement is driven also from the industry itself. Its competitive structure will ensure that suppliers attempt to gain a place in the market by offering something faster, cheaper or easier to use. That the momentum will eventually slacken is apparent from experience in automotive, aeronautical and mechanical engineering when, for whatever reason, an avenue of technology is explored to its limit. Until that limit is reached, or the going becomes difficult, the movement along it will continue because of the common interest of the three prime influences — usage, innovation and supply.

Momentum of System Change

These observations apply as much to the business system itself; not only does a manager expect to be able to buy a better computer next time, he also expects to introduce a better system. The function of the systems analyst is always seen as one of changing systems for the better — greater speed, lower cost, more accuracy, flexibility. Any existing application of computers in a business will always represent the base from which further development is to be launched. It is a reminder that we are not really so very much more clever than our predecessors; we do not discover for the first time what really can be done with computers, we merely take a modest step forward because we can see what has been done and are offered new avenues of advance.

Economic and Social Momentum

The first two factors described might be considered as being the direct influences on business — internal aims and achievements matched to external opportunities and constraints. General economic and social factors may be considered as indirect influences, creating the environment in which change is possible or inevitable. In one sense this goes back to an earlier proposition that it was necessary to invent the computer; it is one of the unfortunate truths about economic society that we always have losses to offset many of our gains.

The comptometer (a manually operated mechanical calculating device), the punched card and the mechanical typewriter have gone; with them have gone the manual skills they required for effective use and, whether we had any reason for wishing them back or not, it is quite certain that we would find no one willing to acquire such skills again. Once an easier way is introduced there is no way back; however deplorable it may be that the school child cannot multiply nine times seven without an electronic calculator, we must plan our systems accordingly. It might be seen as some form of decadence that a side effect of technological progress is to dispose of old human skills and make us more dependent on machines, but it is clear that we have to gear our use of human labour to prevailing attitudes.

Once computer operation becomes an acceptable practice in one sphere it is likely to extend to other spheres. This is not only a question of what makes an easier or more interesting job as far as attitudes to work are concerned, it is also a question of what is easier or more acceptable at the output end of the system. The automatic cash dispenser was introduced to branch banking to provide an emergency service of cash withdrawal because social pressures forced banks to close on Saturday mornings. Since it has now been demonstrated that many customer will happily continue to use the automatic cash dispenser when the bank is actually open, the way also appears to be open for the bank cashier (who has already long since declined in status from a mature, respected senior to a junior assistant) to join the locomotive fireman and the lamp lighter in history.

Adding to social pressures are the economic consequences of rising prosperity. Just as expectations grow and attitudes to work change, so the price of labour increases, driving us towards machine support or substitution. This process is affecting the computer business itself through the growing cost of people who design and operate business systems; it must apply in all work situations once labour cost is pushed by the general movement of incomes above the threshold at which machine support or substitution can come in. If there is a cheaper way to do something it will be adopted sooner or later, unless there is a monopoly supply of labour and we are prepared to pay whatever it costs, directly or indirectly. Otherwise, the occupation and its product or (more often) service, disappears. In contemplating the prospective introduction of the domestic computer terminal which will offer access to the outside world for all messages, enquiries, purchases and decisions, we may dwell also on the relationship between technical and economic feasibility, and the economic and social pressures which eventually leave us no choice.

Constraints of Experience

So far the threads of argument have related to influences which carry us along and encourage us to look forward. Because we associate the computer with future technology it by no means follows that we may not be constrained by past experience in deciding how to apply it. On the contrary, the application of new techniques is always affected by the past and, very often, the easiest way of taking advantage of new facilities is by aping what was done before. Many of the initial failures with new technology have been because the change from the previous system was too great to be absorbed within a reasonable time, resulting in an unacceptable loss of efficiency. Many of the innovations in machines and their application have been economic failures; much of the current prosperity and success of the computer industry is built on a foundation of business failures and huge state subventions. The pioneer is rarely the one who makes the profit (it is to be doubted that I. K. Brunel made any money for many of his financial backers). Thus it should be understandable if the mainstream of business computer application usually follows the easier path of modifying and adapting old systems, rather than advancing fresh, wholly radical concepts not tied in any way to the past.

One can see this cautious attitude as a reflection of fear for the investment in existing systems and of the risk of embarking on radical change. If one looks at what has happened in large business undertakings one may see evidence of steady progression in computer investment, with advantage apparently being taken of each technical advance as it comes along to extend the range and type of computer application as it becomes economically feasible. A closer examination of the actual applications might show that basic systems for processing transactions forming the mainstream of the business activities were very little changed. What often has happened is that more cost-effective equipment has been substituted, and enhancements and additions grafted on to the basic systems but that these systems themselves have changed very little.

In business theory it is argued that one prime criterion for a decision on new investment should be the expected return on that investment, ignoring the potential write-off of any balance of value of the old investment. It has been a frequent criticism of industry in the United Kingdom that it has rejected this argument, retaining old machinery and methods because they still have some 'wear' left, and failing to see that this over-favourable view of the return on old investments leads to the downward spiral of a less competitive future. Yet, curiously, the same thing is often done with computer systems. Perhaps, with the equipment itself, the lesson has been learned; business seems to have moved from the original 10, and then 7 year 'write-off' period for computer equipment to a 'current rental' view of amortisation. But, for software and all the other system costs (which, nowadays, are the greater part of the investment) we do not always seem quite so ready to adjust ourselves to the true economic values of the opportunities open.

Seizing Opportunities

Finally, as a contrast to the comments about the caution which prevents the momentum of computer development becoming a headlong rush, something needs to be said about the occasions when positive advance is achieved through the seizing of opportunities. While a true 'systems' approach to the provision of business information is comparatively rare and the practical application of computers a long way short of the theoretical, there is, nonetheless, a great degree of innovation in information systems which probably owes as much to opportunistic decisions as to deliberate intent. In chapter 13, where the economies of computer systems are examined, reference is made to intangible benefits of computer systems which may not be anticipated at the time an investment decision is made. Most unexpected benefits of computer systems may be as seemingly modest as the examples given, but chance has made a moderate computer investment into a highly profitable one and may well tilt an industry in a completely new direction.

Check List 11

Computer Applications in Business

Cement Manufacture
  Order processing.
  Sales accounting.
  Sales analysis.
  Purchases accounting.
  Payroll.
  Production cost analysis.
  Stock control.
  Office communications.
  Production process control.

Electro-mechanical Assembly Manufacture
  Production management.
  Sales order processing and accounting.
  Sales promotion.
  General ledger accounting.
  Product mechanisms.

Builders Merchanting
  Order processing.
  Branch stock replenishment.
  Sales accounting and analysis.
  Warehouse stock records and replenishment.

Supermarket
  Point-of-sale sales recording.
  Branch stock control.
  Shelf labelling.

Department Store
  Electronic funds transfer.
  Credit control.

Airline
  Passenger check-in.

Electricity Distribution
  Distribution network monitoring and control.
  Customer billing enquiries.

Engineering Design
  Circuit design.

Advertising
  Telephone sales support.

Life Assurance
  Personal sales support.

Further Reading

Hirschheim, R., *Office Automation*, Addison-Wesley, 1984.
Kroeber, D. and Watson, H., *Computer-Based Information Systems*, Collier
  Macmillan, 2nd edn, 1986.
Lee, B., *Data Processing Methods*, Hutchinson, 1984.

12 Organisation of Computing

Computer Installations

The impact of computers on business organisation and management necessarily depends on the nature of the processes and techniques they supplant, and on the extent of change they bring. Between the contrasting extremes of a small personal microcomputer used to make a more efficient personal support tool, and a large computer system installed as part of a machine complex representing the principal capital resource around which the rest of the organisation is grouped, there is a wide variety of size and use of computers and allied machines. Because of this variety in a period of rapidly changing technology, it would be misleading to see business computer systems in any form of organisational stereotype. Situations can be found which mirror those of the first days of business computers 30 years ago, and which seem still to be wholly appropriate; one can also find very recent innovations which challenge most of today's concepts. The 'death' of the mainframe and of the data-processing department have been threatened for some years but both are still thriving. All that can be said for certain is that the computer industry as a whole is in a state of thriving ferment and that it will continue to change.

The Computer Centre

Business computer installations, for the most part, started in accounting departments where they superseded punched card installations or keyboard accounting machines (with their facilities for typing, calculating and limited data editing) to handle Payroll, Sales Ledger and other accounting applications. As computer use extended to other kinds of business application, commercial data processing ceased to be a purely accounting function and grew into a general service to business. The special skills required for computer system design, programming and operation led to the creation of new departmental structures to provide the general data processing facilities required, with the necessary level of skilled support. Sometimes computing would remain part of an administration or accounting function; in other organisations it became a major department in its own right. The growth of this central data processing service concept was also encouraged by the economics of computers which offered advantages from size, and by the technical facilities which opened up the possibility of integrating business systems. This combination of specialist skills, economies of scale and opportunities for system integration caused the Data Processing Department or Computer Centre to become established as one of the primary organisational elements in business.

The technical and economic arguments for this are no longer quite the same but general-purpose computers, providing services to all parts of an organisation, have continued to be predominant in business use and the concept of a data processing department embracing both operating and system planning functions is still representative of the typical medium to large business.

The effect of creating a centralised computer service, in system terms, is that the input and output (user) functions are organisationally separated from processing elements which, with essentially manual systems, would have been within the user department. Aside from the creation of a computer department as a new organisational unit, such changes have not otherwise noticeably distorted traditional organisational structures. Departments which have experienced a significant reduction in labour cost as a result of the introduction of computer systems may have become smaller in number of employees, but their responsibilities are not diminished because they have retained responsibility for the decisions and actions which come from the information system.

Major organisational changes to create centralised computer services did not always come about with ease, nor were problems arising from these changes always settled harmoniously. One difficulty inevitable with (open) business information systems is that they are affected by the systems with which they interface and, if such effects are harmful, operating problems may become disputes. A natural reaction to any mishap, failure or disaster is to seek to lay blame, usually elsewhere. The computer, especially in situations where there has been some resistance to change, is a natural target of blame. Being inanimate (which also is often little understood), it is even more readily blamed by managers or operatives seeking relief or excuse. Only where the computer service is impeccable do such frictions not arise and, since problems in computer installations are as much caused by human decision and action as problems in any other business activity, impeccable service is hard to find.

Although one may deplore any lack of objectivity, it must be recognised that the concept of acceptability applies to the computer installation as well as to the systems which it operates, and it is often found that user departments are ready to accept an opportunity to control their own computer facility in preference to taking a service from outside. When changes in computer industry technology and economics brought down the threshold for effective use of computer facilities, tolerable alternatives to centralised services became feasible; in consequence, there has been a tendency towards reversion to former organisational concepts, bringing computer facilities back within the user functions which they served.

There was a period when the supersession of the 'mainframe' — the large central computer concept — in favour of the 'mini' or 'micro' which would serve the user directly, was firmly predicted. It has been realised that that is nonsense and that there is scope for all sizes of computer facility, but the public view of computers currently is still influenced by the personal micro and the belief that everyone can now do his own data processing. The reality of business computing is that one may find large data processing centres providing universal services to all operating departments in some situations, independent departmental facilities in others, and combinations of the two in all kinds of 'distributed' and 'networked' computer facilities.

User-managed Installations

The attraction of a 'departmental' computer is not just a consequence of the introduction of cheap, powerful systems which can operate economically at relatively low levels of activity; there always have been situations where a departmental computer was more appropriate than computer facilities provided by a general data processing service. Many scientific and technical applications are in this category.

The extending range and versatility of equipment undoubtedly has opened up fresh possibilities for decentralisation of data processing and for special-purpose installations. It has brought computer power within the scope of much smaller organisations and much more varied applications; because of the changing relationship between falling costs of equipment and rising costs of system development and operation, it has also led to the erosion of arguments concerning specialisation which had caused the growth of central computer installation services. Special system consultancies and external software suppliers have offered alternatives to the use of an organisation's own specialists for design and programming. More powerful software facilities have been provided with the computer equipment, including programming and application tools which make it easier for the user to take responsibility for his own system development and computer operation. As a consequence, computers have become accepted by business undertakings in situations where there would be no justification or need for computer specialists. User managed and operated computer installations can now be found for control of industrial processes, as engineering and research tools, and in the management of commercial computer facilities for business administration.

Contract Computer Services

Although there is now much wider distribution of computer power and more decentralisation of responsibility for system development and operation, these changes have neither disposed of the specialist programming and operating functions nor made the computer system a simple matter which can be handled in all respects by the unskilled user. Some specialist functions may have been pushed back to the 'supply' side (bringing computers into line with most other kinds of business machine) but the user still has the problem of making essential judgements about what kind of business system shall be developed, how it will operate, and what equipment and software will best suit its purposes. The necessary knowledge and skill can be purchased from an expert consultant and, indeed, the entire computer facility can be obtained as an external service through a computer service bureau or under a facilities management contract. The computer is really not different in principle from other business services; all business undertakings are fully accustomed to situations where there is a choice of 'employing' or 'hiring'. One organisation will employ its own specialist, another will hire the services of the appropriate expert when the need arises; one organisation may run its own transport department, another will employ a haulage contractor. Neither approach is better; the choice should simply be a question of economics.

Information Service Concepts

In the computer world the economic arguments are dominated by the remarkable (and continuing) reduction in the cost of computer power. This reduction is such that the cost of expert advice and help is often so great in comparison that it has become a decisive element in the economics of smaller business and personal computer systems. If the prospective user of a small computer today finds it necessary to pay for special programs to be written, the system justification is almost certain to be imperilled because programming will cost so much more than the equipment. Where this leads users to buy equipment and packaged software cheaply without expert knowledge or advice, the consequence may be wasted expenditure, and that has been the destiny of a high proportion of personal microsystems. One solution offered to the problem of linking end user with expert without high cost within some of the larger businesses has been the concept of the Information Centre. It implies a recognition of the importance of information, of the need for professional expertise in the creation of systems and, at the same time, of the desirability of limiting user dependence on outside expertise for the development and running of those systems. In its relationship with user-managed small departmental or personal computer installations, or with user access to 'friendly', powerful, remote computer facilities, the information centre can, in theory, offer a source of expert advice in selecting and implementing applications as well as a means of providing system development or other technical or operational help in case of need.

The term 'information centre' has been applied also to the provision of a central database of corporate information to which end users have direct access and which they can analyse and edit to meet their needs, using software tools (such as the 'spread-sheet') available at local workstations.

The growth of this kind of 'end-user computing' may have been in place of some centralised facilities; generally it has either been a question of introducing computer facilities where none existed before in a small organisation, or a more appropriate distributed facility in a large organisation which complements the central service.

A consequence of the 'convergence' of computer and telecommunications technology is that the computer no longer needs to be physically separated from other systems. With appropriate supporting software, it is possible for a business to offer a general data processing service through a communication network and to link this with other central and distributed computer facilities within and outside the organisation. A logical organisational result of this trend has been to bring the management of telecommunications and computing operations together, to provide a general service facility but with the system development functions tending to move away. Thus the 'data processing department' might become an information technology department providing training, technical support and advice and system protection. The business analysts, application software specialists and staff supplying business system help to users might be organised separately, or found from external suppliers and consultants.

Organisation of IT Functions

Differences in size and use of computers and communications networks demand a wide variation in the approach to organisation of these functions, and it is becoming less appropriate to use the specialist computer department containing all planning and operating functions or the head office administrative services unit as typical examples (figure 44).

Nonetheless, all the functions that would have been found in a central computer or communications department must be carried out by one means or another, and need to be identified even though they may be shared between several organisations.

The principal functions are

- General management
- Production control
- Data management
- Machine operation
- Technical support
- System planning
- User support
- Communication services

Computer Management

Using a computer is an investment in new systems which could take years to bring from conception to fully profitable operation. Such computer system proposals should be treated as an important issue and be included in corporate

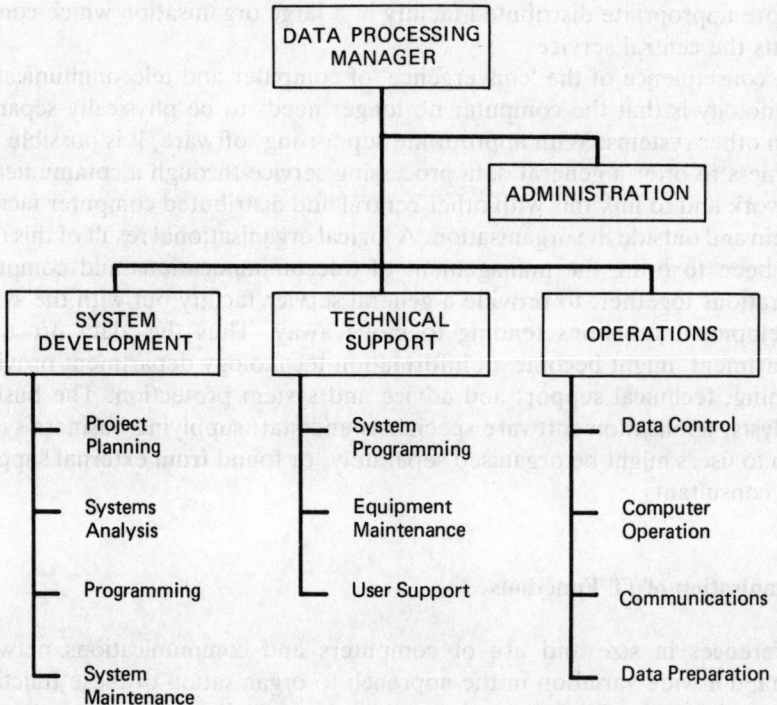

Figure 44   Computer department organisation

planning in the same way as any major proposal for employment of resources or change of business objectives. A computer installation is not a single, non-recurring investment; for a business with a fully developed computer facility, capital expenditure for replacement and enhancement will continue to be substantial, as will the revenue expenditure on operation and maintenance of systems. Figures such as an annual growth in computer investment of 20 per cent and annual expenditure equivalent to 2 per cent of turnover are typical under current conditions and are themselves growing rapidly. Furthermore, many IT applications involve more than one department or function and this also makes it desirable that there is involvement in computer matters at high management levels.

Where computer and communication services are provided as a combined facility and managed as a major department, this organisational status will give IT a voice at higher management level; with a 'user-orientated' approach, although having most responsibilities devolved away from the centre, the economic, organisational, and information considerations should make it no less desirable that higher management be involved. In business today, key management functions must be seen as extending beyond Sales, Production, or Administration to include Information Services; the key management decisions go beyond 'what to buy', 'what to make' and 'what to sell', to 'what information (and what information service) to provide'. It is not going too far to argue that if a new business organisation were to be created today, or an existing organisation completely restructured, then the foundation of that new organisation should be a network of information systems which would be provided by computer-based technology.

The corporate planning aspect of information management, being concerned essentially with policy and major objectives, is a question of looking upwards and outwards. Information technology management is also concerned with the direction and control of communication and computer functions — looking downwards through the organisational structure. In this sense it is like any other major business function, involving decisions about allocating and controlling the use of human and material resources, and about meeting output commitments and financial budgets. Each system within the responsibility of the information function will have some dependence on the performance of other systems feeding data to it; other systems will depend equally on its output. This latter aspect is one which has given computer management some special responsibility because computing is a true 'service' function in that its entire purpose is to serve other parts of the business. The importance of information being so great and the tolerance of any shortcoming in computer-based systems being so limited, it is essential to aim for and achieve a very high standard of performance. If one adds to this the earlier propositions that a computer system represents a large and long-term investment and that the process of changing systems is often fraught with difficulty, then the management skills required must be of a very high order.

Control of Computer Production

A computer is an information machine, and a computer installation can be seen as an information factory with data as raw material being processed to produce information as the finished product. As a factory, therefore, one essential function in a computer department would be the control of its production — work scheduling, machine loading, control of stocks of (data processing) materials — so as to ensure that resources are used efficiently and that customer (computer users) requirements are met at the proper time to the standard specified. In the earlier days of computers one could have found this function easily identifiable in the Computer Centre; the conventional elements of production control, including scheduling and preparation of job tickets and cost and performance analyses, were all primarily clerical functions. Today many of the former manual tasks associated with production control in computing have been replaced by machine facilities — Operating Systems and other software for allocation of resources and management of computer operations according to priorities given. Since many of the cost restraints which would have limited available machine capacity have been removed, there are also many situations where much of the problem of production control has been eliminated. Where capacity provided is sufficient for any authorised use on demand, there is no longer need for scheduling allocation; where there is contention for capacity, setting priorities is all that is needed of the operator. Cost and performance analysis can themselves be computer functions.

In the context of communication facilities which link computers and other machines to provide a multi-purpose information facility, the concept of the computer installation as a factory is too narrow. There may be sequential production processes but such an installation will also be used for large numbers of single transactions and messages, with numbers of different processing operations conducted at the same time. The 'product' of this installation is capacity in the same way that a public telephone service provides a facility which others can use as part of their own information system. There are still questions of production control to ensure that individual jobs are completed satisfactorily and that matters of contention between different users are resolved satisfactorily.

Production control, therefore, is no longer so much a question of allocating machine capacity as of making sure that facilities required are available, and that prompt and appropriate action is taken if anything goes wrong. However, there should be no doubt about the continuing importance of production management; 'interactive' systems, which depend absolutely on communication networks and continuous computer availability, require standards of performance very much higher than could be contemplated in almost any other 'factory' environment. Cheapness and reliability of equipment and sophistication of operating software are not enough to resolve all production problems. One can still find computer system failures caused by equipment or software defects, by inaccurate data or by human error. If output reports from a computer data processing system are late, if the response time on an interactive system to the computer terminal is slow, or if a communication link is broken, there is a production problem and there must be an organisation to deal with it.

Data Management

The first step usually registered in any information system operation is data preparation: the conversion of original data into a form and to a medium suitable for 'capture' by the input device. This could involve transcribing and encoding input data on to a suitable document and introducing various manual and machine checking routines so that it can be captured accurately and quickly through some kind of key-board or other data-entry terminal. The input device itself could be capable of accepting data in its original state with any encoding or validation as a computer function. Data might be prepared and captured at the point of origin, or as the function of a computer department at a central location. There has to be some means of ensuring that complete, accurate data does enter the system at the appropriate time for processing; because it is neither possible to ensure that data presented is always accurate nor to design systems which are totally impervious to corrupt data, there must also be some means of dealing with data problems. This may be through control features within the system or through 'reject' and 'queries' functions which interface the computer service and the system user, or the system user and the originator of data for processing.

In business information systems which handle substantial volumes of data, cost of data preparation and entry is likely to be a key factor in the financial viability of the installation. With each advance of technology it has become economic to transfer more input functions from people to machines (notably, by eliminating stages of data preparation and pushing back the point of data capture towards the transaction origin) but data input is still of critical importance — not least with the smallest business systems.

Data management is also concerned with data that is in the system. There must be a means of ensuring that all data input has been processed correctly, and there must be a protection for data which is held on computer files. Business systems which hold data files for interrogation by users, or which build up large numbers of records for production of periodic management and action reports, need management functions to ensure that data cannot be lost or corrupted, or that access to it cannot be obtained without authority. Much of this aspect of data management has become part of the programmed functions of computer systems; the 'database' concept of integrated computer files has assumed its present importance because of the software facilities developed to handle data management.

The database has become a central feature of many computer systems; business undertakings with substantial investment in such systems have found it necessary to create a special management function to look after the security of data, and to advise those concerned with its use or with the development of new systems requiring the database. This function of 'database administration' has become a key responsibility in large computer installations. If one considers the situation of a business organisation with millions of business records held on computer files which are used in information systems throughout the organisation and which are manipulated and stored under the control of large complex software modules, the need for some specialist data management function is understandable.

One point to consider is that items of data held on computer system files are now usually stored under the control of the computer programs. Automatic allocation of storage space undertaken by database management software systems means that, unlike manual filing systems, the user or computer operator does not know where an item of data is actually stored in the computer memory. To the layman that is often more alarming than it need be, but it does add point to the argument for proper technical management of computer system data.

Machine Operations

The operating function proper in an IT installation comprises direct control of computer equipment and of any machines and facilities for communications, data preparation and distribution of information output. Computer techniques have advanced from the position where it was always necessary for a specialist operator to load programs, files and new transaction data on to the computer before the job was run; now programs and files often may be stored permanently and transaction data fed in directly from points of origin. In a similar way, telephone exchanges have depended less and less on manned intervention, as have all the ancillary machines and facilities attached to information systems which have come under computer control. With such mode of use, the machine-operating function has tended to become less demanding. There are still many installations employing professional operators to handle magnetic storage units and to supervise printing machinery, as there are still manually operated telephone exchanges but, with the growing proportion of 'interactive' user-controlled systems, these operating functions have become semi-automatic or are devolved on to the (end-user) terminal operator. The remaining specialist operating functions may be limited to monitoring equipment performance and intervening in case of failure or other problems needing expert attention.

In small and medium sized business computer installations even this kind of support may not be needed; there may be no professional operator at all. A computer can be switched on in the morning, setting off a program-controlled checking and preparation process to make the system ready for user operation, and then be activated entirely from terminals. In the event of any problem which cannot be resolved by the user (with the help of programmed facilities available in the system), expert help would be sought from the supplier. This does not mean that small installations must necessarily operate at a lower standard of performance than large; suitable equipment and software, obtained from reputable suppliers and used competently by a sensible organisation, should mean that a cry for external help need not be raised as often as once a year.

The need for professional operation is partly a question of the way the information system has been put together and partly a function of its size and complexity. A dedicated installation which uses standard equipment and packaged software, or which has systems precisely tailored to a particular need, might run with very little professional attention indeed. A large installation (in terms of volumes of data, numbers of different applications, numbers of users, or numbers of units of computer equipment) is likely to require some elements of specialist operational control to monitor installation performance, and to provide means of communicating with users and of resolving problems whenever the need arises.

Brief reference has been made to the supervision of printing. Whether in a centralised or distributed mode of operation, printing is still a sizeable proportion of output in spite of the substantial growth in use of other kinds of information access device. Printing means mundane tasks such as paper-handling and report distribution, which are minor matters if only control reports and answers to *ad hoc* enquiries are involved; with large volume data processing activities, such as billing, the associated end processes of printing, separating, checking, folding, enveloping and despatch in a large installation continue to be comparable with a conventional factory situation. No doubt the need for printing much of this type of computer system output will diminish as alternative means of information distribution are exploited, but new techniques are also bringing new print applications. At two ends of the scale the extension of the computer into office systems and the application of the computer-controlled laser printer to direct mail and general printing must ensure the continued need for some level of attended operation.

Technical support

Technical support used to be the function of the supplier or else would be absorbed along with other installation responsibilities in the Operating, System Development or Management functions. It emerged as an important function in its own right because of the expansion in the number of different communications and computer hardware and software facilities an installation might use which, although bringing many new benefits, needed separate organisation of technical support to provide the necessary level of expertise. One of these support functions is the management of 'systems software' — the control of operating systems and the specification of computer job descriptions which allow software to manage control of computer jobs without operator intervention.

The joining of communications and computers, and the increase in numbers and types of machine, have caused relationships with suppliers to change in many large installations from dependence on a single source to use of products from a number of different suppliers. The judgements involved in making such selection, combined with the more frequent change of equipment facilities now considered desirable and the great increase in use of packaged software, have led many organisations to see a need to employ their own specialist technical advisers.

Maintenance of equipment is still largely a supplier function, although the need has declined more or less in proportion to the decline in cost of machines because reliability has improved. Demand for contract maintenance of software has expanded because so much more is used and, particularly, so much is purchased from external suppliers.

System Planning

When computer departments were created to manage large central installations, responsibility for system development was usually brought into the organisation because of its close relationship with computer operations, but it has never been essential that it should be so. The technical elements of system planning — equipment and software specification and programming — involve expertise which is obviously closely linked with machine aspects but the investigation of system problems, definition of the business system, its linking with other systems and its implementation extend to different, complementary skills.

The combination of skills required and the way they are brought together is necessarily dependent on the nature of the applications. One may find variations in approach from the provision of all the skills by external consultants and suppliers of packaged software products to the allocation of all development tasks to internally employed project teams of analysts and software specialists. Whatever the location and relationships of the participants in system planning, they will usually come together under some kind of project team management. Having said that, one must also remember that information system development is, of course, never finished in the sense that, once implemented, a system will then require maintenance until it is replaced. Such maintenance may be provided by own employees or on contract by external suppliers, as with equipment and software; it might, in the end, cost more than the original planning task.

User Support

The user is the customer of the IT installation, the participant in the planning of systems and, more and more, the operator of the equipment and the builder of the systems. Responsibility for computer-based systems has moved towards the end user because of the high costs of specialist skills (in contrast to the lowering costs of equipment) and because of the introduction of software facilities which can be managed by 'unskilled' users. Where user support as a defined installation function remains, as it will with a large installation, it will still include some element of the following

- General liaison with users on 'production' queries
- Resolving data errors
- Advice on systems and packaged application software
- Operator training
- Advice on feasibility and choice of system solutions.

The Information Centre concept mentioned earlier can be an extension of user support to a formalised service, offered particularly in support of personal and other user-managed systems. User support is one of the most important fuctions that the computer specialist can perform because the effectiveness of a computer operation ultimately depends upon the user being able to decide and act competently. It may be possible to buy software and hardware as completely packaged installation facilities but the judgements necessary to choose wisely and to get the best out of such facilities do need professional (as opposed to purely technical) advice.

The Information Technology Industry

The computer having become useful in almost any work situation, in association with almost any kind of machine, it is difficult to determine a generally acceptable boundary for the industry. Even a general definition of the industry as including those businesses which are wholly or substantially concerned with design, manufacture, distribution and operation of computer and communications equipment, software and systems not only takes in a very large number of business undertakings but also encompasses widely differing organisations which do not fit readily into precise categories. For convenience, the industry is described, briefly, in this section under the following headings

- Computer manufacturers
- Equipment distributors and dealers
- Software suppliers and consultants
- Component and ancillary equipment suppliers
- Communication services
- Other IT service undertakings.

Computer Manufacturers

The computer industry has tended to grow both through the expansion of established manufacturers and through the entry of new businesses which have set out to supply new computer markets. The greatest number of new entrants has been at the lower end of the market where manufacture of the micro-computer is often at the level of assembly of standard components. There are many hundreds of businesses concerned with small computer systems but the industry is dominated by manufacturers of larger systems, and there are probably no more than 20 of these which are of real economic significance. These large international businesses represent most of the world-wide supply of computer equipment and, of the 20, one is clearly of outstanding importance in every sense. It is not possible to give even the briefest meaningful description of the computer industry without a mention of International Business Machines. IBM is one of the largest business corporations in the world, and very substantially the largest in the computer industry. It provides more than half the sales of computers in nearly every country in which it operates; only in the United Kingdom, Japan, and a few other countries does IBM not have a majority of the local market.

IBM and ICL (the two largest suppliers to the United Kingdom market) and some of the other leading names in business data processing have evolved from earlier roles as manufacturers of punched cards, key-board accounting machines and other types of business machine to become manufacturers and suppliers of general-purpose business computers. They offer to meet most business needs for computer equipment and software but their true significance in the market is really their relationship with customers as providers of computer solutions to business problems, rather than simply as manufacturers of equipment. It has been argued that the strength of IBM comes from its recognition that true needs are not for computers but for the benefits that they can bring, and its marketing policy has been directed rather to sell its services than to argue the technical merit of its products.

Not all the large manufacturers of computers are of this type; there are other major suppliers whose origins are in engineering, such as the Digital Equipment Corporation which developed primarily as innovators in computer technology, supplying specialised equipment for engineering and other technical applications, and Fujitsu, which is an example of the more broadly based Japanese manufacturers who are extremely influential in many aspects of electronics. These companies are typical of manufacturers which have expanded rapidly in new markets and which (with a number of the second-rank suppliers) have secured leading positions in particular segments of the computer market.

Equipment Distributors and Dealers

As with most industries, the computer manufacturer has a choice between selling equipment directly to the ultimate customer through his own (retail) selling organisation or through an intermediary organisation of some kind. Generally speaking, business machine companies started by selling equipment with software and system advice directly to users (and, for most of their sales, still do) while the manufacturer for the 'technical' market sold directly where only the machine was required, or through distributors where additional equipment, software or service was needed.

The practice of selling through distributive outlets was predominant from the outset with the personal microcomputer which can be purchased by the ultimate customer from computer service specialists, from retail suppliers of office equipment and domestic electrical products, and from toy shops. 'Wholesale' distribution for microcomputers and other small business systems has now extended to the larger manufacturers (including IBM). This change is a logical consequence of the evolution of the business computer into a packaged product which can be installed and operated by customers without close technical supervision. An additional cause is that selling prices for this kind of equipment are so low that the manufacturer is left no margin for expensive and elaborate direct selling in small numbers. Reduction in manufacturing costs also has made it progressively more difficult for a manufacturer to operate comfortably purely as a supplier of 'hardware', except where the scale of manufacture is very large.

The manufacture and sale of personal microcomputers started as a section of the computer industry separate from the general business market because unit cost of equipment was so very low and also because the principal sales were to 'hobby' rather than to 'business' customers. At this lowest end of the price range, some microcomputer systems are sold for business uses (such as education) but the great majority of the very high volume of sales is truly for personal entertainment. The conventional marketing approach for domestic consumer goods of using television and other media advertising to create demand which is then satisfied through retail outlets meets the needs of personal customers, albeit in an unstable, fiercely competitive market but, for the potential business user of microsystems, it will not do.

The business customer requires expert advice and the product purchase decision for software must come before that for equipment. The microcomputer started to attract business users partly when it moved closer to the mainstream of computing facilities in technical terms but principally when appropriate software became available. Remembering that the real cost to a business of a personal microcomputer is primarily the operator's labour and secondly the software, the prospective business user would find that a low price for equipment without system advice or software support — which was all that the typical retail dealer could offer — was not satisfactory. The prudent purchaser would choose the (initially) more expensive path of seeking the kind of comprehensive service available for larger systems. One source of this service is the 'software house'.

Software Houses and Consultancies

The many types and size of business to be considered under this heading are not confined to the personal microsystems market; they extend right through the range of computer size and application. They include individuals who sell their own services directly or through other consultancies, and international businesses with sales income greater than that of many computer manufacturers. Some are independent; some, including many of the larger ones, are associated with other businesses in the computer industry or with large industrial corporations. The range of services offered varies widely. The professional consultant sells advisory services, embracing functions similar to those undertaken by the internal business computer system analyst, such as feasibility studies and preparation of system proposals; software and equipment will be left to recommended suppliers. The specialist software house may be more closely comparable with the equipment manufacturer, designing and selling software products directly or through other outlets. There are also many businesses under the software house and consultancy labels which aim to offer the business user a comprehensive service — a complete business solution including systems advice, software and equipment, which may include many machine elements other than computers.

The software houses, as designers and suppliers of packaged or tailored software, and as 'turnkey' suppliers of complete equipment and software solutions (with which all the customer has to do to use them is 'turn the key') have been taking an increasing share of the computer market. Part of this growth has been due to the need for an expert intermediary between the manufacturer and the supplier of small business systems and part to the increasing attractions for end users of 'buying in' system development resources for particular projects. Buying these professional services has been found to be a more economic course than to recruit, train and manage 'in-house' system teams whose services were not likely to be required at the same level after system implementation.

Some of the most successful have been specialist system houses which, having acquired some expertise and reputation in a particular industry or application, are able to offer customers in that industry better, lower-cost solutions to systems problems than they could provide themselves. This approach is being adopted wherever the number of potential customers justifies development of application-specific solutions or where the solution is both complex and specialised. Examples include monitoring systems for electricity distribution, 'command and control' systems for police or ambulance services, data management systems for libraries, banks, building societies and hospitals, and systems for automated plant operation.

Component and Ancillary Equipment Suppliers

As in many industries, the names of major manufacturers which symbolise the IT industry are the centre of a large and complex structure of ancillary businesses including many suppliers of electronic components, storage, printing and other devices and machines (including complete computer systems) with which the manufacturer's concern may only have been the design specification and the marketing. The electronics industry which, for a brief period, held the major share of the business computer market, is still involved in a very substantial way through the provision of components from which computer and communications facilities are created. For the most part, basic components such as integrated circuits are bought from other suppliers by computer manufacturers, and most of the manufacture of microsystems is a question of assembling other suppliers' components. Specialisation in manufacture of the peripheral units necessary to a business computer system has also produced benefits in technological advance and economies in scale of manufacture, such that a large proportion of peripheral devices like visual display units, printers and magnetic stores are common to a number of computer products. The largest scale at which these engineering suppliers operate is in the substitution of complete systems: the 'plug compatible' devices which ape IBM products, offering better performance at lower price to tempt computer users who are committed to IBM software but are willing to use some other supplier's equipment if it be compatible.

Around the fringes of markets created by the primary businesses, too, are many other businesses of varying size which depend on them — suppliers of furniture and of 'consumables' such as stationery, flexible discs and technical literature.

Communications

The communications and computer industries have been moving closer both in technology and in application. The telephone exchange and Telex terminal are now as much computer-based machines as are business computers and their terminal facilities. There has been a difference between the industries because the provision of telecommunication services was in the hands of designated suppliers. Supporting these statutory telecommunications authorities have been manufacturing specialists of telecommunications equipment. With few suppliers and customers, the industry neither fully reflected market requirements nor technological possibilities until the convergence of computer, communications and other information technology brought these many elements together and, with it, a liberalisation of policy related to telecommunication services. For the most part, provision of the telecommunication service itself remains in designated hands for obvious economic and social reasons, while the range of facilities offered is now much wider than the original speech and telegraph and there are new kinds of service using these facilities which are attracting new entrants. This is the area of 'value-added' services which involve sale of information through the medium of the telecommunications network. Expansion of telecommunications into computer data transmission and electronic mail has opened new opportunities whereby organisations other than the telecommunications authority now use the public service networks to provide information services — the 'value-added' element of information superimposed upon the data transmission costs. Value-added networks (VANs) are being introduced for many kinds of specialist information service, linking suppliers and users with common interests in industries such as insurance, retail groceries, pharmaceuticals and banking. There is no doubt that such information services, whether provided by consortia of information users or by professional third party organisations with special skills in telecommunications, are bound to grow substantially.

The manufacturers and suppliers of equipment and cables for telecommunications have been predominantly general electrical manufacturers or specialist manufacturers for the telecommunications market and, until the closer association of computers and communications, had been only marginally concerned with the computer industry itself. The changing character of telecommunications has both altered the nature of the products (from electromechanical to electronic) and caused a rapid expansion in the size of the industry through a combination of increased total demand and specific requirements for many new types of terminal and control device to attach to communications networks. It is becoming more appropriate to see the communications and computer supply industries as the information technology industry because the boundaries are sufficiently blurred that differences are now at the level of the individual firm rather than of any industry segment.

Other IT Services

Aside from the general consultancy and software services, the largest elements of the growing support service side of the information technology industry are

- Computer service bureaux
- Facilities management services
- Third party maintenance
- Education and training
- Recruitment services

One group of existing businesses in the computer industry which has been moving into the value-added market has been the Computer Service Bureaux, which have found their original businesses declining from earlier heights because the thresholds for justification of 'in-house' computer facilities have fallen as computer systems have become cheaper and easier to manage. The bureau does still have a place in the computer industry, notably in the provision of computer services which are required by users on an *ad hoc* or infrequent basis that is insufficient to justify the cost of owning a computer installation. This might be for occasional complex calculations which demand very substantial computer power, for regular services such as payroll which an expert specialist supplier can offer at a lower price and higher standard by serving many customers, or in situations where the services provided are the bureau skill and software rather than equipment capacity.

Expertise in managing computer operations has a value, just as do skills in system development; the 'facilities mangagement' service, whereby a complete working installation is provided by outside specialists, may be used in the same way as a business might employ a specialist transport contractor.

As with equipment and software, the computer service category also has a large number of lower-level supporting services, including technical services for maintenance of equipment, the supply of professional staff such as programmers or operators on short-term contract, and the provision of training services through the supply of materials or the running of courses and seminars.

Check List 12

The computer has ceased to be physically separated from other systems by the need to translate data into computer-compatible information for input. The joining of communication facilities to computer systems and the development of supporting software have made it possible to provide general data processing facilities at the centre of communication networks and to link general and specialist computer facilities within and beyond organisation boundaries for transmission and processing of data.

Types of Computer Installation
Computer centres — data processing departments.
User-managed — departmental installations,
Contract services.
Information centres.

Computer Functional Organisation
Management and administration.
Production control — operating system management.
Data management — database administration.
Machine operations — computers and communications.
Technical support — software and hardware advice and maintenance.
System planning and software development.
User support — liaison, training, technical guidance.

The Information Technology Industry
Computer manufacturers — IBM.
Equipment distributors and dealers.
Software houses and consultancies, turnkey suppliers.
Component and ancillary equipment suppliers, plug compatibles.
Communication equipment and services, value-added services.
Computer bureaux, and facilities management.
Maintenance.
Education and training.
Staff supply and recruitment.

Further Reading

Awad, E., *Introduction to Computers*, Prentice-Hall, 1983.
Oliver, E. C. and Chapman, R. J., *Data Processing, An Instructional Manual*,
    D.P. Publications, 6th edn, 1983.
Silver, G. and Silver J., *Data Processing for Business*, Harcourt Brace, 1981.
Zorkoczy, P., *Information Technology — An Introduction*, Pitman, 1985.

13 Economics of Computer-Based Information Systems

Although it is usually a requirement that computer systems be justified at the proposal stage on cost grounds, savings are not necessarily the main reason for deciding to introduce a computer, nor the sole criterion for cost effectiveness. Where a computer project is likely to involve substantial financial commitment, it is proper that it be subjected to evaluation against normal investment appraisal criteria and that the proposal be rejected unless there is a prospect of acceptable risk and reasonable return. To make a financial appraisal, it is necessary that some value be placed on the costs and benefits expected throughout the life of the system. However, there is often a special difficulty with computer-based information systems in that cost and (particularly) benefits cannot be quantified with any accuracy. There always will be some elements susceptible to subjective evaluation which tend to be interpreted more favourably at the proposal stage than proves justifiable in the outcome. For the system analyst there is the personal risk that a desire to 'sell' a computer project may overcome professional objectivity in evaluating imponderables; for the computer project there is the certainty that, of these imponderables, it is the unfavourable factors which will always be felt.

Nevertheless, although it may be said that the initial impact of computer projects often fails to match financial expectations, it is also a fair generalisation that the typical computer installation tends to show a steady improvement in cost effectiveness during its life, often in unexpected areas such that the viability and then the indispensibility of the installation usually become firmly established. If the first computer installation is sometimes a financial disappointment, the second should really pay its way.

Reasons for Introducing Computer Technology

Financial justification for computer applications is now much easier than it was because of changing economics and because of the experience acquired by so many businesses which have made use of computers over the last thirty years. There is much more readiness to recognise the many important arguments for computer-based systems other than the achievement of new, tangible financial savings.

The argument for computer-based systems should not be seen in simplified financial terms unless these are actually contained in the business objective. The ultimate reason for employing any kind of technology should be to further the business objectives: to assist survival, expansion, profitability or other objective by enabling the organisation to make more effective use of its resources. This may well be capable of interpretation in financial terms but the introduction of new machine systems in place of manual or other less advanced machine systems can achieve results in ways other than through direct reduction in operating cost. In furtherance of business objectives any one of the following reasons may be advanced for introducing computer technology

- To save money
- To save time
- To improve data management
- To improve information for decision-making
- To increase revenue
- To improve the competitive position
- To allow expansion
- To remedy system defects
- For emotional reasons.

Substitution of machine for manual operation is one potential source of financial saving through reduction of direct labour costs in such applications as office clerical tasks, the automatic control of machine tools, the monitoring and control of industrial processes, and personal support in selling and customer services. Direct savings also may apply to other kinds of resource, such as greater efficiency in the use of energy, reduction in stocks, or reduction in requirements for working capital.

A computer may be designed to process data at the rate of 20 million instructions per second or more, and one of the prime characteristics of computer-based information systems is the potential ability to produce information at a faster rate than can be achieved by other means. This saving in time can be a very powerful argument for a computer solution; it can permit tasks to be performed which were not possible before, or indirectly bring improved revenue because customer satisfaction is increased, or permit operation at reduced costs because there are fewer complaints or special problems to be handled. In the processing of sales transactions, faster production of bills may result in earlier receipt of cash, thus saving the cost of working capital. Saving time in the production of management information may enable managers to take decisions more promptly, either to resolve problems or to seize opportunities which may bring more tangible benefits.

Improvement of accuracy and control in the management of data, another of the factors taken into account in system design, is also a potential source of major benefit from a computer-based system because machine systems can be designed to sustain a higher level of accuracy in operation than can any human being. This demonstrates itself in relation to all other kinds of manual task. The computer-controlled robot is not just a potential means of reducing labour cost; it can offer an improved standard of performance. With the right system design, the human failings of fatigue, forgetfulness, carelessness or lack of skill can be replaced by a uniformly high standard in repetitive, routine situations and by effectively better judgement in decisions based upon experience. Human experience is not always applied objectively, whereas a computer database cannot deviate from its determined logical path.

The ability to produce better business information in general is an increasingly plausible argument for introducing computer technology. A business decision may be based on inadequate information because full information would have been too costly, or have taken too long to produce. Any of the information system requirements found in typical business planning or operating situations, whether to analyse existing data with thoroughness, to explore possible consequences of a range of hypotheses or to focus attention on matters of significance, might be better met by a computer information system; it can even make possible the production of information which simply could not be contemplated before. Rapid digestion of masses of 'raw' data, easy application of scientific method to achieve a balanced conclusion, or simply the ability to transmit an item of information to the right place at the right time, can make a radical improvement in the running of a business activity, open the possibility of anticipating future events, or scale down the risk attaching to a business venture.

Increased revenue may come as an indirect result of time-saving, better accuracy or fuller information. It may be the direct consequence of an operation which creates a new product (such as a computer-based information service) or which improves the sales potential of existing products (as with direct mail or point-of-sale systems). It may improve the performance of sales representatives by helping to eliminate waste of time or by making the sales presentation more attractive. From another angle, any of these system improvements may be seen to result in revenue gain by generally improving competitive position as opposed to improving industrial sales performance. Competitive position might also benefit from service improvements, as with systems which facilitate customer transactions outside normal hours or at distant locations, or which deal more effectively with queries and complaints.

It is also a valid aim to help a business expand without proportionate rises in cost. This is probably a more common experience than direct cost reduction because introduction of a new computer system is very often the prelude to or coincident with a period of expansion. It is at such times that existing systems show their weakness; expansion beyond normal capacity may result in system failures or disproportionate increases in cost. Ability to lift the optimum size of a system or an organisation as a result of the introduction of computer techniques has been demonstrated in such differing situations as booking systems, control of traffic and production processes, and even in the management of computer systems themselves.

The economic arguments are not always constant; business users are less excited than they used to be by the proposition that the computer never seeks a rise in pay, but there are always other reasons why the marginal costs of expanding a computer-based system are likely to be relatively small. The cost of system development (including the specification and assembly of software) is not directly proportional to the volume of transactions handled nor is the demand on equipment capacity. A proposal for system development which implies a substantial degree of change must be designed to provide some spare capacity or flexibility to provide room for economical expansion in case of need; if this expansion occurs, the system can then absorb it economically. Remembering, too, an earlier axiom that the use of computers tends to improve, it is likely to be found that adding new applications to an existing installation is proportionately less costly than the initial investment.

From a negative viewpoint the introduction of information technology may be seen as a means of remedying defects in an existing system. Although a business which is properly managed to meet its objectives will be constantly seeking better ways of operating its systems, the reality for many organisations is that they react under pressure of events. For such businesses, development of new systems is likely to be a response to weaknesses or deficiencies which have been identified in current systems, and which are now beginning to threaten the achievement of important objectives. This is in itself a perfectly valid justification but it does also hold the danger that a new system arising out of such necessity may well be out-of-date very soon because it is fixed on present needs and problems rather than related carefully to future requirements.

The reason for introducing computer technology as a part of the general business environment, such as the creation of a general communications or office automation infrastructure, could be a deliberate response to an identified need or an opportunistic decision resulting from some larger change, or it could be associated with a general policy of renovating the fabric of the business — the kind of policy decision which should normally come out of a long-term corporate plan. There is no doubt that one of the essentials for business prosperity is the ability to look beyond the current condition of the business, including any pointers to the possible need for system change, to a situation where some new approach may be needed, or some better way be opened. With information technology this will be a relatively bold decision where such systems are not commonplace, because there is no doubt that complex computer and communications services must require a longer period of development to optimum efficiency than any system which operates over a narrower and more clearly defined area. A project for the development of a communications infrastructure to serve a complete business location is clearly one which would be taken as part of a strategic policy, on which specific information systems will be constructed with more precise objectives in mind.

One aspect of human behaviour must not be forgotten in considering reasons for introducing a computer: the decision may not be based on economics or any other objective assessment but primarily on emotion. Just as competing businesses ape each other in their products and promotional campaigns, fearful lest the other be right, so those concerned with developing information systems or making decisions about the use of business machines may be as much influenced by the actions of competitors and rivals as they are by the logic of any independent evaluation of their needs. Decisions are also influenced by the marketing activities of suppliers of computer equipment and software, who certainly may be expected to have no intention of allowing potential customers to remain complacent about their existing systems once a 'bridgehead' sales argument has been established with a new product or in a new industry application.

Elements of Cost

Whatever reason is advanced for proposing to introduce information technology, and whether or not that differs from any subsequent justification for its installation, the business user cannot escape the economic implications of a computer project. As has been said, in the design of any kind of new system cost must be a factor — if not dominant, then certainly acting as a constraint — and this clearly must apply to any system using computers or communications equipment. The expected costs and benefits of a computer proposal must be evaluated, as far as is possible; they must be monitored carefully and ultimate actual results reconciled with projections if there is to be any chance of securing sensible control over the progress of the project and in ensuring the achievement of the original objectives. Even with the least cost-sensitive project it is essential to be aware of the cost elements which have to be taken into account, and these are now examined under six convenient headings

- Planning
- Capital investment
- System operation
- System maintenance
- Change of system
- Profitability.

Planning

System planning, from the study of feasibility through system design to implementation, can add up to a substantial part of the total system cost; moreover, it is a cost which will be incurred before the system brings any return. Development cost is mainly the cost of people; software is largely the product of people's time. Apart from analysts, programmers and other planning specialists wholly engaged on the project, there is the time of the people concerned with running the present system, and of those who will be running the new system. If professional services are brought in, the planning cost is still incurred but appears as purchase items rather than on payroll. Planning involves equipment costs, too; computer facilities will be used for testing and proving new systems as well as for training and operational experience until new procedures are fully operational.

Capital Investment

Since IT systems and software function as revenue-producing assets, it may be considered appropriate to treat them in accounting terms as capital items, although it is rather more difficult to evaluate their cost and depreciation than it is with tangible assets such as machines. There is no real difference in nature between the cost of a set of programs which have been paid for through the labour of employees who have written them and the cost of an equivalent packaged software module which has been purchased from an outside supplier in the same way as one might buy a piece of equipment. The comparison with machines as capital items is even closer when one recognises that an item of computer equipment often contains computer program elements which are sold as integral parts of the 'hardware' deal. Whether or not a financial distinction is drawn between planning activities and acquisition of revenue-earning assets, expenditure on the machine facilities and their environment is clearly a capital investment, and a business will expect to spread its costs over the life of the system whether the equipment is financed by outright purchase, through leasing or rental.

There needs to be provision for accommodation of the 'hardware' (computer equipment, communication facilities and other machines which make up the installation), including items such as power supplies, environmental control, security systems, and the furniture for operating and supporting staff. Information technology equipment makes less demand on space and environmental conditions than in the past, but there are still many applications (notably for integrated systems) where special accommodation has to be created or adapted at high cost.

System Operation

The costs of operating include the actual or proportionate share of the cost of all elements of running the system, including any data preparation, the operation of the computer and communications equipment, the control and handling of output, and the resolution of data problems and various supporting facilities. These costs are made up of direct and indirect labour salaries and overheads, consumables such as tapes, flexible discs and stationery, line costs for communication systems, maintenance of the operating environment and power consumption. Equipment in the installation requires maintenance and repair which is usually provided through contractual arrangements with the supplier at a fixed annual charge or on a 'time and materials' basis.

Systems Maintenance

Just as the facilities which the system uses must be maintained, so must the system itself, represented by the investment in systems design and software. General information facilities such as a communications network might run for some time without the need for system attention, but business systems for data processing and information retrieval are unlikely to be able to function efficiently for long without frequent intervention for maintenance. Apart from the necessity to provide for repair (in the way that hardware performance must be supported), most business systems are likely to undergo continuous modification and development through their life as requirements change and as experience shows how the systems may be improved. Maintenance costs obviously must vary with the type of support required but a typical annual contract charge for maintaining a packaged software module would be around 10 per cent of its original cost, similar to that which has been applicable for equipment maintenance. An organisation undertaking its own system development must expect to have to allocate at least equivalent resources.

Change of Systems

Although it is not always the largest element, the cost of change is usually substantial; it is frequently ignored, despite the apprehension frequently engendered by the very considerable differences in organisation and procedures, and the individual job skills often required by a computer system. It is an unavoidable hazard of system change that the first effect is a loss of efficiency; knowledge and experience are essential ingredients in human competence, whether the activity is manual or intellectual, and a change in system must always have some disruptive effect. Apart from disturbance to existing activities leading up to the point of 'cut-over' to a new system, there follows a period of learning during which people have to adapt to new tasks and, through training and experience, become proficient. This loss of personal efficiency has been indicated as one reason for a tendency to resist change. People who are judged to be efficient in their existing jobs may give the appearance of incompetence if moved suddenly into an unfamiliar environment. The learning curve from the point of change to the plateau of 'normal' efficiency may be shallow or steep, depending upon the nature of the change and the care given to retraining, but there always will be some effect which must show itself through a simultaneous loss of efficiency and increase in workload.

System change is not only a matter of 'changing horses in mid-stream'; apart from the work of those involved directly in planning a new system, the process of implementation itself imposes additional tasks. Setting up new files involves the transfer of data from different media, with checking and reconciliation necessary to ensure that the new system is not burdened by errors at the outset. This can be an expensive process where large files are involved and may be beyond the capacity of the organisation to handle without outside aid.

Alterations to accommodation for new system facilities, and preparation of procedural instructions and operational documents, training and trials, all add items of cost. It may also be that the need to ensure a smooth changeover rules out any question of an abrupt change from the old to the new. Extended testing, 'prototyping' and parallel running might be considered necessary to ensure that the old system is not abandoned until the new system clearly meets all requirements. There will be few organisations with such spare capacity that the extra work-load involved in overlapping old and new systems can be absorbed without added cost and convenience.

Profitability

An improvement in profitability may be a deliberate objective or a fortuitous result of introducing an IT system; whatever account may be taken of results in full operation, profitability must also be seen from the cost angle because there is likely to be some negative effect until normal efficiency is reached. The consequences of change discussed in the preceding paragraphs have some effect on profitability because they increase costs with no likelihood of compensating increases in revenue at that time. Hidden elements may have some effect on profitability — notably those which can depress revenue. An interruption to production to permit a change in the system to be carried through, or a reduction in output as a result of temporary loss of efficiency, may affect both costs and revenue. A move to new premises or a delay in billing are examples of situations where cost must be measured in terms both of resources used and of revenue lost.

The cost of money may be a crucial element. Increased need for working capital as a consequence of delays in billing or production is one aspect; there is also the question of the return on capital invested. The judgement about what constitutes a reasonable rate of return will vary from business to business and from time to time but some investment-return criterion needs to be set, against which the expected net return from the project can be compared. Comparison must be either with the cost of borrowing funds used to finance the project, or with the return which might have been received if funds available had been used for a different investment.

Assessments of Costs and Benefits

Some assessment of likely costs and savings is needed at a very early stage in the planning of a computer-based system and, by the time the proposal has been adopted, there must have been a careful evaluation of all the financial elements. In that planning estimates will be based on the theoretical system and must include projections extending over its expected life cycle, there is bound to be some element of subjectivity and margin for error at the beginning.

Where the plan is to buy a complete solution which is immediately available, a substantial part of the cost estimation can be made with some precision; it may be an attraction to accept a fixed price offer from an outside supplier rather than to rely on the uncertainties of time and cost estimates of using one's own resources. If a proposed system compares closely with existing computer applications, estimating can also be made with confidence; like any other project, the greater the speculation and uncertainty about the shape and impact of the new system, the greater the financial and physical risks. It would be too sweeping a generalisation to say that the typical computer-based information system is always uniquely complex, but there is no doubt that few are absolutely predictable. One virtue of a well-designed computer system is being adaptable to unexpected change in system requirements, which is itself an indication of the difficulty in anticipating financial influences on a system in operation.

Financial appraisal of any investment which seeks a return over a period of years must take account of such questions as possible changes in the cost or value of money, and thus of the possible prices of resources likely to be required during the investment period. If the physical circumstances in which a system operates differ from those at the time of planning, it may be very difficult to know whether or not the original forecasts were reasonable. If there are larger transaction volumes than expected or changes in operating requirements and in interfaces with other systems, any evaluation may not be comparing 'like with like'.

Theoretical appraisal of planning and operating costs often assumes that a computer system is somehow to be physically separated from other systems so that clear estimates of cost can be applied to it. In practice, if one considers a typical business operation which uses computer facilities, a number of different information systems will be found to share common resources such as computer and communications equipment and operating software. Transaction data may be common to a number of systems also.

Appraisal of benefits can be equally taxing. To apply some financial value to better information when this is offered as justification for a computer system, it is necessary to make assumptions about how the information is to be used and what the consequences will be. In reality, information may be misused or used in a different (and possibly better) way. Chance may lead to the discovery that information available from the system is much more valuable than had been thought.

In the face of such uncertainties, the system analyst, accountant or user manager may tend to avoid placing an absolute value on such things and instead make assumptions — such as deciding that the computer project will be viable if it produces an x per cent increase in revenue or a y per cent decrease in losses. In the event, there may be sufficient evidence of tangible costs and benefits to provide sufficient confidence in the scheme as a whole without considering the imponderables.

One argument which relieves the uncertainties of projects related to information systems to some extent is that they will be capable of modification to improve economics if they are sensibly planned. A computer system should become steadily more valuable throughout its life; those concerned with its operation can become more proficient, defects and weaknesses in the system can be eliminated, useful enhancements may be added at low marginal cost and fresh uses for information available in the system may be discovered.

System Failure

This is not to say that a computer-based system cannot lead in the opposite direction — to a disaster. While there is now less concern about problems of high capital costs and relative inflexibility of equipment and software which were an unavoidable aspect of earlier computers, the ability to develop highly complex networks and integrated systems for 'real-time' operation do offer the temptation to embark on high-cost, high-risk projects which may have a material effect on the success or failure of the business as a whole. More and more, business organisation structures and business undertakings themselves are being designed round computer-based information systems. Any failure of design or operation might terminate business operations or impose unbearably heavy penalties.

Three essential criteria for cost-effective systems in general are that, apart from meeting the business objectives identified at the outset, they should have the virtues of reliability, simplicity and flexibility. In computer terms this means that no failure should have any material effect upon the physical or economic performance of the system, that it should be easy to manage and not be over-sensitive to other system deficiencies or otherwise difficult to operate at optimum level and that, if affected by any external change, it could be adapted quickly to the new circumstances. In the context of such problems as industrial unrest, when dependence on a computer offers easy opportunities for those wishing to exert pressure on business management, the logic of putting all computer eggs in one basket is open to question.

It is also relevant to consider the implications of compatibility with its environment as applied to computer systems. In theory, dedicated systems for automatic monitoring and control usually pose inherently easier design tasks for the system analyst than information systems which have to handle very varied data and processing requirements. When one considers that these kinds of automatic system depend on collecting data with precise accuracy from engineering plant, machines or vehicles in all kinds of operating conditions, it may be realised that the physical problem of capturing that data with certainty can be much more difficult and intractable than it would be for a system which operated in a protected electronic environment. It is difficult enough to have reliable communications in a system for controlling a model railway, let alone for wagons in a grimy marshalling yard.

A direct cause of failure of a computer-based information system can be an insoluble technical problem, but this is becoming comparatively rare outside the category of specially designed automatic systems. With the general range of business systems, the main cause can usually be found under one of four heads

- Excess cost
- Time over-run
- Shortfall of capacity
- Deficiency in output.

A system may exceed its estimated costs so that it will never become economically viable, but failure causing abandonment of the system is likely to relate to continuing costs which could be avoided rather than to expenses which have already been incurred. Time over-run can occur both during the planning process and in the actual operation of the system, and either might be decisive. Bringing the new system into production might be so delayed because of planning problems that further work on system development is abandoned. In production, if the system does not meet specified time criteria and is producing output responses or reports too late for useful action and without possibility of remedy, then a fundamental purpose of the system will be frustrated.

Shortfall of capacity is a common consequence of over-optimism about system performance, underestimation of data volumes, or simply of unwise choice of the cheapest solution. No doubt there are bargains to be had in the world of computers, and some equipment and software may offer better value than others; on balance the potential user of computer facilities is wiser to assume until proved otherwise that price does reflect performance characteristics when choosing a computer. Capacity shortage as a cause of total failure should be comparatively rare these days since there is usually the means of adding capacity. The situation in which such failure is likely to be irredeemable is one associated with highly specialised machinery or software which has been designed and manufactured to order for a system demanding rigid adherence to performance standards.

If a computer system does fail or does not produce the anticipated benefits one cannot say that the fault must lie with the equipment, or with the suppliers, or upon unavoidable consequences of God or Government. The first place to look for fault is in planning. Planning cannot make it possible to measure precisely all the influences and consequences but it should provide the means to identify potential hazards and evaluate alternative courses of action. It should also make it possible to progress towards system improvement with confidence, because each step has been selected with care. Good computer systems which produce the best economic results are those which have been planned to professional standards with professional skill. Planning is a management function and this responsibility is not in any sense separate from that of evaluating other proposals. A manager who commits himself to a project which fails has himself failed somewhere in judgement.

Check List 13

The ultimate reason for using any kind of business machine should be to further the objectives of the organisation: to assist survival, expansion, profitability etc. by enabling the organisation to make effective use of its resources.

Reasons for Introducing Computer Technology
  To save time and money
  To improve information handling and provision.
  To increase revenue.
  To improve the competitive position.
  For expansion.
  To remedy existing system defects.
  For emotional reasons.

Elements of Cost
  Planning — specialists, users and equipment use.
  Capital investment — machine facilities and their environment.
  Operations — installation management — labour, consumables, maintenance.
  System maintenance — system and software modification.
  Change of systems — testing, training, conversion.
  Profitability — efficiency loss, cost of money.

Criteria for Cost-effective Systems
  Meeting business objectives.
  Reliability.
  Simplicity.
  Flexibility.

Causes of Failure
  Bad planning.
  Cost and time over-run.
  Shortfall of capacity.
  Output deficiency.

Further Reading

Awad, E., *Introduction to Computers*, Prentice-Hall, 1983.
Silver, G. and Silver J., *Data Processing for Business*, Harcourt Brace, 1981.

14 System Development

Given that better business decisions need better information systems and that information technology has become a necessary means of bringing those improvements, the remaining question is, how can the transition to better systems be achieved? One cannot mutter "magic" in the dismissive manner of the amateur breed of managers who, baffled by the first computers, considered that any knowledge of information technology was somehow demeaning. Nor can one call round the corner and buy all that is needed, which amounts to the same thing. Neither those who think that their management decision to acquire a computer is the most difficult part of the project and that the remainder is the easy 'nitty gritty', nor those who are so daunted that they do not know where to start the exercise of system planning, have IT projects in proper perspective.

IT Development Strategy

If we were to concern ourselves only with the tasks and techniques involved in developing new computer-based information systems, then it would be convenient to start with the systems 'problem', whether the reference was to developing a new system where no computer system existed before or merely to the enhancement or modification of an existing computer-based facility. However, the potential applications of information technology are now such that the 'problem' can no longer be dealt with on the piecemeal basis of a specific function, system or organisational unit. It must be considered first at the level of the business itself; furthermore, whether or not it is a specific business problem which triggers the decision to consider system change, it now must be a function of management to ensure that there is an overall business information strategy. This strategy should take proper account of the implications of information technology both for the internal structure and activities of the business and for the possible external influences on the vital interests of the business.

The day-to-day reality of most business affairs will still be a preoccupation with system change at detailed levels and will not give the appearance of involvement in an IT 'revolution' but, because information has become the most important business resource, the concept of the communications 'infrastructure' and the possibility that information technology can bring change in any aspect of systems, organisation or objectives make it an urgent necessity for any business which has not done so to examine itself totally in information terms.

Before the advent of the computer, the most expensive business machine was probably the telephone exchange. There is much merit in the argument that the telephone exchange, if not the most expensive, is still the most important business machine and a proper IT strategy should start with an intention to ensure that it is capable of handling all the IT requirements whether of voice, image, data or text. The strategy should also determine the extent to which computer-based information systems might be applied and the potential organisational and technical relationships between them. Because such an examination would have far-reaching implications, it would be difficult in the extreme for many organisations to reach clear conclusions on strategy into which 'tactical' decisions could then be fitted, even if there were no continuing change in technology or business needs. It is much easier to visualise a total information approach in circumstances where a move to a new location for plant or office can be argued but, in the typical business situation, the implications of change would be daunting.

The key factor is the acceptance of the proposition about the significance of information. Once that is accepted then the criteria which are applied to judging decisions about the other resources can be seen to be no longer important. Thus the kind of review of business activities which could lead to a decision to close one operation, create another or embark upon a radical change in organisation should be contemplated as readily for information. The justification for a move to a new location, for example, could be to provide the appropriate information infrastructure.

At a more detailed level, determination of information strategy will lead to decisions about the organisational allocation of functions. At the service level, the relationship must be determined between the computer and communication functions provided by data processing and office administration departments and, at the system development level, between the professionally designed applications, the general user facilities, and the end-user driven system applications. It must lead to decisions about IT investment policy, equipment and software technical standards, procurement procedures and technical support. It must provide a framework of information policy within which decisions may be made about the provision of general and specific information services and, possibly above all, it must allocate senior management responsibility, giving appropriate weight to the management of change. This is not only because management of change is a vital and often underestimated problem applying to any computer-based system, but also because the implications of integrated IT systems may be so far reaching that management of change must be a corporate responsibility.

Development Policy

A computer-based system is intended to improve the effectiveness of business in achieving its objectives and, viewed in this light, any system change should be approached with respect. Computer systems operate through the precise observance of rigid rules; in consequence their design itself must be precise, requiring a careful, disciplined and objective approach. Perhaps one may exclude some of the many users of small computers as personal support facilities but the computer which is to be used as part of a business system, for a useful end-product, should not be conceived purely as something requiring a casual adjustment to a changed environment through an instinctive reaction based on general business experience. The system development process should sensibly be treated as a project in which the system problem needs to be investigated first and a new system design specified and implemented through a planning procedure which follows carefully framed rules.

On the other hand, one must not view the development of a computer system only as a series of complex technical tasks. Seen through the eyes of the systems designer this will sometimes (wrongly) appear to be so, but it must be remembered always that it is not the systems designer alone who determines the outcome of the computer project, it is also the user of the system. The user should decide whether the project is to be undertaken, determine how it is to be carried out and what the end result should be. It is now fashionable to see the (unskilled) user as analyst, or as programmer as well as machine operator and, although this is an exaggeration, it does reflect some truth. Easier paths to system development are opening, in the same way that self-help has become possible with other business problems which had once been the exclusive preserve of the specialist.

Whether the user takes the primary role in all aspects of computer system development or not, it still can be asserted that proper account should be taken of all elements contained in the various theoretical stages of system development, and that the resulting system should have been designed according to professional standards and design criteria. The distinction being made is that while what must be done is similar for all types of system, there will be differences in the ways chosen to complete the projects.

In this chapter the process of developing a computer system is examined from the theoretical viewpoint of the planning stages from conception to operation, and from the practical standpoint of the choices open to user management and system designers in producing a satisfactory computer solution to system problems. Behind such a brief survey, of course, must lie a great weight of detail which forms the professional content of the systems analyst's work: the techniques to be used in the definition and the specification of computer systems, the technical considerations necessary for selection of hardware and software, and the means by which IT systems can be constructed and implemented.

System Planning In Theory

The 'Structured' Approach

The 'classical' approach to system planning involves dividing the total task into separate stages, each one of which has its own objectives, tasks, resources, constraints and time-scale specified at the outset. Starting from a preliminary identification of the system problem, the planning process is carried through successive stages of

- Feasibility study
- Logical system definition
- Physical system specification
- System construction
- Implementation.

Each stage represents an expansion and continuation from the previous stage, breaking the development task into greater detail, and culminating in the preparation and testing of computer programs and their implementation in association with manual and other machine procedures in a 'production' system.

Most computer-based system development work falls naturally into stages and there are clear advantages in this approach. It provides a logical sequence of planning activities and makes possible a clear allocation of responsibilities and specified planning tasks. With larger projects, where many activities may overlap, a sophisticated 'networking' approach may be advantageous but, whether the project be large or small, a vital aspect of formalised system planning is that all the main activities can be identified separately and sequentially.

At the end of each planning stage there is a requirement for formal reporting to the authority responsible for supervision of the project, to review progress, to examine proposals and to approve recommendations before moving on to the next stage. This clear definition and the provision of break points between stages make it easier to exercise control over progress and direction of the project. They also make it possible to anticipate, identify and cure problems before they reach harmful proportions and, through defined approval procedures, to obtain agreement and commitment to every aspect of the project so as to give assurance that the ultimate solution will be acceptable. The long-term investment in a computer system may be significant both in its cost of development and in the time it takes to complete the development work. The creation of a formal structure for systems analysis and design places heavy emphasis on the use of carefully defined standards and formal documentation to ensure coherence and control throughout the stages of the planning process.

By such techniques as introducing precise definitions for each element of data in the system at the earliest stage, it both reduces the risk of mistake in development of system plans and makes possible the maximum use of computer facilities to accelerate the system development process. It is aimed generally at the three risk areas in system planning: of cost and time over-run, and of failure to achieve user planning objectives.

Planning Assignments

The first step in the development of a computer-based information system is the assignment of the project. The assignment brief is usually drawn up as a joint task by those responsible for authorising the project (often the prospective system users) and by those providing the planning assistance. Its purpose is to provide terms of reference and guidance for the project leader assigned to the first stage of the investigation.

The assignment brief should describe the background to the investigation, the scope of the enquiry defining the boundaries of the system, department or function within which the investigation is to be conducted, and the nature of the problem to be examined. Most important, however, are the user objectives which state the outcome required from the study and from any consequent system change. These objectives, which express the essential aim and purpose of the study, must identify in measurable terms the expected effects of the new system. These must be precise, measurable and easily understood so that it will be possible, ultimately, to see that they have been achieved. If the system does not achieve the objectives for which the project was launched, it has failed. For this reason it is vital that there is reference back to those objectives at each stage of system development to ensure that they are still being maintained.

The terms of reference contained in the assignment brief must also indicate any limitations to the enquiry: the timetable to be followed in carrying it out, the resources available in terms of assistance, facilities and information which may be used in the study, as well as the constraints which will limit both the scope of investigation and the solution. These constraints might be limits affecting access to people and records for enquiry, exclusion of particular kinds of solution or (as is likely in an organisation which already has a computer installation) restrictions affecting the technical specification of hardware or software.

Feasibility Study

Although the initial terms of reference may give information related to the complete project, the first stage of planning, assuming that there is not a prior commitment to a particular solution or that the assignment does not allow for the immediate preparation of a detailed system specification (as with the modification of an existing system), must be to determine whether or not there is likely to be a machine solution which can meet user objectives.

The first step in a 'feasibility study' is usually to obtain information about the existing organisation and systems. Information must be collected about all relevant parts of the existing system — inputs, processes, files and outputs. It must be analysed so that system problems can be identified, the validity of user objectives confirmed and the feasibility of an acceptable solution determined. It must be both quantified and qualified. Information is needed about organisation, job descriptions, decision and action responsibilities and information flows, including volumes, patterns and content for all kinds of data processed through the system. Rules and procedures governing system operation must be understood and, where not available in verified, written procedures (as is quite probable), must be derived from a study of the system in action. Exceptions to the data flows and procedures must be noted and evaluated, as must any defect or constraint which is affecting system operation.

The resources used in running the system must be identified: the people, machines, materials, accommodation, and their costs. It may be necessary to examine historical information: past data volumes, trends and previous system changes which have led to the present situation and which may be helpful both in understanding present policy and procedures and in making estimates about the future. Any planned or expected future change which could have bearing upon system requirements must also be noted. The analyst conducting the study must have an understanding of the personalities of those involved in the present system because their attitudes will shed light on the existing system and its problems and the path to finding an acceptable solution.

Logical System Definition

The completed feasibility study should state conclusions and recommendations in such a way that, at the very least, a decision can be taken on the next planning stage. This may be to define a computer system proposal or to propose changes other than the introduction of a computer, or it could be to abandon the project because no system change is justified. If a solution involving a computer is identified as feasible, the project may be expected to progress to the definition stage. This stage is the most important since it culminates in a proposal which, once accepted, will commit the business to implementing the recommended system. Whereas the feasibility stage might be limited to establishing broad elements of the solution and evaluating the economics sufficiently for further planning steps to be taken with confidence, the definition stage must include a full examination of all aspects so that an informed management judgement can be made on the resulting proposal. All elements of the proposed system must be defined and documented so that the user can see exactly how system requirements will be met, what will be the effect of the proposed system, including financial implications, and what must be done to implement the proposal (figure 45).

> Statement of system objectives and user requirements
>
> Description of the proposed business system
>
> Effect of the proposals on the organisation
>
> Constraints on the design of the new system
>
> Factors to be considered in changing the system
>
> Development and running costs
>
> Planning and operating timetable
>
> Formal recommendations for action
>
> Activities in the next stage of development

Figure 45   Content of the system proposal

Physical System Specification

The physical system comprises equipment and computer software which will carry the logical system defined in the previous stage of planning. Physical system design includes preparation of detailed technical specifications of all the system elements for which equipment and software can be selected or constructed. Whereas, for example, the logical definition of a computer file is concerned with the data it has to hold and the information that it must be able to provide, the physical specification is concerned with the nature of the storage element, how the data is held and the means of access. The logical stage is concerned with systems analysis and specification, the physical stage with carrying out what has been decided. In that sense, this technical phase is less demanding than the analysis phase since it is generally easier to resolve problems of which one knows the outcome.

System Construction

To meet the software needs this stage may be carried out by taking a detailed program specification, coding each module in the chosen programming language, testing the coded modules and linking programs together to form complete machine processes. It may be accomplished also by choosing a prepared set of programs which meet the design criteria, or it may be put together as a combination of tailored and packaged program elements or from the wide range of system-building software facilities. The construction stage is completed with the creation of a system which exists physically and which now requires to be accepted and put into operation.

Any computer-based system comprises more than the application software element; the operating functions (the 'man–machine interface') and any clerical or managerial functions associated with system input and output will require appropriate physical development in the form of detailed procedures, documents and physical elements. Many IT systems make use of machines other than computers; often the computer is the minor part of the machine element. There may, therefore, be questions of constructing accommodation, plant, communication systems and information-handling facilities. Many of these activities will involve users, and many will require professional expertise comparable with that of the computer systems analysts and programmers.

Implementation

The implementation stage converts this theoretical system into practice through processes of system testing, training and conversion, bringing the new system into operation in place of the old. The system-testing process itself may go through a number of stages, joining computer and other elements of the system and running them under controlled conditions which simulate live operation, and culminating in formal trials in which the system is offered for approval and acceptance by the user.

Before a system can be put into operation it is necessary to ensure that everyone concerned with its running has received adequate training and operating instructions, that procedures for end users have been prepared and that any other equipment, materials and facilities are in place. The remaining tasks are to set up the new system in its starting mode with files ready for processing where required, and 'cut over' from the old system, taking account of any problems of timing and accuracy arising in such conversion processes.

Finally, there is a period of 'bedding down' when latent defects and problems are resolved and the efficiency of the system in operation is brought up to a standard of normal running. The development then may be considered to be complete, and results may be evaluated and the actual achievement reconciled with the original objectives.

Project teams

It is part of this concept of system planning as a staged project that organisation of work be on a team basis. Bearing in mind the widely differing types of problem for which computers are used, one cannot be dogmatic about composition and organisation of planning teams but, to be successful, they must bring together three separate groups of skills and interests. These three groups are the 'user', for whom the system is being developed, the 'operations' function which is concerned with running the system, and the 'design' function which provides the skills for systems analysis and design, programming and other disciplines necessary to meet the technical requirements. It is essential that the project team be properly managed and it will be usual to designate formally a project leader who undertakes all appropriate management responsibilities: allocation of planning tasks, preparation of schedules, supervision of team members, liaison with managers and users, and formal responsibility for the conduct of the investigation and for its successful conclusion.

Systems Analysis and Design

The term 'system analysis' has come to be concerned specifically with the development of computer-based business systems. This is not self-explanatory and it might have been better if systems analysis referred generally to all kinds of business system without being linked necessarily to computers. The concept of using professional skills to investigate and analyse business problems and to design new systems is as relevant to situations which do not involve the use of computers. For those who study clerical and factory systems, equally inappropriate labels such as 'organisation and methods' and 'work study' have been attached. We have to become accustomed to such labels because they are applied in theory and practice, remembering only that the labels change their meaning. For example, new kinds of information technology now applied to computer systems and the computer-assisted techniques for system design and construction which are tending to supersede the formerly more detailed approach are bringing with them new kinds of label. The terms 'business analyst' and 'systems engineer' have come into common use, reflecting the increasing emphasis on first establishing the essential business framework for the information systems and then of taking an engineering approach to the question of its construction. The observation that a prospective computer user cannot escape from the systems analyst is intended to indicate that the 'business analysis' function remains vital, however easily the 'system engineering' function can be obtained in ready-to-use form.

It is quite possible that systems analysis would have assumed much of its present importance even if computer-based business systems had not evolved during the past 30 years, since this period has been associated also with a steady increase in the professionalism applied to business management and services generally. However, it is not difficult to see why systems analysis became associated with computers. When business computers were new and relatively expensive it was hard to justify or make effective use of them without having undertaken a complete review of existing systems. It is still true that system objectives and requirements should be properly identified, and that new computer systems should meet them with optimum efficiency; this was mandatory with early computers because the economics were so finely balanced. There was also the very important consideration affecting early computer systems that, to select the equipment, design and specify the systems, write the programs and operate them all required new, highly specialised knowledge. The business proposing to use a computer would be buying a piece of machinery with little of the kind of built-in or additional software facility which now translates much of the technical complexity into forms easily understood and managed by people without experience.

Now that there is more often a choice between employing technical specialists and buying the results of their services in packaged form, it is becoming appropriate to make a clearer distinction between the 'technical' and 'business' aspects of system development. The intention to use the resources of information tchnology to construct complex systems to provide an information service or product which uses computers, communications equipment and other machines carries with it also a commitment to complex design structures. The resulting system may still be composed of package elements although these and the design skills which created them may be drawn from a number of different disciplines, of which computer system design will be one. In these systems, the technical element is likely to be sharply distinguished from the business element. Regardless of the method of system construction it is the business aspects which continue to be of concern to the computer user: the establishment of feasibility, the investigation, analysis and synthesis functions necessary to define the extent and detail of the systems proposal, and the various tasks involved in turning completed 'technical' products into fully operational and effective business systems.

Part of the business function, too, is the relationship with people. Systems analysis is essentially about people and whether a system is concerned with manual activities or only with automatic responses from machines, the objectives and requirements of a system and its logical functions will be influenced primarily by the behaviour and attitudes of people concerned with system inputs, processes and outputs.

Work of the Systems Analyst

A system analyst employed on a business computer project will have six principal groups of tasks, related to the classical system development stages

- Preliminary investigation of existing organisation, functions and systems
- Detailed analysis of data about existing systems, identification of system requirements, evaluation of alternative courses of action and identification of feasible solutions
- Definition of logical elements for a new system and preparation of system proposals and implementation plans
- Design and specification of physical system elements to implement approved proposals
- Co-ordination and supervision of system construction including computer programming and other specialist system engineering tasks
- Supervision, co-ordination and support for the implementation of tasks, including testing, training and conversion to the new system operation.

To carry out these tasks the analyst needs knowledge and skill appropriate to all the functions and techniques involved with the system project. These will include

- Sympathetic understanding of the organisation and systems with which he is dealing
- Skill in applying systems analysis techniques
- The ability to communicate with management, operating staff and other participants
- Technical knowledge of the relevant equipment, software and other facilities used in a system
- The ability to visualise and construct theoretical solutions to systems problems
- The capacity for an orderly and disciplined approach to system planning tasks.

This list can present only a superficial impression of the analyst's function. The system analyst's profession is to be an agent of change. He must be able to take a system which may have developed and run over many years and replace it by something totally different, changing organisation, procedures, jobs and techniques so as to create a better system in a changed environment. He must be able to achieve this without the benefit of substantial experience within the existing system, be able to secure the support of people who may be reluctant to change and hostile towards new technology, and then guide development of the new system through design and implementation processes which may be complex, lengthy and detailed.

This demands a richer mixture of skills than do many occupations, although it would be unrealistic to see the systems analyst as being able to handle any kind of computer system application. Technical expertise may mean a general appreciation of computer products and their characteristics but detailed knowledge and experience within much narrower ranges. In relation to business systems themselves, knowledge of essential system theory concepts may be general but practical experience will be confined to particular applications. Anything with a special flavour such as database management, telemetry, management accounting, or microsystems, will require special expertise. Systems analysis is a heading, not a universal job description.

System Planning in Practice

The means by which a system project is brought to fruition and the path followed by those concerned in its planning and implementation inevitably can vary, depending on the nature of the problem and its solution. A project may be completed in one day by one individual, or may require many man-years of planning effort by a large number of people with different specialist skills. The relation between cost and time for each planning stage is not constant. A very lengthy feasibility study may be followed by rapid progress towards implementation; on the other hand, a system may be defined and specified quickly whereas implementation may occupy more effort and time than all the preceding stages together. These planning stages themselves may be subdivided or brought together and it may be extremely difficult to relate examples of practical application to theoretical concepts. The combined pressures to reduce cost of planning and to shorten the time between assignment and implementation may lead to short cuts, or to the modification of professional standards of documentation and control in planning.

As in all business activities, a commonsense view should prevail. There is no sense in the observance of detailed formal procedures where these have no real virtue and serve only to bring unnecessary elaboration, nor is it undesirable to take the opportunity to achieve planning objectives more efficiently. However, there is a distinction between finding equally effective but less costly techniques for system development and abandoning sound planning principles in a desire for haste or short-term economy. As a general rule, if planning in haste for a computer system involves jumping to conclusions, then a price will be paid in poorer system performance, inflexibility, or failure which will lead to some repentance at leisure.

The concept of formal planning stages and project team organisation associated with precisely defined planning procedures and documentation standards was, and still is, most appropriately demonstrated in relation to the development of large business computer systems where planning is handled internally by the systems and operating functions of a computer service department, in association with other departments and functions which will use the new systems. The realities of system development in many other business undertakings may, at first sight, be very different, not only because applications and the technical elements in computer-based information systems can vary so much but also because the chosen means of achieving system solutions also vary.

With every wave of technological development in economic history there has been a general progression from hesitant acceptance by the mystified user of an innovation proffered by the technical expert, to technical expertise being employed to meet special user requirements, and then to the user being able to select the most appropriate from prepared solutions. That is an over-simplification, of course; even where 'ready made' is the norm, there is still ample demand for special solutions to special problems. For a realistic view of IT system development we have to look for both aspects: the detailed, formalised processes of creating 'tailor-made' systems in which all the technicalities of system planning are evident, with the focus of attention on the professional designers, and the (now) typical business situation where many technical elements of the computer system are the concern of the (external) supplier, and the focus is on the user. The principles of computer system development still apply and all the planning elements are there; they are simply hidden within a packaged product.

The Packaged Solution

At the feasibility study stage, the business manager's choice may be to undertake his own design study or call in a consultant instead of employing a systems analyst. System definition can be handled in the same way, or be provided by a hardware/software supplier in response to a specification of requirement. Construction of the system, instead of from specially written programs, can be through the purchase of ready-made programs providing a packaged solution, or by means of software facilities so designed that the end user can create programs without needing to acquire specialist programming skills. If desired, the complete solution can be bought from an external supplier as a 'turnkey' proposition — ready to run as soon as the equipment is unlocked.

The attractions of totally packaged solutions can be seen most easily with small business systems, where the employment of one specialist programmer could cost more than all the equipment and software put together. The business manager would be foolish to pay for special programs if, with acceptable compromise, a ready-made or easily adaptable packaged solution were available instead. An unskilled programmer paid at manager's rates is likely to produce a most expensive and unsatisfactory product and many first-time users of personal computers, attracted by the suggestion that everyone can become his own programmer and operator, often dissipate the benefit of computer facilities in the cost of these 'amateur' programmers and typists. Good management decisions depend on good information and a manager can be his own expert only if he is as well informed as the expert; otherwise he should seek advice. An architect is employed to build a house to special requirements; if a house exists already which meets those requirements, the architect is not needed. 'Do it yourself' is for quick and easy solutions, or for people whose time has no cost. Thus, with the small or simple business problem, the need for specialist help may be minimal and general management ability may be sufficient for a sensible choice to be made between prepared solutions. For large, complex projects which will be beyond the technical expertise of any user, and which will not fit any standard packaged solution, the alternative to employing a specialist planning team is to employ that expertise through a contract with a professional supplier experienced in solving similar problems.

Constructing the Business Model

The first consideration in systems analysis always is to establish clearly what are the user objectives. This is not simply a matter of understanding and interpreting objectives stated by the user: it is also one of making sure that these objectives are both compatible with the system problems identified during the feasibility study and are achievable through changes in systems.

It may be that the user's wishes on which the whole project is founded are not reconcilable with the needs identified as a result of the system investigation. It is possible that the user has neither a proper understanding of the working of the present system and of its defects, nor a clear view of the objectives which should be set for a new system. Such objectives must themselves be compatible with the overall objectives of the business; while it would be a rash assumption for any systems analyst to assume that a user is incompetent, the existence of a system problem itself might indicate some lack of understanding either at operating level or at policy or organisational level. In the context of speculation about the user as analyst, it must be reaffirmed that it is a management function to have a clear perception of systems matters for the general identification of objectives, and of the decisions and information which provide a path to those objectives. The improvement of systems that provide the information is also a management responsibility but to be able to identify accurately the link between symptom and cause of system deficiency and define essentials for a solution is beyond normally required management skills and experience.

When user objectives have been determined and existing system problems identified, the next task should be to construct a business model from which the new system requirements can be formulated. The idea of the business model is that it will show the primary data flows and relationships which make up the business, from which it is possible to draw clear conclusions about the information needs and other essential requirements which must be taken into account in designing new systems. It provides the outline and foundation for specifying system requirements, defining data and identifying system modules from which more detailed definition and specification can follow.

The business problems which were the reason for commissioning a computer feasibility study may be readily apparent to the business management, but they may not necessarily reflect the true systems problem which may remain obscure until a detailed system investigation has been carried out. The true problem so revealed may not be capable of resolution by a computer system; even if first views of the system problems prove to have been a correct interpretation, it may not follow that information technology will offer the best answer. Where a computer solution can be found, it is still quite likely that the user will not have understood at the outset what the costs or the potential benefits might be. Careful examination and appraisal of facts and intentions is needed to reach an objective conclusion about what is wrong and what needs to be done so that it becomes possible to construct the theoretical framework for a viable new system. This will be the model for the new system and this first outline should purport to offer a whole solution, identifying the principal elements including boundaries and interfaces with retained existing systems and appearing capable of operating effectively in the business environment in which it is to be used.

At this stage the shape, or even the possible existence, of a computer solution will not necessarily have been defined in any way. In relation to the classical steps in system development, construction of business models represents the first stages of investigation and analysis leading towards conclusions about feasibility and system requirements. This view of the systems approach can be held whether or not the task is handled by the user alone or principally by professional analysts, provided that system planning skills and experience of the existing business structure and operations are brought together, with all misconceptions removed through the use of objective analysis techniques.

From this point onward the practicalities of computer system development are not always easily related to the theoretical necessities of staged project planning, or of the ordered distribution of tasks between user management, operating staff and technical specialists.

'Structured' Design

On the technical side, there are three aspects which have to be brought into consideration. The first of these is the professional skill to be able to recognise and take into account all factors likely to influence the design of the new system — questions of cost, time, acceptability and so on. The second is the knowledge to decide whether or not a computer solution is feasible and then to determine which form it should take. The third is concerned with the technical processes of definition, specification and construction of the new system. However well-qualified the user may be in the first two fields, it is most unlikely that anyone but a professional specialist will be able to handle all aspects of the technical stages and development. Yet, if the process of system development is to be carried through in the most efficient way, it is desirable that the technical stage be started at the earliest possible time — as soon as commitment to the end result can be safely anticipated, or is confirmed.

The current view of systems design techniques is still that the process of system development should be formalised, but that this 'structured' approach should start from as early as the stage of setting up the business model, with definition of data and its relationships in a way that can be maintained right through successive stages of planning. Each stage represents effectively an 'explosion' or further detailing from the preceding stage, in conformity with the classical approach but combining all the benefits of rigorous standards of control and procedure with the maximum use of assistance from the computer itself in the form of software tools for development, such that the process of system design links logically and coherently with the stage of software construction or programming.

This can be fitted into the concept of the specialist project team in which the user participates as customer and supplier of raw data. It is also compatible with a situation in which the user buys the services of external specialists to develop the system either in the same way as would an internal development team or through the acquisition of a packaged solution. However, there are two aspects of system development from the user viewpoint which complicate relationships with computer specialists: the user may not necessarily accept the expert view nor know what he wants until he has it. One of the great criticisms of computer systems and of computer specialists which has persisted through each computer generation has been that the computer does not provide always what the user wants. From the analyst's viewpoint, the counter argument is that the user frequently does not know what he wants. Both of these criticisms can be found to have been true, sometimes as a failure in communications, sometimes as the result of a lack of comprehension. In the period when computers were relatively expensive and new systems had to 'fit' the computer to be economic, the degree of change from existing procedures could be very considerable. The resulting forced compromise could turn itself into a deficiency of machine or designer in the eyes of the user, particularly if the system in operation proved less beneficial than the (inexperienced) user had imagined it would be. There is less need for economic compromise today and user discontent is more likely to show itself in objections to the time taken to produce the desired result, rather than to the result itself.

New Solutions

The problem of the user 'who does not know what he wants' is not a phenomenon associated only with computers. Any professional specialist concerned with business systems is likely to regard this as one of the burdens of his occupation, and be familiar with the situation where, while the salesman claims he will be happy with any information offered and the accountant is determined to have nothing less than every detail, neither wants what is offered when he actually gets it.

The idea of programming to precise specification at considerable expense, with additional expense and delay if subsequent modification were needed, led computer system planners at a very early stage to attempt to resist any change in specification once formal proposals had been agreed, until after the system was fully operational. The analyst would attempt to ensure that the definitive system did meet user need by taking great care to confirm objectives and requirements, and by seeking formal authority through approval of detailed proposals and specifications. This may be justified in logical argument, but it has never been enough because only exceptional human beings can sustain acceptance of such constraints. However much desired, system requirements rarely remain unchanged from start to finish and people are rarely able to commit themselves with certainty to what they want until they actually see it. These kinds of pressure, as much as those from the actual costs of system planning, have channelled much of the economic and technical advance of computers into making the process of system development easier, so as to allow changes of mind or other lapses from impeccable system development standards without incurring the severe penalties that once would be applied.

One must not push such generalities too far because the ultimate disciplines of computer-based systems cannot be denied as yet, but there are now easier ways to many business computer applications in which the user can retain, in belief as well as in reality, a much greater degree of control over progress towards the solution than used to be the case. Large systems still demand highly professional project management but there are many smaller business applications which do not involve very high risks or special technical problems. With these smaller systems any need to interpose specialists between user and objectives could result in disproportional delay and cost, which would cause irritation to the user. The user's ability to construct his personal microcomputer system using simplified languages and 'parameter-driven' application packages makes economic sense. With a slightly larger installation, some professional advice and a 'ready to use' system might be appropriate at the beginning, but it need not take long before the user has sufficient experience and confidence to devise his own systems and software for future applications. It is not surprising that there are increasing numbers of installations in small businesses or departments which have ceased to depend on professional operation or systems development support. Even where the complexity of the problem demands the services of the system planning specialist, that specialist can build the system himself without the assistance of a skilled programmer by using some of the current advanced software tools. In the development of any system, the relevance of programs coded by specialist application programmers is diminishing steadily as the high level languages are superseded and, with this trend, the days of the application programmer are also numbered.

There are professional suppliers who have also discarded the formal processes of defining logical systems on paper before committing them to the machine, in favour of a co-operative process of constructing systems with user and designer creating files, inputs and outputs through computer screens: a sophistication of the self-build approach used with the small business microcomputer. However much it may shock the purist and appear to contradict the propositions that secure progress by stages is the best approach, it does answer the question "what do you want the computer to do;" when the report format displayed on the terminal screen satisfies the user, the design can become firm. Moreover, it can be changed with relatively little fuss, such is the flexibility of the sophisticated software tools that are available.

The conclusion that one should reach about the evolution of techniques for the application of information technology from the viewpoint of business management is that there is no fixed way towards the best results. Certain underlying principles must be preserved: the normal financial and other criteria which should apply to any business investment, careful analysis of system requirements, and evaluation of all the influences on good system design. Beyond that, provided the manager is sure the definitive system cannot create a situation beyond his control, the method by which that system is developed may be as varied as any comparable good engineering practice, whether involving delegation to professional advisers and specialists, the construction of prototypes or experimental models, or other means. The empirical approach could be just as valid as the ordered sequence of stages from plan to action.

Check List 14

For the development of effective computer systems, the planning process itself must be orderly and a 'structured' approach from problem definition through analysis and synthesis to implementation is vital. However, there is nothing in the concept of computer system development as a process involving skill and discipline that is incompatible with the aims of economy, speed and user convenience in the application of system planning techniques.

Stages of System Development
  Feasibility — investigation.
  Analysis — definition of the logical system.
  Design — specification of the physical system.
  Construction — system building.
  Implementation.

Responsibilities and Tasks of the Systems Analyst

Practical System Planning
  Packaged solutions.
  'Structured' design techniques.
  End-user system development.

Further Reading

Daniels, A. and Yeates, D., *Basic Systems Analysis*, Pitman, 1984.
Gore, M. and Stubbe, J., *Elements of Systems Analysis*, Wm C. Brown, 1983.
Martin, J., *An Information Systems Manifesto*, Prentice-Hall, 1984.
Squire, E., *Introducing Systems Design*, Addison-Wesley, 1980.

Index

Index